AF269986

Dick Laros, a man who ultimately became my most influential mentor during my career in the hunting industry, spoke those words to me about a year after I started my outfitting and wildlife management company. For the next two-plus decades, Dick and I spent a lot of time on many occasions exploring why the hunting business is so unique. Now in this book, I am sharing my knowledge and insights gained during my 36 years in the profession that stirs the imagination of many. So join me as I examine what it takes to succeed in the hunting business as well as the current and future challenges our hunting community faces. Plus, there are business and life lessons throughout the pages of *The Hunting Business* that most anyone can apply to their own professional development regardless of their chosen field. Welcome to my world…

Greg Simons

"A PECULIAR VIRTUE IN WILDLIFE ETHICS IS THAT THE HUNTER ORDINARILY HAS NO GALLERY TO APPLAUD OR DISAPPROVE OF HIS CONDUCT. WHATEVER HIS ACTS, THEY ARE DICTATED BY HIS OWN CONSCIENCE, RATHER THAN THAT OF ONLOOKERS. IT IS DIFFICULT TO EXAGGERATE THE IMPORTANCE OF THIS FACT."

—ALDO LEOPOLD

"IN A CIVILIZED AND CULTIVATED COUNTRY WILD ANIMALS ONLY CONTINUE TO EXIST AT ALL WHEN PRESERVED BY SPORTSMEN. THE EXCELLENT PEOPLE WHO PROTEST AGAINST ALL HUNTING, AND CONSIDER SPORTSMEN AS ENEMIES OF WILDLIFE, ARE IGNORANT OF THE FACT THAT IN REALITY THE GENUINE SPORTSMAN IS BY ALL ODDS THE MOST IMPORTANT FACTOR IN KEEPING THE LARGER AND MORE VALUABLE WILD CREATURES FROM TOTAL EXTERMINATION."

—THEODORE ROOSEVELT

"WHEN SOME OF MY FRIENDS HAVE ASKED ME ANXIOUSLY ABOUT THEIR BOYS, WHETHER THEY SHOULD LET THEM HUNT, I HAVE ANSWERED YES— REMEMBERING THAT IT WAS ONE OF THE BEST PARTS OF MY EDUCATION— MAKE THEM HUNTERS."

—HENRY DAVID THOREAU

"MAYBE STALKING THE WOODS IS AS VITAL TO THE HUMAN CONDITION AS PLAYING MUSIC OR PUTTING WORDS TO PAPER. MAYBE HUNTING HAS AS MUCH OF A CLAIM ON OUR CIVILIZED SELVES AS ANYTHING ELSE. AFTER ALL, THE EARLIEST FORMS OF REPRESENTATIONAL ART REFLECT HUNTERS AND PREY. WHILE THE ARTS WERE MAKING US SPIRITUALLY VIABLE, HUNTING DID THE HEAVY LIFTING OF NOT ONLY KEEPING US ALIVE, BUT INSPIRING US TO ABHOR HUNTING IS TO HATE THE PLACE FROM WHICH YOU CAME, WHICH IS AKIN TO HATING YOURSELF IN SOME DISTANT, ABSTRACT WAY."

—STEVEN RINELLA

"I HAVE ALWAYS TEMPERED MY KILLING WITH RESPECT FOR THE GAME PURSUED. I SEE THE ANIMAL NOT ONLY AS A TARGET, BUT AS A LIVING CREATURE WITH MORE FREEDOM THAN I WILL EVER HAVE. I TAKE THAT LIFE IF I CAN, WITH REGRET AS WELL AS JOY, AND WITH THE SURE KNOWLEDGE THAT NATURE'S WAY OF FANG AND CLAW AND STARVATION ARE FAR CRUELER FATE THAN I BESTOW."

—FRED BEAR

3-12x56
STOP THE HUNT
NO MORE HUNTIN

THE HUNTING BUSINESS

GREG SIMONS

THB PUBLICATIONS

THE HUNTING BUSINESS

PUBLISHED BY THB PUBLICATIONS, LLC.

P. O. Box 5121, San Angelo, TX 76902

DISTRIBUTED BY GREENLEAF BOOK GROUP

For ordering information or special discounts for bulk purchases, please contact Greenleaf Book Group at PO Box 91869, Austin, TX 78709, (512) 891-6100.

EDITING BY LORIE A. WOODWARD

COPYEDITING BY CHRISTINA TEWES AND LAUREN CARSWELL

FOREWORD BY LARRY WEISHUHN

DESIGN AND COMPOSITION BY LAURET JARVIS

PRIMARY PHOTOGRAPHY BY GREG SIMONS

COVER PHOTOGRAPHY BY CHRIS DOUGLAS

PHOTOGRAPHY CREDITS PAGE 278

Publisher's Cataloging-in-Publication data is available.

ISBN 979-8-9877635-0-6 (hardcover)

ISBN 979-8-9877635-1-3 (ebook)

Printed in China on acid-free paper.

Greg Simons can present at your live event. For more information or to book an event, contact Wildlife Systems, Inc. at (325) 655-0877 or visit WildlifeSystems.com.

DEDICATION

This book, which reflects my lifetime vocation and avocation in the hunting and wildlife business is dedicated to my family. My wife, Deborah, has not only been patient, understanding, and supportive of my crazy work pace for the past 36 years, but she has been instrumental in the success of Wildlife Systems, Inc. Day after day, year after year, she has worked alongside me and putting her prodigious accounting and business skills to use on our behalf since the company's launch. Our two kids, Tyler and Erin, allowed me to be away from home during a large percentage of their childhoods, an absence which I now regret because time gets away too quickly. Rarely did they give me any grief, which is a testament to their understanding the duties and obligations that go along with owning a business particularly in this industry, and a reflection of the great parenting that Deb provided often as a sole practitioner.

This dedication to my family also includes my amazing mom and dad, who both left this world way too soon. My mom cleaned houses so that she and Dad could afford to send me to college to study wildlife biology. Prior to her death when she was just 48 years old, she helped with some of the first hunts I outfitted, cooking and providing unsurpassed hospitality in those camps. While I was growing up, my dad taught me, by example, the importance of being passionate and dedicated to your profession. His leadership style and his generosity inspired me in many ways, and still do today. Dad guided for me for several years after I formed Wildlife Systems, Inc. in 1987 and he was my biggest fan until the day he died. Together, Mom and Dad made many sacrifices for us three kids so that we could enjoy things that expanded our opportunities, but stretched our household budget. I am forever grateful for their selflessness that put me on a path that led to where I am today.

My father-in-law and good friend, Bruce Ingram, who recently passed away, was central to my growth as a business owner. Bruce was one of the most instinctive and effective businessmen who I have ever spent time around. The things he knew and freely shared were essential to the development of Wildlife Systems, our team—and me. Plus, his caring, genuine, and generous nature left an indelible mark on me forever as did the special times we spent together in hunting camps across Texas and beyond.

And last but not least, this book is dedicated to my maternal grandfather, Gene Gillam. Any time I contemplated writing a hunting book, even in my earliest days, I vowed to dedicate it to Pawpaw. Although he passed away when I was six years old, Pawpaw loomed larger than life in my eyes. The self-taught horticulturist, rattlesnake wrangler and beekeeper, harvested big mule deer and elk on public land in Colorado and taught me how to catch trout on salmon eggs and worms. During his brief tutelage, Pawpaw left a deep imprint on my life. I still feel his influence some 52 years after his death. I suspect that it is his outdoor-loving DNA that is so deeply embedded in mine that pushed me to become a professional wildlifer—and I am eternally grateful.

CONTENTS

FOREWORD

BY LARRY L. WEISHUHN

"It'll be easy," he said.

And then Greg Simons, who was putting me on a sizable West Texas mule deer he had spotted about a mile away, went onto explain.

"All we have to do is crawl on our hands and knees past those first three mule deer bucks, slip through that herd of javelina, and skirt around those three whitetails. Then we'll crawl the last quarter mile, on our bellies, through the brush. At that point we should be within easy rifle range."

After describing the five by five muley with a kicker as "massive and tall, and the best buck we've seen," Greg asked, " Care to give it a try?"

If he thought we could do it, who was I to question? I had learned long ago, "Never guide the guide."

Greg and I belly-crawled, undetected within arm's reach of mule deer, javelina and whitetails en route to the big buck. By the time we got close to the buck, it was nearly sundown and the buck had bedded.

We spotted antler tips. I cautiously moved into a sitting position. "Our" buck was just seven steps away as I pulled the trigger. Greg had perfectly orchestrated our stalk—and an exciting, fun, satisfying and thoroughly successful hunt.

We finished quartering and caping the buck well after dark. With the meat, antlers and cape loaded on our pack boards we headed toward our vehicle, parked six miles away.

Heavily overcast and moonless, the night was darker than dark. My flashlight's batteries played out just as we finished dressing the deer. By the time we finished, Greg's flashlight batteries were severely "fatigued." To save the remaining battery life, we walked in total darkness, Greg in the lead.

It's still a mystery how we avoided being impaled by the desert's sharp array of thorns and spines. Greg amazingly seemed to know when to walk straight and where to step left or right.

About a mile from the vehicle, Greg suddenly commanded, "Stop!"

He knew we were approaching a deep ravine. The weak beam of Greg's flashlight proved his memory, sense of direction and unerring knowledge of the landscape correct. Had we walked another three feet, the ground would have dropped out from under us and sent us tumbling down into a rocky chasm that was at least 20 feet deep. Our magnificent day could have ended in a nightmare of broken bones or at least fun-stealing sprains, scrapes and deep muscle bruises.

We couldn't see our hands in front of our faces and yet he knew exactly where that ravine was. Even after all these years, I'm still not sure how he managed it. Suffice it to say, it made quite an impression. I knew right then and there his future in the hunting business was golden.

From the beginning, Greg always seemed to innately know "when to do what." He became a knowledgeable manager of wildlife, business, and equally important, people.

Stepping back, I met Greg shortly after he graduated from Texas A&M University with a degree in wildlife science. At the time he referred to himself as a "practicing javelina skinner." (I'll expound on his self-proclaimed moniker a bit later.)

Freshly out of college and recently married, Greg and his wife Deborah moved to San Angelo, Texas. Using their "life savings" and the business plan he had prepared as a college senior, Greg and Deb formed Wildlife Systems, Inc. They invested countless hours, hard work and dedication. In a very few years, Wildlife Systems became one of the most widely known, best managed and highly respected hunting businesses in North America and beyond. It continues to be lauded by hunters, landowners, and wildlife conservationists alike.

There is little having to do with hunting and wildlife conservation, in which Greg has not been professionally involved. Today, he and Wildlife Systems serve as the example of how things should be properly done to create and maintain a highly successful hunting business.

Greg did not stop at creating a highly successful and respected outfitter/guiding business. He and the knowledgeable professionals who work as part of his team establish and maintain quality wildlife management programs on the properties where Wildlife Systems directs the hunting programs. Their programs continually improve the health, quality and variety of wildlife that live on the properties. He and his team of professional guides and camp cooks, continually strive to find ways to improve the outdoor experience for their clients.

Success, in part, comes from paying attention to and handling minor details. Wildlife Systems excels at planning and customer service. Nothing within the team's control is left to chance. The collective goal is putting a smile on every client's face.

While The Hunting Business centers on hunting, wildlife and people, it provides a path to the success of almost any business.

Thankfully Greg has also been an active leader in the wildlife conservation community. He has served as president of the Texas Wildlife Association and the Texas Wildlife Association Foundation, and a member of the Dallas Safari Club board of directors, and on many other wildlife-oriented boards and committees. Because of his expertise in the fields of wildlife conservation and people management, these organizations as well as all wildlife, and, we the people, have greatly benefitted.

Several years ago, Greg told me, "I'm going to write a book about the hunting business to share what I've learned being involved in the best industry in the world."

Periodically, I would ask how the book was coming, to which he replied, "Working on it, but keep learning things I want to include. Bear with me, it will happen." And I knew it would.

Now, it has. Greg has completed his book, the most comprehensive book ever written about the hunting business, which also includes a host of topics beyond day-to-day operations that will likely shape the future of our beloved tradition.

His narrative is neither forced nor dry. It is sprinkled with personal anecdotes, insights and great photographs. The book manages to be enjoyable while expertly covering the hunting business down to the tiniest detail.

The Hunting Business is educational and informational whether you are a hunter, an entrepreneur interested in the hunting business, or someone who simply loves the outdoors and appreciates learning from someone "who has ridden the river."

When Greg asked me to write the foreword, I was honored to the point of being speechless. When I regained my ability to talk and told him what the request meant to me, he replied, "As you know, I'm just a javelina skinner."

He continued, describing a Jeremiah Johnson-esque movie starring him and me. According to his mental screenplay, when we meet for the first time in the film, I ask him, "Can you skin griz, Pilgrim?"

He replies, "No, I skin javelinas."

We meet again 35 years later.

I ask, "Pilgrim, you ever learnt how to skin griz?"

At this point in the movie, he pulls out some javelina jerky, rips off a bite and replies, "Nope, but I've determined them Crows and just about everyone else is scared as hell of a man who makes his living off a javelina."

That, my friend, is Greg Simons.

For all he was, is and will be... for all he has done for wildlife, hunting and wildlife conservation and will continue to do in the future, Greg Simons truly is my hero. After you read what follows, I know he will become your hero as well. Enjoy and learn!

GREG SIMONS

Growing up in a rural household of modest means in Kaufman County, Texas, Greg Simons often dreamed of working in the hunting and wildlife management profession, but he never imagined he would someday own and co-own several successful businesses encompassing so many facets of hunting and conservation. In 1987, immediately after graduating from Texas A&M University with a Wildlife and Fisheries Sciences degree, Simons scraped together a small amount of start-up capital and launched Wildlife Systems, Inc. (WSI). WSI has grown into one of the largest and most recognized outfitting and wildlife-related businesses in the U.S., currently operating hunting programs on almost 1 million acres in Texas. He also co-owns Wildlife Consultants, LLC, which provides wildlife management services to more than 50 private landowners in several states. In 2018, he helped fledge Conservation Equity Partners (CEP), LLC. Currently Simons serves as a principal in CEP, which places large sums private equity into ecosystem service markets including environmental mitigation, forestry management, natural resource-based recreation, and other emerging ESG (Environmental, Social, and Governance) markets.

Previously Simons owned businesses involved with booking agency services for international hunting companies and publishing a hunting magazine. As a freelance contributor, Simons has had over 75 articles published in popular magazines. His work in the wildlife-related field has stretched across 15 states and several foreign countries.

Simons is past president of Texas Wildlife Association and Texas Wildlife Association Foundation, where he still serves on boards for both organizations. He is currently on the board for Dallas Safari Club, National Deer Association, and serves on appointed advisory committees for Texas Parks and Wildlife Department as well as Texas A&M University's Rangeland, Wildlife, and Fisheries Department. Simons is a past officer of Texas Chapter of The Wildlife Society, past board chair for San Angelo Convention and Visitor's Bureau, and served on the board for San Angelo Chamber of Commerce. He co-founded the West Texas Deer Study Group. He has also served on many other appointed boards and committees as well as being active in the public policy arena, where he works with elected officials and lobbyists helping to shape state and federal legislation and testifying when needed.

Few people have crossed over between commercial hunting and natural resource conservation as broadly and successfully as Simons, while also actively donating time and money to help support causes important to him personally and professionally. While he is entering the twilight of his professional life, Simons' appetite for civic engagement and professional achievement remains strong and his commitment to serving as an advocate for wild things and wild places is unwavering. *The Hunting Business* is offered as the capstone of Simons' career.

INTRODUCTION

The Hunting Business was originally intended to serve as a signature on my life's work in the hunting and wildlife business. Along the way, I found myself trying to create a book that would not only be a tool for those interested in the business side of hunting but would also appeal to other interests as well. I was also compelled to share my thoughts about the direction we, as a community of hunters, and as professionals trying scratch out a living in this industry, appear to be heading.

Some of my information is expected boilerplate material, while other parts of the book are esoteric or perhaps philosophical. I included plenty of personal anecdotes and select photographs to help illustrate various points and add to the information's impact. The book is intended to be more than a "how to" book. I am unaware of any other book that takes such as deep-dive look at the many facets (and some of the weird nuances) that make the hunting business like no other.

The first chapter is titled, "There's No Business Like the Hunting Business," and there's not. Some features of the hunting business fit within the standard sideboards of most other businesses, regardless of the industry, but there are many unique characteristics that add strange dimensions to this complex business. I hope that *The Hunting Business* does a reasonable job of identifying and explaining many of these features.

Good, bad, or otherwise (and I could pro and con it either way), my experience of being an entrepreneur from the day I graduated from Texas A&M, inspired me to share some thoughts that are relevant to most business start-ups. As a result, some sections apply to most entrepreneurs, business owners, managers, and professionals regardless of their field. I do not claim to be the brightest business person, but I've worked with and around many who are. Our association has served as a great learning platform where I have gleaned invaluable pieces of knowledge. Ultimately this knowledge, shaped my business practices and philosophies, many of which I have woven into the fabric of this book.

The hunting industry in the U.S. has a glaring need for businesses that are operated with excellence. On many occasions over the years, I've mentioned that people tend to get into the hunting business for the wrong reasons, which often leads to proprietors who cut corners and ignore basic business principles. In some cases, this lack of applied business sense can be attributed to owners who have not done their basic homework before launching a business, while in other cases, the proprietor lacks business savvy and is unaware of the need to build core business principles into the new company's normal operating procedures. A portion of this book is intended to create convenient touchstones that anyone who is embarking on a career in this field can use as compass points as they navigate their way through the fundamental and subtle, unique challenges that characterize this business.

The U.S. hunting industry is also plagued by a lack of professionalism. Some of the information found in *The Hunting Business* is my attempt to provide proven information for hunting professionals who want to implement best management practices in order to raise their businesses to new heights of professionalism. This is the information that I would have loved to have had when I was fledging and growing my business in the late 1980s.

Much of *The Hunting Business* examines the basic mechanics of operating a business in this space. If this book helps rookie outfitters and guides avoid basic mistakes by shining the light on the fundamental aspects of the business, then that's a great win. I also hope that veterans who have been involved with this industry for many years will appreciate the detail that I have put into certain portions of this book, as they, more than anyone, understand the challenges associated with consistently producing quality experiences for hunting clients.

Those who know me well, know that I have a philosophical side. I have included some thought-provoking material in this book because I think all professionals, regardless of their chosen field, are well-served to force themselves to think deeply on a regular basis. Whether such deep thinking involves introspection, spending time exploring management-oriented solutions, or reflection on life's subtleties, it is healthy for everyone to explore their deep mental and emotional capacities. Along those lines, Chapter 18, titled the Eight M's of Hunting, is an esoteric look at elements that make hunting unique and important. Some will appreciate this chapter more than others, but I hope that many of you will relate to this portion of the book in a meaningful way and find that it adds value to the scope of the work.

In business and in life, there is no replacement for trial and error. With more than 36 years of experience in the hunting business, time has taught me the importance of constant adaptation as I try to stay at the tip of the spear in business strategy. I think it is human nature to become more entrenched in our ways as we age, but a paradoxical truism is that many of successful veteran business owners also recognize the need to adapt to changing times.

The material I built into this book is not beyond reproach and is also subject to the influence of changing times. And times are changing more rapidly today than ever. The COVID pandemic, alone, has been a huge change-agent. Societies around the globe have connected and reconnected to the outdoor world in ways that would have been hard to anticipate during pre-COVID periods. Only time will tell if the effects of the pandemic triggered a permanent paradigm shift and heightened appreciation of the outdoor world. Regardless, I feel we are on the frontend of the most profound environmental movement that this planet has ever witnessed. Emerging ESG (environmental, social, and governance) pressures alone are forces that seem undeniable. With ESG, societal expectations will define practices that are deemed acceptable as well as those that are not. How will these ESG pressures influence hunters and hunting? How will these pressures impact the hunting business? I do not claim to have those answers, but I am confident that as a community of hunters, we must learn to play the game smarter if we are to remain relevant and prevent from having the life squeezed from its already frail body. With these evolving demands, it is even more urgent that the hunting industry refine its business practices to stay within the parameters of the day's new norms. We have proven to ourselves that activities and values that do not cleanly fit within the tolerances of mainstream USA will eventually run their course and pass from the scene like dinosaurs.

One of the chapters explores the role that NGOs play in hunting and wildlife conservation. In my opinion, efforts to play the game smarter must begin with the vast number of conservation/hunting groups that are out there. I currently serve on boards of three premier conservation groups and I hope that my experience across these organizations allows me to eventually better understand how the NGO community can do a better job of leveraging their efforts, creating synergies and ultimately becoming a stronger voice for hunting and conservation.

I struggled with the closing chapter, "The Future of Hunting." Finding words to adequately put a bow on the book project was a bit more difficult than I anticipated. As you might expect, I wanted my closing messages to be strong and thought-provoking, especially as things relate to my "crystal ball" projections of where we appear to be headed as a hunting community. This alone forced me to be more discerning and demanding as I worked to capture and express my thoughts clearly.

Another thing that made this chapter so challenging was the fact that things are changing so rapidly these days—regionally, nationally, and globally. Trying to rationalize and understand such dynamic times, times that are profoundly affected by so many conflicting pressures and resulting pressure points, and then anticipate what all of this will look like as we work our way into the future, is tricky to say the least. I would like to think that the future represents plenty of sunny slopes and green pastures for hunters and hunting, but there are certain shadows in tea leaves that are concerning. Only time will tell.

I hope that you will find *The Hunting Business* to be a useful resource. But, most importantly for me, I hope that you will find this book to be an enjoyable read and that you will find pleasure and adventure as you work your way through the book. It was a monumental, marathon undertaking from start to finish, but I am pleased that I completed this journey. I am grateful that you have taken the time to travel alongside me through these pages and share my life's work in the hunting business.

MARLIN, MAYODAN, NC · USA

THERE'S NO BUSINESS LIKE THE HUNTING BUSINESS

1

YOUNG PROFESSIONALS NEED MENTORS.
I WAS FORTUNATE TO HAVE SEVERAL KEY
PEOPLE WHO HELPED SHAPED MY CAREER
DURING ITS FORMATIVE STAGES.

OPPOSITE
Dave Frankfenfield
1992 Mule Deer
Las Animas County, Colorado
Guide - Greg Simons

One such individual was Dick Laros from Allentown, Pennsylvania. Becoming friends with him is a remarkable story, and one of good luck and great fortune for me.

I founded Wildlife Systems, Inc. (WSI) in 1987, shortly after graduating from Texas A&M University with a Wildlife and Fisheries Sciences degree. During the business's first year, I focused on developing hunting programs that centered on seasonal leases as well as inexpensive day hunts, such as one-day dove hunts. In the 1980s, fee-based hunting programs underwent a huge shift. The industry transitioned at providing access and perhaps rudimentary lodging to a service-based industry that offered fully-outfitted packages, including guiding, meals, comfortable lodging, and other amenities. I'm not saying that outfitted package hunting programs did not exist prior to the 1980s, but it was during that era that the inertia behind commercial hunting programs put stronger legs under outfitted hunts across the country and globally.

Initially, I began the business in the North Texas area around Albany and Breckenridge. In April 1988, my then new bride, Deborah, and I moved to San Angelo. At that point, I decided that I wanted to dabble with offering some outfitted hunts. At that time, WSI had no customer base, but I knew America's East Coast was home to many hunters who actively traveled abroad and spent large sums of money on their hunting trips. Not knowing where to start, I decided that having an outdoor writer from the East Coast attend one our WSI hunts would be a good way to get some attention through a publication.

I was unsure of who to contact, so I called the Philadelphia Chamber of Commerce and asked what the largest newspaper in Philly was. It was the Philadelphia Inquirer. Next, I called the daily paper's main number and asked who the outdoor columnist was. The receptionist patched me through to Ben Callaway, who covered that particular beat at that time. Cutting to the chase, I explained to Callaway that I was new to the hunting business and wondered if he might have some interest in coming down on a white-tailed deer hunt in exchange for providing a newspaper article. Callaway was accommodating. In his pleasant voice, he explained that there were internal newspaper policies that prohibited him from accepting my offer. However, he kindly provided me with the names and phone numbers of three other Pennsylvanians: a booking agent, a freelance outdoor writer, and a taxidermist. (Yes, I know, this sounds like the start of an Aggie joke, right?)

My first call was to Jim McCarthy, a well-established booking agent from the Harrisburg area. Jim was all business and, in a matter-of-fact tone, he promptly told me that he did not represent any outfitters who he did not know. He was direct and cold. My next call was to Jim Fitser, a freelance writer, who was also from Pennsylvania. The conversation was similar in tone and content to the earlier one I had with McCarthy. Fitser explained it was somewhat unethical for an outfitter to offer a writer a free hunt in exchange for some positive press. He went on to explain such a "free hunt" arrangement might yield some coverage and it might not. I still remember thinking that if I was going to give away a free deer hunt, then I darn well should get an article out of it. When I hung up the phone with Jim Fitser, I will admit that I had tucked my tail a bit. Two cold calls and two strikeouts.

ABOVE > I credit much of WSI's success to the close relationship I developed with Norma and Dick Laros approximately one year after forming the company. Fledgling entrepreneurs are well-served to have mentors they can rely on for advice, counseling, and inspiration.

Sheepishly, I made the third call to Dick Laros, the taxidermist on my list. In addition to owning Laros Taxidermy Studio in Allentown, Pennsylvania, he was also the proprietor of the Lehigh Valley Outdoor Expo Sports Show and an "informal" booking agent, who, for many years, sent hunters abroad on various excursions. On the other end of the phone, I found a warm, inviting person who I connected with immediately. After talking with him for about 30 minutes, Dick told me that he had never hunted in Texas and that he would love to do so. He also volunteered to put together a group to come hunt with WSI and gave me the option of discounting his hunt if I wanted to. And so, the foundation of an amazing relationship was laid. Our friendship lasted until his death in February 2016, 28 years after our first conversation. Although my first two calls were strikeouts, the third call was a grand slam that forever changed my life.

Not long after our initial visit, Dick offered to host a social for me at his house so I could visit with some of his clients. My dad and mom, who were active in my business then, and I made the long drive to Pennsylvania. I met with some hunters who would later book a hunt with us that fall. More importantly, I immediately bonded with Dick and his wife, Norma, forging a relationship that grew into deep, lasting friendship. Over the years, I personally guided them on more than 50 hunting trips in Texas, Colorado, Oklahoma, and Alabama.

By the time Dick and Norma arrived for their first hunt with me, which was a whitetail hunt on the Butterfield Peak Ranch in Coke County, Texas, I had realized that Dick was a real pioneer and a well-respected person in the hunting industry. As you might expect, I was looking forward to learning as much as I could while he was on his inaugural hunt with WSI.

On perhaps the second day of the hunt, Dick and I were sitting on a hillside overlooking a flat during the early afternoon, waiting for deer activity to begin. I was doing my darnedest to glean as much knowledge as I could from this gentleman who had so much to offer, and Dick was kind enough to oblige. After a somewhat extended Q&A session, Dick looked me in the eye and said, "Listen son, there's no business like the hunting business!" He then went back to scanning the flats with his binoculars while I sat there waiting for more of an explanation. In retrospect, I think he intentionally left me hanging after he made that comment because he wanted me to figure much of "it" out on my own. Over the next 28 years, we spent a lot of time discussing the fact that "there's no business like the hunting business" and examining what makes this business so peculiar.

Over the years, I have spent an immense amount of time reflecting on why the hunting business is unique and, perhaps more importantly, how its atypical features can be leveraged to help ensure an enterprise's success. I have given presentations at field days and conferences on this topic; it is an annual discussion at our WSI in-service meeting, and I occasionally add my reflections to conversations that center on the business side of hunting. While I certainly do not claim to fully understand the peculiar nature of this crazy business, I am going to share some of my thoughts on why "there's no business like the hunting business."

UNIQUELY DIFFERENT EXPECTATIONS

When a television is purchased, consumers' expectations are relatively narrow, based on the price they paid for it and how they anticipate it will perform. If the remote control works and the audio and visual are reasonably good, the consumer is generally happy with the product. When people buy a gun, if it functions as advertised and shoots well, the owners will normally feel that they got what they paid for. Typically, restaurant patrons are happy if the food tastes good, is served hot, and the service is reasonably good because that is what they expect.

One of the complex features of outfitting is that all people who book hunts have a broad—and likely different—set of expectations for the hunting experience based on the price and the elements they are anticipating.

As you can see from these questions (and this is just a small sampling), the features that comprise a client's expectations are almost endless. Trying to cater to all these unique expectations can be challenging. It becomes even more difficult if the business is hosting a large mixed group. While it can be tempting to try to tailor services to each individual in the group, this strategy carries an inherent risk: some clients may feel as if some other clients are receiving preferential treatment.

My best advice? Develop a customer service strategy that recognizes the unique expectations of every client but balances them against the need for services to be delivered consistently and equitably. In other words, address the expectations of each client to the best of your ability, but do not compromise the process that is structured around the greater good of the overall group.

VARIABILITY OF CLIENT EXPECTATIONS

- What is the weather going to be like? How many deer will they see on an average day?

- What size buck might they take?

- Will they have to sit around camp during the remainder of the hunt if they kill the first day?

- What will the meals be like, and will the food meet their special dietary restrictions?

- Will their guide be friendly and accommodating?

- How much experience does their guide have?

- How much should they tip the guide and cook?

- What will the other hunters in camp be like, and will everyone get along?

- How will they get their meat home?

- Should they use the outfitter's taxidermist, or will the outfitter be able to ship their trophy to their taxidermist back home?

- Should they bring their own liquor?

- Will the outfitter allow them to have a cold beer at lunch if the hunt is still in progress?

- Will they have to do much walking, or will the physical demands be minimal?

- Will sleeping space be shared? If so, will the other hunters snore loudly?

LOOMING PERILS

Each year at our WSI in-service meeting, I always make it a point to say, "There are certain mistakes that we cannot afford to make. Otherwise, it may cost someone their life." This is a harsh statement, but the hunting business is fraught with risks and perilous liabilities. The risks come in many shapes and sizes, including food allergies that may result in something of minor discomfort to something life-threating. Then there are the obvious potential risks, such as firearm accidents, venomous snakes and bugs, walking in the dark across broken terrain, fatigued guides shuttling clients to and from the airport during early or late hours, ATVs, horses, knives and other sharp tools, loading heavy dead animals onto truck beds, consumption of alcoholic beverages, disputes and frustrations, gas leaks in cabins, and aggressive livestock. And the list goes on. Unlike some other businesses, putting a sound risk management plan in place is essential in the hunting business.

EMOTIONS

Make no mistake about it, when it comes to issues relating to hunting and wildlife, emotions can ramp up quickly. This human dimension of the hunting business is an amazing feature. According to human behavioral scientist E.O. Wilson, people have biophilic tendencies, meaning we are hardwired to want to connect to other living creatures, such as wildlife, domestic livestock, and pets. Additionally, our modern human DNA was shaped by the success of our hunter-gatherer ancestors. In my opinion, most humans desire a personal connection to wildlife and hunting. This inherent desire often prompts heightened emotions in hunting-related matters.

These hunting-related emotions are expressed in a variety of ways. In the case of the actual harvest, the emotions may range from euphoria to sadness and remorse. Sometimes the emotions are cloaked in opinions on hunting strategies that directly conflict with their guide or differing opinions related to the hunting weapons of choice, such as bows versus centerfire rifles. Emotions spill out in discussions between those who hunt and those who do not. Discussions between hunters on equitable allocation of game resources and inequitable access can become fraught with emotion.

An outfitter's support team should be trained to anticipate and handle this human dimension of the business without getting too emotionally charged themselves. Embracing and nurturing the joy is fun and important, but be prepared to work objectively and calmly through the more volatile and challenging side of situations. Effectively working through the emotional spectrum is equally—and oftentimes more important when it comes to customer service strategies as it is when placing the client in a position to take a quality animal or collect a bag limit of birds.

INTIMATE INTERFACE

The hunting industry is one of the very few businesses where a client and vendor share a protracted, personal interaction. The outfitter's staff essentially lives with the client for several days, or perhaps even weeks on some of the international hunts.

In the hunting business, the vendor takes care of the meals, looks after the safety and well-being of clients, provides entertainment, and supports the guides whose workmanship and technical assistance undergird the entire endeavor. Camp staff, on all levels, provide "listening ears" and act as friends and often confidants

so clients can vent and get things off their chests. Hunting guides often wear many different hats in their seemingly straightforward job. Camp staffers must bring their A-games, especially when dealing with difficult clients. In addition, they must perform well, even if they are tired, which, thanks to a hunting camp's typically long hours, is often. All while consciously managing their own emotions.

As Benjamin Franklin once said, "Guests, like fish, begin to smell after three days." Most hunting packages are at least three days long and many are longer. The extended "forced togetherness" of a hunting trip can create its own brand of "weirdness." There is no doubt the vendors and their people will make an impression on the clients. Hunters walk away from their trips with personal opinions and impressions about the staff, the hunting, and the overall outfit. From the staff's perspective, the key is to learn how to gauge the clients' reactions during the hunt and channel their energy into a productive exchange that benefits the clients and, ultimately, the enterprise.

LETTING THEIR HAIR DOWN

Outfitters and their staff see the sides of people that are often not on display in other aspects of the clients' lives. When people choose to remove their masks, it can be a bit unpredictable. Some clients decide to cut loose and party, while others may morph into greedy "game hogs," and still others may become more introspective, caring, and empathetic.

TOP-LEFT > Focusing on the details under one's control, such as the cleanliness of facilities and the quality of food, is the basis for ensuring great outcomes in hunting camps.

TOP-RIGHT > Uncontrollable variables, such as vehicle issues, can present frustrating challenges for guides and outfitters. African Professional Hunters (PH) set the industry standard when it comes to resourcefulness and capabilities in the face of unpredictable problems.

As many of my industry colleagues have noted, we get to see people's "true colors" when we take them hunting. If the clients' behavior is harmless, friendly, and fun, then camp staff can just sit back and enjoy the interaction. If, on the other hand, the behavior is somewhat dangerous, destructive, or threatens to drown the camp in negativity, the staff must adapt and actively try to steer the behavior toward a positive outcome.

I suspect that I am not the only hunter who has witnessed behavior change during an outing. You do not have to be a professional outfitter to see people transform drastically in a hunting camp or when they have a gun in their hands in the field. After all these years, I continue to find this phenomenon fascinating.

UNCONTROLLABLE VARIABLES

One of the hunting business' more frustrating aspects is the large number of variables that are, for the most part, outside of the outfitter's control. For instance, weather, not just during the hunt but events such as drought or floods that take place months prior to the hunt, can affect antler production and the nesting success of game birds. For guides, it can be extremely frustrating to present opportunities to clients who are unable to harvest the animals. The chemistry between the people in the camp is mainly beyond the outfitter's control. Unusual dietary needs, delayed flights, lost luggage, unreasonable or unmanageable clients, and even bad luck are all uncontrollable variables.

Not a single feature that I have discussed in this chapter makes the hunting business extraordinarily difficult, but when all these aspects are combined, they create a dynamic and complex business framework that can be challenging. From my perspective, the outfitters who are most successful in the industry focus on variables that are within their control and stay flexible to address the variables beyond their control. It would be maddening to get too caught up in the uncontrollable; it will waste valuable time and yield more frustration than results. Maintain perspective; try to see the big picture, all while realizing that details matter. As I have often said, there are easier ways to make a buck than outfitting or guiding. Many individuals who venture into the hunting business end up miscalculating the inherent challenges, and some just get into this business for all the wrong reasons. The hunting business is like the proverbial onion: as you peel back layers, you discover features not apparent from the outside.

Of course, hunting has a romantic allure. Almost any outdoor-oriented person who ever read a well-written adventure story about a hunter packing into the wilderness to pursue elk or grizzlies or got lost in one of Robert Ruark's stories about tracking Cape buffalo through the African mopane shrublands has entertained the notion of becoming a professional hunter or an outfitter. Some countries in Africa have enjoyed the safari industry for more than 50 years. Because of the maturity and the structure of those industries, aspiring outdoorsmen in Africa can consider a possible career as a professional hunter with some sense of confidence in their ability to make a successful go of it.

Due to a variety of pressures and circumstances entering the guiding and outfitting business in the U.S., there has never been a "safe bet" in terms of developing a lifelong career. Domestically, those who find success and long-term satisfaction in the hunting business are often individuals who work part-time or seasonally, or they are retirees with a nest egg or pension plan who opt to work as a guide to keep busy. Not to say that there are not opportunities for someone in the U.S. to solely focus on guiding and outfitting as a lifelong profession, because there are plenty of people who have done so successfully. But I will say it again, there are easier ways to make a living.

As I will expand upon in greater detail in the final chapter, the heyday of outfitted hunting is likely behind us. With that said, there are still years of good opportunity ahead. In recent years, the international pressures

on hunting have diminished what was once considered robust hunting opportunities in many international locales. Because of society's changing values and the loss of wildlife habitat to development, it is all we can do, as they say in tennis, to "hold serve" here in the U.S. and elsewhere.

Despite the innumerable challenges that characterize this business, I have found immense pleasure in working as an outfitter for my entire professional life, 36 years and counting. While I would like to think that I have sorted out most of the pitfalls for succeeding in this business, I, on occasion, get stumped. I will admit that my patience comes and goes.

As I proceed along my professional path, perhaps entering the twilight of my career, I find great pleasure in reflecting on all of the trials, tribulations, and good times that I encountered along the way. I occasionally ask myself, "If I had a second chance, would I follow the same path?" Honestly, I am not sure. But one thing is for certain, as my mentor Dick Laros would say, "There's no business like the hunting business."

ABOVE > While memories of successful hunts, as demonstrated by this magnificent mule deer taken by Dick Laros, characterized our relationship, a single statement made by Laros on our first hunt in 1988 stayed with me and shaped my career. Laros opined, "There's no business like the hunting business." And, indeed, there is not.

2 THE VENUE

THE LAND ON WHICH COMMERCIAL HUNTING PROGRAMS TAKE PLACE GENERALLY SHAPES MANY OF THE OPERATION'S FEATURES.

For the start-up hunting business entrepreneur, this aspect of the fledgling business may be the most difficult part of the process. In order to be successful, the hunting proprietor must have access to an amount of land that will support a certain level of hunting activity at both an ecologically and economically sustainable threshold. It comes down to simple math based on acreage and game numbers.

Depending upon the game species of interest, along with a few other variables, the amount of acreage required to meet client volume goals can vary greatly. On what many call "game farms" or "game preserves," where animals are released onto the property and hunted that season or that year, the amount of acreage necessary may be smaller than on properties where the surplus animals available for harvest are naturally produced. (The next chapter takes a deeper look at some of the differences between low-fenced properties, high-fenced properties, and game farms.) Wild game populations can only produce a limited number of surplus animals and remain sustainable. If proprietors need to increase their hunter volume to maintain business viability, the hunting area's scale becomes a consideration.

Though a considerable amount of hunting (in the U.S. and elsewhere) takes place on public lands, much of this book is focused on operations that are tied to privately-owned lands. With that said, I have included some information in this chapter that touches on some proprietary features of public-lands hunting operations.

PRIVATE LANDS
OWNED

Private landowners, whose families have owned the land for several generations and continue to actively farm and ranch their properties to generate income, tend to view their game resources as an alternative cash crop. Because these landowners rely on the land's yield to generate a profit and, perhaps, to support their families, they are often resourceful and thrifty. Historically, these landowners saw their game resources as a potential secondary source of income, but did not emphasize game management to develop them.

The landowner culture has changed over the last 20 to 30 years as agricultural profit margins have shrunk continuously. Now, landowners who own property in game-rich areas are actively looking for ways to manage their wildlife as the value of these resources has increased during this time. In many cases, these landowners consider hunting to be a profitable resource equating to, or more than, traditional agriculture. The paradigm has shifted. On many ranches, game now is as important, or even more important, than livestock.

Then there are "new" landowners who have purchased rural ranches or farms in recent years primarily for recreation. Lands with good wildlife potential are especially appealing to these new landowners. Generally, these new landowners do not buy their properties planning to host commercial hunts, but as the economic realities of land ownership set in, it is not terribly uncommon for some to look for alternative income streams to defray or offset operational expenses. Hunting is a viable alternative. In this case, fee-based hunting programs tend to be an afterthought.

Regardless of the length of ownership, the obvious advantages for owners who run commercial hunts on their own property is the avoidance of the annual financial burden of leasing land to obtain hunting rights.

Additionally, proprietors operating on their own land are not at the mercy of a potentially fickle landlord who may decide to not renew their hunting lease. Sometimes landlords change the rules after the deal has been struck, which can be frustrating and costly. Hunting proprietors who own their own land are also more likely to invest in significant capital improvements because they are able to benefit from these investments in a broader way than a lessee. This is particularly true of permanent improvements such as lodging.

One of the downsides of running a commercial hunting operation on land that you own yourself is the fact that the business is limited to the game species and the game populations available on that location. Furthermore, the scale of the operation is proportional to the size of the property, so if the proprietors want to continue to grow the operations, then they may be forced to lease other land or work as a third-party contractor with other landowners. Most outfitters who own hunting lands do not have enough acreage to grow their business to a larger scale, so as their hunting clientele grows, they need access to more acreage.

Ironically, when operating fee-based hunting programs on land owned by several family members, it can be a struggle to maintain harmony. It is common for various family members to have different values and ideas about hunting on those properties. Sometimes certain family members may want to retain some hunting privileges for themselves and perhaps their guests, while other family members may want to maximize the potential income potential by capitalizing on all hunting activities on that property. The process of resolving such disparities among family members can be arduous and can tax family members' relationships, so it's not uncommon for such families to seek third-party assistance to help work through such divisive circumstances.

I was recently retained by a family to serve as a mediator to resolve an inner-family conflict. The mediation yielded an operating agreement that provided a frame of reference to help resolve any disagreements on how the livestock and hunting operations were to be run. This kind of family turmoil, which can become polarizing and emotional, can occasionally result in legal proceedings and partitioning of family-owned properties. I anticipate that conflicts between family members on how to operate their ranches and monetize these resources will continue to become more common as there is a growing disparity in lifestyles among family members who live on the land versus those who are absent. Different experiences and expectations affect value-driven ideas on how to operate these properties.

ABOVE > Around the globe, much of the finest hunting takes place on privately owned lands. Although some hunters, especially those who live in places with deep public-lands hunting cultures, are offended by landowners charging access fees for hunting on their land, private landowners often hold the key to diverse wildlife habitat and sustainable wildlife populations.

HELPFUL CONSIDERATIONS ON FAMILY-OWNED, FAMILY OPERATED HUNTING PROPERTIES

HUNTING PRIVILEGES

If certain hunting privileges are going to be retained by family members, then these should be clearly identified and understood by everyone involved. Please note, perceptions of inequity arise when it comes to these types of family business details and decisions.

OPERATING AGREEMENT

Create an operating agreement that clearly outlines the vision for the hunting program, including who is responsible for various duties, functions, and financial obligations, how profits will be dispersed, and how disputes will be addressed.

FAMILY BOARD

While it may be perceived as too formal for families who equate casual dealings as a sign of a strong family relationship, creating a family board that is made up of appointed family members, and perhaps at least one non-family member, can be a logical, objective way to vet issues and to make decisions that hopefully are good for the whole family. This board-governed approach appears to be more common on larger properties with more assets, but I have seen this management structure work on smaller properties as well.

BUSINESS ENTITY

Forming a business entity that serves as an operating corporation or company is common with family-owned properties.

LEASED HUNTING RIGHTS

When a family member is granted the hunting rights to the property or is designated as the hunting operations proprietor, it is common for that family member to lease the hunting rights from the family-owned company or to pay a percentage to the company for those rights. The family member with those rights is treated as a third-party contractor or tenant. This can be a reasonable way to keep things clean and to approach these family matters in a businesslike fashion.

CONFLICTING INTERESTS

It is wise to recognize that when mixing recreational pleasure with business, there is an inherent possibility of conflicting interests.

THIRD-PARTY EXPERTS

When it becomes obvious that there are potential disagreements between family members on the structure and operation of a family-owned hunting program, I suggest enlisting a third-party expert to help guide discussions and assist with constructing an operational plan. Using an objective third party can help prevent soured family relationships while also giving direct access to an experienced professional who may be able to provide information to help make smart decisions.

PRIVATE LANDS
LEASED

For people who do not own land but are interested in offering commercial hunting opportunities on private land, the primary option is to secure hunting rights on a landowner's property. I am most familiar with this arrangement and have worked with more than 100 landowners during the last 33 years. I currently offer fee-based hunting opportunities on approximately 1,000,000 acres, involving approximately 25 landowners.

Our company spends approximately $1.5 million annually securing hunting rights on these lands, so the lease costs to operate on a large-scale in this business can be significant. Regardless of the size of the financial commitment, any outfitter is well-serviced to make sure that their deal structure with their landowner(s) is sound and well thought out.

ABOVE > Healthy, long-term relationships between outfitters and landowners hinge on many variables including best practice standards where the operation is run like business.

AN OUTFITTER SHOULD CONSIDER MANY THINGS WHEN SECURING HUNTING RIGHTS FROM A LANDOWNER AND BUILDING THE RESULTING HUNTING PROGRAM

LEASE DOCUMENTS

I continue to work with many landowners where the basis of our arrangement is essentially a handshake. However, best practices should include some form of a written agreement that covers the most important features of the deal, which should include the following:

- Name of parties included in the agreement

- Equipment and facility use provisions

- Description of the area

- Harvest allocations or hunter number restrictions

- Lease rate or fee schedules

- Client protection clause or non-compete

- Rules and conditions

- Term of the agreement

- Waiver of liability

These hunting agreements are rarely used during legal proceedings. However, recording certain details can serve as a valuable frame of reference should there be any disputes or uncertainties. It is not common for such documents to be notarized or witnessed, but signatures by both parties are customary.

Email history can also be a useful frame of reference if there are questions or uncertainties. The focus here is preventing simple misunderstandings from clouding an otherwise friendly and functional relationship.

A CLOSER LOOK

1) DESCRIPTION OF AREA

Occasionally this provision may be more important than initially believed. It is not unusual for certain pastures, specific items, or areas of a facility to be excluded as part of the agreement. To avoid misunderstandings, it is helpful to have sufficient descriptive details under this agreement provision.

2) HARVEST ALLOCATIONS AND HUNTER NUMBER RESTRICTIONS

The details of this provision are especially important so that both parties understand the harvest or hunting pressure restrictions. It is also not unusual for some big game species to have harvest allocations with restrictions on the number of animals taken and also the size and age of those animals.

On properties where the landowner is actively managing the wildlife resource, the parameters defining these harvest allocations become more imperative and more descriptive. One "sleight of hand" to be aware of is allowances that relate to "number of hunters" versus "number of animals." Some outfitters "recycle" spots when a hunter does not shoot the primary animal of interest. When this happens, the outfitter may resell that spot later, which may or may not be consistent with the spirit of the allowance within the agreement. This is one of the agreement's finer features that needs to be fully explored by both parties to avoid misunderstandings.

3) FEE SCHEDULES

The financial arrangements between outfitters and landowners can vary immensely. In arrangements where there is an agreed-upon annual lease fee, it is customary for 50 percent of those fees to be paid in the spring, usually March or April, with the balance being due just prior to the start of the fall

"""

hunting season. In arrangements where the outfitter is paying per hunter or per animal, those fees are often due within seven to ten days of the hunt's completion. Each deal can be different, but having a clear understanding of the fee structure and the payment schedule is important. When it comes to the money end of business deals, people are highly focused on complying and making good on one's commitment or obligation, so honoring the deal in this category is super important.

4) CLIENT PROTECTION CLAUSES

It is not unusual for some type of client protection clause to be built into the agreement that guards against clients being "poached" from the outfitter by the landowner. Some outfitters invest a great deal of money and spend years developing client portfolios. Regardless of the reason, if the business relationship between the outfitter and landowner ceases, it occasionally can be a "natural progression" for the landowner to solicit the outfitter's clients who have hunted the property and carry forward with the hunting operations by tapping into the market that is already developed and most convenient. For an outfitter who has lost access to a property "for no good reason," this can be incredibly frustrating. I have personally experienced this on multiple occasions. At a minimum, it creates heartburn and can, on rare occasion, result in legal action depending upon the client protection clauses included in the agreement.

5) RULES AND CONDITIONS

To ensure that all parties are on the same page, it is wise to define in detail and in writing who is responsible for what, the provisions included, etc. Some of the details that need to be discussed and spelled out may include costs for utilities, lodge cleaning, equipment maintenance, and game feed as well as various other details such as muddy road use, campfire acceptability/guidelines, guide access prior to hunts, pet provisions, and artifact collecting.

6) TERMS AND TERM PRESSURES

Most term arrangements between outfitters and landowners are typically one to three years, with five years being considered long. Regardless of the agreement's terms, the business deal between a landowner and outfitter is only going to remain in place if the relationship lasts. Thus, it is imperative that both parties feel comfortable with one another before commencing with the business deal while also working at maintaining a good relationship through the process.

When they grant the outfitters and their hunters unsupervised access to their cherished private property, many landowners feel vulnerable. Likewise, outfitters are taking a leap of faith by trusting that if they provide an honest and successful effort to build a quality hunting program on their landlord's property, the landowner will honor the deal and not undercut the outfitter's efforts and investments by "stealing" the outfitter's clients or voiding the contract for frivolous, capricious reasons.

While there is an endless supply of egregious examples of outfitters taking advantage of landowners and vice versa, there is an equal number of examples of productive and friendly relationships between landowners and outfitters. I have been working with one family for 32 years, another for 24 years, and several others for more than ten years. Long-term relationships are possible when people are honest and are willing to adapt when necessary, with adapting and flexing often being a key ingredient in relationship life. One of the key ingredients is making sure that all parties are compatible and are in sync from the beginning of the business venture, setting forth a smooth path and then nurturing the relationship as things move along.

7) LIABILITY INSURANCE REQUIREMENTS

In today's litigious world, it is not unusual for the landowner to require that the tenant or outfitter carry a certain amount of insurance coverage. The landowner can often be added as an additional insured for little or no extra expense beyond the normal premium. Many landowners often carry their own farm and ranch coverage, but upon close examination, these policies generally exclude the activities and risks that are directly tied to commercial hunting practices, thus leaving landowners more exposed than they prefer. (hunting insurance is covered in more detail in the "Risk Management" chapter.)

PUBLIC LANDS

Admittedly, I do not have any personal experience developing or operating commercial hunting operations on public lands, but there are some generalities that apply in this arena. Very few commercial hunting programs exist on public lands in Texas. However, there are many enterprises that have been in place for decades in some western states where national forests and Bureau of Land Management lands abound as well as in many foreign countries, including Canada and several African countries.

Here in the U.S., the largest obstacle regarding outfitting on public lands is understanding the permit and registration requirements at either the state or federal levels. On public lands, outfitters must often navigate more regulatory hurdles, so understanding these regulations is necessary for proprietors to effectively and legally operate within a strict framework. Tutoring from a seasoned outfitter with experience in a region can shorten the learning curve, while some of the basic information can be acquired through simple internet searches.

Compliance standards that allow an outfitter to legally provide commercial hunting services on public lands vary between the jurisdictional ownership of those lands. The majority of outfitters will, at a minimum, be required to carry certain limits of insurance and bonding. Certain states may also require state outfitter registration to outfit on those lands.

Land-use fees will typically be required, but these fees are generally significantly less than the costs associated with obtaining hunting rights on private lands. In addition to user fees, outfitters may also be required to pay a site reservation fee for reserved campsites that ensure exclusive use of the sites, and may also be required to pay grazing fees for transport and pack animals such as horses or mules.

Outfitting on public lands can be unpredictable due to the institutional bureaucracy, which varies

from state to state and can differ between individual regulators who hold the same or similar positions. As a result, the way governing regulations are administered can be inconsistent. Regulations may be changed, voided or new ones added at any time, which can add a level of uncertainty and frustration for the hunting proprietor.

Though circumstances can vary, one of the other downsides for outfitters who are operating on public lands is the lack of control over who is hunting those lands concurrently with the outfitter and his clients. It can be almost impossible to coordinate all hunting activities on those shared areas, which can then create frustrating interruptions in the client's hunting experience. In the past, outfitters often accessed the more remote areas of these lands to escape the crowds making the experience more peaceful and enjoyable. These days, it is common to find other hunters who are hunting on their own using the same strategies of accessing these remote locations, which makes it less likely to find secluded places where the hunting may be better.

In addition to the challenges of overcrowding and lack of coordination, there are also resource management issues associated with what is commonly called the "tragedy of the commons," as described by Garrett Hardin in his 1968 article of that name. According to the philosophy of the commons, there exists a tendency for humans to act independently of one another in a system of shared resources and for those shared resources to eventually be depleted due to the inherent tendency of individuals to act in their own self-interest, taking whatever they need or want without regard for anyone else or the sustainability of the resource. This self-centered approach creates user patterns that are not good for the whole.

Certainly, state or federal regulations can create a regulatory framework that is intended to help manage these "shared" game resources on public lands. Nonetheless, the agency management culture and the land-use system are generally not as conducive for quality game management on public lands as those management systems on private lands, where both the quality of the habitat and the harvest are more controlled.

LOW FENCES, HIGH FENCES AND GAME FARMS

3

FOR HUNDREDS OF YEARS, HUMANS HAVE BUILT FENCES FOR VARIOUS PURPOSES. TWO OF THE PRIMARY FUNCTIONS ARE DELINEATING PROPERTY BOUNDARIES AND CONTAINING LIVESTOCK.

Some of the earliest fences were constructed from natural stones and tree branches. By the late 1800s, especially in the U.S., wire became the principal building component of fences. Over time, fencing became a common landscape feature serving as a livestock containment tool. These fences not only allowed ranchers to contain their animals but to move them from one location to another more easily, doctor animals more easily, and control breeding activities within their herds. They also expanded the overall husbandry capacity of livestock managers. Fences became a game changer in taming the land. They forever altered mankind's ability to force the land to work for them and, at times, forced the land to work against them.

As fee-based hunting programs began to gain traction during the mid-20th century, fencing as a game management tool began to appear on the landscape. These game fences were considerably taller than conventional fences used for livestock and were used to contain or exclude certain game species, especially white-tailed deer as well as some exotic ungulates that had been introduced. Although some of the early game fences were approximately 6' in height, most of the game fences installed in the last several decades are 8'–8.5' in height. High fences are most common with big game species and are found in many states and various countries, such as New Zealand, Canada, Mexico, Argentina, several countries in Africa, and many more.

Though one could debate the technical and philosophical impacts of fences on hunting, I have chosen to keep it simple. The remainder of this chapter will explore some of the pros and cons of offering commercial hunts on low-fenced lands, high-fenced lands, and those that I classify as game farms.

LEFT > Humans have been attempting to contain wild and domesticated animals for hundreds of years. Some of the earliest efforts relied on stone fences. These remnants are from a stone pen at Fort Hudson, near Juno, Texas, used by the U.S. Army in the mid-1800s to temporarily hold camels. The Army was determining the practicality of camels as military-related transportation. Obviously, fencing technology has changed in recent decades.

LOW-FENCED HUNTING PROPERTIES

Though it varies highly between states, most commercial hunting in the U.S. and other countries as well, takes place on low-fenced properties. The fences, which are often 4'–5' tall, are generally used for property boundary delineation and livestock purposes.

Since most upland and migratory birds do not distinguish between low fences and game-proof fences, the character and description of any fencing found on these bird hunting properties is normally moot. Wild, native game birds come and go freely.

On bird hunting operations, game fences rarely serve as a tool in bird management. Sure, there are many examples of bird hunting occurring on high-fenced properties, but typically the fences are being used to manage the big game animals on the same property.

Actively and strategically managing big game herds found on low-fenced areas has its limitations. Simply, on smaller acreages, most of the animals that frequent these areas are also "shared" by neighboring properties to some degree. If the neighboring areas implement management practices that are contrary to the property in question, then the ability to effectively manage or manipulate the local big game herds for targeted or desired outcomes is generally compromised.

Wildlife cooperatives (co-ops) offer an alternative option. Neighboring landowners in an area aggregate their individual properties to form a larger management unit. This creates scale thresholds intended to make managing the wildlife and land resources more effective across the co-op. Wildlife co-ops are only as effective as the level of buy-in and commitment of the collective group of participants.

Successful co-ops require good leadership, sufficient communication, education efforts, morale and enthusiasm cultivation, and sufficient long-range vision that identifies and showcases the intrinsic values which incentivizes the sustainability of the cooperative efforts. Independent, third-party leadership can be a great way to allow objective experts to provide unbiased direction for their management program, which may also help keep peace within the co-op. Here in Texas, whitetails drive the formation of co-ops that are most common in areas of the state where property holdings are smaller and more fragmented, such as East Texas and a few in Central Texas.

I have seen landowners become frustrated when they have invested time and money in game management efforts, such as supplemental feeding programs, culling strategies, and various habitat improvement projects, but ultimately see little gain in their game resources' performance. These expensive, futile efforts often lead landowners to consider the option and merits of high fences as a management tool.

Another reality for outfitters or proprietors who rely on low-fenced areas is that the business's volume is often defined by the amount of acreage available to the operation. While applied management practices can occasionally increase the volume minimally, the primary option available to scale up the hunting business is adding additional acreage. To some degree, high-fenced areas and game farms are independent of this limited acreage factor. As a result, outfitters can elevate their game numbers in the high-fenced areas to an artificially high density, which is often supported through an intensive feeding program.

From a cultural perspective, low-fenced hunting operations are generally more broadly accepted across both the hunting and non-hunting communities. The idea of animals moving around their habitats and home ranges in a relatively "unrestricted" fashion is simply less contentious and polarizing than those where high fences are incorporated. For some commercial hunting operators, using less contentious methods is appealing while other operators do not place much, if any, weight on these considerations.

HIGH-FENCED HUNTING PROPERTIES

High fences have been used to manage big game species for several decades, but they began to gain widespread traction in the U.S. in the 1970s. Initially, high fences were found most often on exotic game ranches, more so in Texas than anywhere else.

Interest in managing for quality whitetails accelerated in the mid-to-late 1970s when Al Brothers and Murphy E. Ray, Jr. published *Producing Quality Whitetails* in 1975. That same year, the Texas Trophy Hunters Association was founded. In 1977, acclaimed outdoor and hunting columnist John Wootters published *Hunting Trophy Deer*. By 1980, interest in hunting and producing quality whitetails gained even more momentum. By 1990, commercial hunting programs and values associated with big game in the U.S. were garnering more attention with landowners expressing more interest in growing big whitetails for their own recreational pleasure. From approximately 1995 to 2010, the number of high-fenced properties spiked as people focused on whitetails and exotics.

During the same time span, high-fenced operations emerged in the western states, and elk received most of the focus. However, high-fenced operations in the western states never gained as much traction as they did in other areas of the U.S. Some of this can be attributed to state regulatory restrictions as well as cultural pressures that were—and are—different in many areas of the west.

As a game management tool, high fences are expensive. Installing a high fence requires major capital investments, especially on large properties. Construction costs vary greatly depending on the materials used and the land's topography. In more recent times, game fences can cost between $30,000 and $35,000 per mile. Other features that increase variable costs include water gaps, turns, angles, and gates. In addition to the capital costs, there are also some costs associated with regularly checking these fences, repairing holes and water gaps as well as maintaining these fence lines to avoid encroachment of vegetation.

Arguably, there is no other game management tool that is as profoundly impacting as a high fence. A high fence essentially transforms the land from an "open system" to a "closed system." Managers of high-fenced properties should look at their duties with a more heightened sense of obligation regarding how their management practices impact the ecological health on the high-fenced property. Regardless of what the manager may or may not do, the wildlife and habitat resources on this closed system are generally going to begin to respond much more readily than they did prior to the fence's construction. In some ways it is like trying to grow big largemouth bass in a pond compared to growing that same species in a lake or the backwaters of a river; it is easier to grow big fish in a pond, but it is also more common to have stunted fish in a pond depending on the habitat's features and how the fishery is managed in the pond's closed system.

Throughout my career, I have frequently been told by deer managers that their high fence serves primarily to keep other deer out as opposed to keeping "their" deer in. Quite honestly, I think that this claim is overstated, and in some cases it is a psychological placebo to make some people feel more

comfortable with this tool. And indeed from a management standpoint, there are distinct and real advantages to controlling the entry of other animals, but I believe preventing animals from dispersing onto neighboring properties is generally a greater motivator. However, movement in either direction has possible consequences for the program.

From a herd management standpoint, high fences often allow the manager to manipulate herd characteristics more readily, including animal density and herd composition, such as age structure and sex ratios. Selective culling on high-fenced areas tends to be more effective at enhancing genetic profiles of a deer herd than on low-fenced properties, but people tend to overestimate the ability to manipulate the genetics of a relatively large deer herd that is spread over a relatively large area.

In some cases, the improvements within the deer herd are a function of improved buck maturity and improved herd nutrition. Also, by aggressively culling bucks with "undesirable" antler traits, managers can end up with a "sculpting" effect where the buck herd has been cleaned up, and the animals with undesirable characteristics are no longer part of the herd's "look." What appears to be genetic enhancement may simply be an enhanced look of the current crop of bucks that resulted from sculpting instead of genetic improvement. In this case, when the aggressive culling ceases, the antler characteristics tend to revert back to what they were prior to the culling process within five years. Many culling programs alter the deer herd's phenotype more than its genotype. The ongoing research being conducted on the massive Comanche Ranch in South Texas is yielding some interesting results that support what I just described.

Do not get me wrong, I am not saying that a deer herd's genetic profile cannot be manipulated. I do think deer managers tend to oversimplify this aspect of their management programs and do not fully and accurately understand their deer herd's response, especially when other management practices are being applied concurrently.

High fences can be a major concern when you consider the restricted movement of certain ungulate herds that have seasonal changes within their home range and distribution patterns. In recent years, radio telemetry has found that mule deer, pronghorn, and elk in some areas of the country have had significant changes in their home ranges, often resulting in migration or dispersal where animals may relocate as much as 50-plus miles within the same year. Changes in home ranges and migration are generally a response to habitat and resource needs, which can vary through the year. When an obstruction, such as a new highway or a high fence, becomes a barrier for normal movement patterns, it raises many questions from both an ecological and herd fitness standpoint. If certain individuals or groups of animals are denied the habitat resources that they rely on, it is safe to assume that there will be negative consequences for the physiological health of those animals and for the future viability of those populations.

From a broad wildlife and hunting community standpoint, concerns like these, in my opinion, should be central topics of discussion, and these considerations should not only shape personal and individual decision-making but should, on occasion, shape regulatory and statutory policies to ensure the long-term and sustainable health of wildlife resources. These can be contentious issues that raise hard questions and create volatile discussions which can result in industry in-fighting, but at the end of the day, we must consider the sustainable health of these important wildlife resources while also looking for solutions that balance needs for stakeholders.

From a commercial hunting standpoint, operators can more readily scale-up their operation's volume on a set amount of acreage when they are working with a high-fenced, enclosed area. By combining a closed system with a supplemental feeding program, the land's carrying capacity can be artificially inflated, thereby increasing the area's annual harvest yield and ultimately increasing the volume of hunts that can be sold on that area.

Depending upon other variable costs, in particular labor costs, the increased volume of paying hunters associated with the inflated yield capacity may not always equal a greater profit at year's end, as the feed and labor costs may exceed the added revenue potential. This economic aspect raises the question of whether a high-fenced operation is more profitable than a low-fenced operation, the answer to which is highly debatable. The truth is that "it depends"—and it depends on many different variables, including how the accounting practices are being applied.

One major variable that creeps into this equation is economies of scale, especially how these scale issues affect labor costs. On smaller operations, where one person is the general manager or caretaker and sole employee, that person may be able to tackle the added workload associated with feeding and checking fences on top of their regular workload. However, on a larger property which will have more feeders and more fences to tend, the additional workload may outstrip the ability of one person to handle it all and require hiring more people, thereby increasing labor costs. The financial metrics associated with scale interact with cost efficiencies, and together they ultimately shape the operation's profitability.

The age of the existing livestock fence is another variable in determining whether a high fence is cost effective. If the traditional fence needs to be replaced, some operators justify the costs of installing a high fence by looking at the additional cost of the added height of the fence instead of viewing the full cost of the high fence as a stand-alone capital investment. While some of this boils down to financial semantics and the nuances of accounting practices, these are legitimate considerations when evaluating the long-term financial justification of a high fence as a game management tool.

When it comes to hunting behind a high fence, there are generally two market cultures that exist: those who are fine with hunting in an enclosure, and those who are not. However, it is not as black and white as some may think. When it comes to the hunting marketplace, some hunters are okay with hunting in an enclosure if it is a relatively large area. This scale factor varies from hunter to hunter and is also influenced by which game species is being pursued. As a rule, it seems that a thousand acres is a psychological benchmark for some, but there are others that require a much larger enclosure to meet their personal threshold of acceptability.

Another factor that influences the comfort zones of some hunters is whether the animals were bred, born, and raised on these enclosed hunting areas or whether they were released on it. I will explore this a bit later in this chapter. Many hunters are simply not interested in hunting in an enclosure, regardless of size or circumstance, and a significant percentage of these hunters actively advocate to prohibit hunting behind high fences.

The differing opinions and perceptions can prompt deep, complex discussions when organizations, hunters, and wildlife managers openly discuss issues related to hunting and wildlife management on high-fenced properties. These discussions can turn emotional and confrontational. Personally, I think it is good for our hunting and wildlife communities to be introspective and to evaluate the short-term and the long-term impacts of what we do and how we do it. With that said, these discussions often draw blood, so these conversations may not be for the meek and mild.

Hunting behind high fences seemed to gain market strength over the last 30 to 40 years, but that trend seems to have decreased in the last five years. I suspect this market retraction in recent years is to some degree a result of a waning percentage of hunters who favor this style of hunting and is also perhaps a reflection of a societal movement that is more sensitive about fair chase hunting practices and animal welfare matters. Also, we have gone far enough down the road of highly intensive game management practices that some of these practices look more like livestock husbandry than they do traditional game management, which has resulted in its own deterioration of market strength from hunters who feel comfortable with participating in those type of highly intensive operations, most of which occur on high-fenced properties. Hunting proprietors who can adapt to these market changes, or offer multiple options, are better positioned to respond to these changing market forces.

PUT/TAKE GAME FARMS

There are many variations of practices related to introducing outside animals onto a property; some may be for genetic enhancement purposes while others may be trying to increase the size of the breeding populations of game on these places. With that said, there are also high-fenced properties that introduce animals raised at a different location as a means of providing "shooter animals" to be hunted during a single season, often during the season or year that those animals are released, sometimes within a day or two after release. For the sake of discussion in this book, I am going to define the high-fenced game farms that use this system as "put-and-take" (put/take) operations. In other words, they are put/take operations, stocking introduced animals with the express intent of taking those same animals through hunting. We also refer to these operations as "game farms," although this nomenclature can vary across states and across countries, but for the sake of this book, put/take operations and game farms are viewed as one and the same.

Put/take game farms have been in place in the U.S. for many decades. During the early days, these types of hunting operations were more common with game birds, such as pheasants, quail, and chukar. For a wing shooting operation, these birds are propagated in small pens and, in some instances, are flight conditioned in larger pens. Then they typically are "planted" during the morning of a scheduled hunt. Most birds shot on game farms during a single hunt have been released that day, but some birds, a much smaller percentage of the bag, may have been released a few days earlier for other hunts and "carried over." Only a very small percentage of released birds survive to the next year. Typically, the released birds add little to the reproductive capability of the population of native, wild birds found in these locales, though there can be some exceptions.

At the same time the put/take bird operations were becoming more common, the exotic big game market began to increase. Much of the early exotic game hunting took place in Texas, and this is largely still true today. While Florida, Ohio, Missouri, and a few other states have seen these exotic game hunting operations emerge, Texas is the preeminent location for this type of hunting by a huge margin. Some of these exotic hunting operations strictly rely on animals born and raised on these areas, including high and low-fenced properties, while other operations partially rely on shooter animals purchased from sale barns or from other ranches who are selling stocker animals trapped from their pastures. Again, put/take practices vary greatly.

As the whitetail hunting markets increased during the 1980s and 1990s, and as high-fenced whitetail hunting operations grew in numbers, so did the captive breeding of white-tailed deer. For the sake of this discussion, it is important to distinguish between these different game management and hunting-related practices. When I refer to captive breeding or deer breeding, I am referring to those operations that are registered or permitted to raise native cervid species in pens that may later be sold, traded, or released. Deer breeding-related laws vary immensely between states, and some states do not allow any captive breeding of native cervids. Captive breeding of whitetails grew tremendously from around 1995 to 2010. Once again, Texas dominated the deer breeding scene, but other states such as Michigan, Ohio, Missouri, and Pennsylvania left a large footprint on this industry during that time as well.

Deer breeding, from my perspective, changed the landscape of commercial whitetail hunting forever. In 2009, a paradigm-shift occurred when the Texas economy temporarily tanked, and the price of these pen-raised bucks softened for the first time in the history of deer breeding. Prior to 2009, bucks in pens were generally worth more alive as stockers to be sold to new breeders who were entering the business and needed inventory or as breeding stock to be sold and released onto ranches in the name of genetic enhancement.

OPPOSITE-TOP > Commercial white-tailed deer hunting changed drastically when captive propagation became an accepted practice in the hunting industry in the ten years between 2005 and 2015. However, chronic wasting disease is creating a paradigm shift as deer movement qualifications become more demanding and complex.

In 2009, this all changed when the shooter buck market erupted. At that point, many commercial, high-fenced whitetail hunting operations recognized it was easier, cheaper, and more predictable to buy shooter bucks and release them to be hunted that season instead of trying to produce big deer on their own property. Plus, by then, the size of the bucks in pens were much larger than those that were being reared in the pasture. The ceiling of the antler size on pen-raised whitetails has continued to rise every year. Using intensive animal husbandry methods, breeders are producing whitetails that are now in excess of 800" on the Boone & Crockett measuring system.

From a hunting proprietor's standpoint, a distinct advantage of the put/take deer hunting is that the number of hunts that can be hosted is no longer tied to the operation's acreage because the number of animals available is not dictated by habitat; proprietors simply purchase and release as many bucks as they anticipate needing that season. I know of properties smaller than a thousand acres that have hosted hunts for almost a 100

deer hunters in a season, meaning they are turning out 100-plus bucks on these areas. As part of the financial efficiency strategy, proprietors assess their hunt bookings around September and then decide how many shooter bucks need to be purchased and released. As a cushion, many put/take hunting operations will add a few more animals into the inventory to allow for death loss and to perhaps allow for additional hunts that may be sold after the purchased deer are released.

Some put/take proprietors who analyze this aspect of their business operations shop around between different deer breeding operations, finding the best prices and selecting deer of various sizes and antler configurations based on their clientele's preferences and expectations. This is the closest thing to supermarket shopping that exists in the hunting world. In some cases, hunters can pick out the bucks they will likely shoot before the hunt begins, creating the question of how much mystery and magic remains in the hunting experience.

As deer breeding grew and was eventually integrated into commercial deer hunting, confusion and chaos followed. A significant percentage of hunters and non-hunters fail to recognize the difference between basic high-fenced properties that are relying on deer that are born and raised on those areas and high-fenced operations that are buying and releasing their animals to be hunted; the practices are distinctly different, but they often become muddled in the mind's eye of hunters and non-hunters.

To add to the confusion, the deer breeding industry practitioners have done a good job of cloaking themselves by creating the perception that they are just another high-fenced operation. Part of this sleight of hand is creating greater acceptance of the deer breeding industry by creating an appearance that put/take practices and high-fenced properties are essentially one and the same. They are not. They are often very different in terms of the practices that characterize the management of the resources and the details associated with the origin of the deer that are hunted on these properties. Lack of disclosure has, at times, taken on a form of snake oil in terms of creating false understandings of what is actually being sold/bought, but that's a whole matter in itself, and one that I'll touch on later in this book.

TYPES OF FEE-BASED HUNTING PROGRAMS

4

PART OF THE BUSINESS WORLD'S BEAUTY IS THE FREEDOM FOR BUSINESS OWNERS AND MANAGERS TO USE THEIR CREATIVITY IN DESIGNING PRODUCT OR SERVICE CONCEPTS THAT EITHER SUIT THEIR TASTES OR PERHAPS GIVE THEM A COMPETITIVE ADVANTAGE; THE HUNTING BUSINESS IS NO EXCEPTION.

Many variables can influence what type of hunting arrangement may be best suited for a particular hunting operation. These include game species, available facilities, support staff expertise, game resource management goals, financial goals, time constraints, demands of supervising clients, and the amount of time the landowner is willing to allow clients access to the ranch.

Most conventional fee-based hunting programs fall into one of four major categories: day hunts, seasonal or year-round leases, hunting clubs, and outfitted hunts. There are many variants and hybrid arrangements that encompass these four categories, but this assembly characterizes the general make-up of how most programs can be lumped. Over the years, I have actively been involved with hunting programs that fit within each of these four categories. I personally prefer outfitted hunting programs, but seasonal lease operations are where I initially started in the industry. Even today, I continue to work with many programs that fall within these two categories.

Currently, our dove hunts are the only true day hunts that we offer, and I have found this arrangement works well with this species. I have spent the least amount of time working with hunting clubs, but hunting clubs are a great cultural fit in some areas of the country, especially in the Southeast and, to some degree, in the Northeast. Each of these programs have pros and cons, and they each serve important niches in the marketplace.

DAY HUNTS

Basic day hunt operations charge a daily fee or perhaps a fee for a relatively short duration such as three or four days. These hunts may have no, or very few, added services or amenities. Thus, the day hunt option is a fairly simple arrangement where the hunting proprietor charges a trespass fee for the hunters to have access to the property for a given amount of time that is often no more than a day or two.

Day hunts are one of the earliest forms of fee-based hunting programs on private lands in the U.S. I have heard of day hunt operations in Texas dating back to the 1930s, but I suspect there was money exchanged for hunting privileges even before then. Day hunts for big game animals were common in the U.S. during the 1960s and '70s. By the 1980s, many private landowners began looking at alternative ways to monetize their game resources. During that era, commercial hunting programs around the globe began to greatly increase in number and intensity.

Today, day hunts for doves continue to be a common offering and represent one of the more economical options for hunters. There are some major dove hunting operations that focus on day hunters, generally charging $75 to $150 per hunter, per day. Pheasant and waterfowl hunting are often offered under this type of arrangement as well, but the group sizes and total hunt volume are generally less than dove hunting. Day hunts for bobwhite quail used to be common, but as wild quail populations have dwindled in some areas, so has this type of fee-based hunting. Feral hogs are commonly offered under a day hunt basis, as are javelinas in Texas.

If you are the proprietor, I suggest you provide some degree of supervision or have some checks in place that minimize the possibility of irresponsible hunters who abuse the resources or engage in dangerous or reckless behavior. Combine this with the need to steward the game resource with the various risks associated with turning strangers with guns loose on private properties, and it obviously points toward it being poor discretion for the proprietor to walk away from the activity and assume that "it all will be good."

ADVANTAGES OF DAY HUNTS

- Appeals to a large market due to lower price structure

- Requires little or no hunting expertise from the support staff and does not normally require a large staff base

- Hunters generally have fewer expectations because of lower price points

- Easy access to markets through internet, social media, classified advertisements in newspapers, and flyers posted at local sporting goods stores and other outdoor-related or high-traffic storefronts

- Quick and easy

DISADVANTAGES OF DAY HUNTS

- Generally, this business model relies on volume of hunts and/or hunters instead of profit margin; therefore, it requires dealing with a larger number of hunters

- Day hunters are generally not deeply vested, so they are more prone to leave trash, be poor stewards of the land and wildlife, and be less diligent in taking care of their surroundings

- Not an effective option for selectively harvesting big game animals because clients will tend to be more opportunistic

- Someone must meet with each hunter or group to show them the property and perhaps periodically check on the hunters, which creates a larger demand for staff's time

- Day hunters tend to be unsupervised and unfamiliar with the hunting area, which can result in hunters straying into wrong areas, perhaps leading to trespassing

- Due to the lack of direct supervision, liability exposure for the proprietor or landowner may be greater

ABOVE > Day hunts, especially for game birds, remain popular in some areas. One downside of day hunts is hunters are often less vested and tend to lack a stewardship mentality, which is demonstrated in many ways, including not picking up their own trash.

SEASONAL OR YEAR-ROUND LEASES

Seasonal and year-round leases have been a common fee-based hunting option for several decades. This is an arrangement where landowners lease the hunting rights on their property, or a portion thereof, to a group of hunters. Lease arrangements provide the hunters unrestricted access to the property during the hunting season or perhaps year-round. Lease details and structure can vary greatly. Some leases include cabins or lodging while others simply include hookups for campers and RVs. Still others provide no lodging amenities. Certain leases will include exclusive hunting rights for all game species while others may split seasons or retain certain hunting privileges. While a few leases include hunting blinds and feeders, most properties require that the hunting lessee furnish these items.

The bottom line is hunting lease agreements' terms, conditions, and features vary across the spectrum. Generally, the agreement's provisions are spelled out in the lease at the beginning of the term, but there may be some occasions where adjustments that are in the best interest of all parties need to be made during the lease's term. Using the "F" word—flexibility—can be the difference that keeps all the parties working together.

Leases became commonplace during the 1970s and '80s. Then, from about 2000 to 2010, I noticed a downturn in lease numbers as many landowners opted to host outfitted hunts. In relatively short order, landowners began to encounter difficulties marketing and selling their outfitted hunts. Landowners also learned that outfitted hunts require intensive preparation and a large time commitment and more overhead for staff, food, lodging etc., which can reduce the profitability of outfitted hunts. For many landowners, the less demanding lease programs were more profitable. I saw—and continue to see—landowners going back to traditional season leases.

Lease hunters tend to be on the property for a longer time and are generally unsupervised; therefore, it is crucial that the landowner and lessee be "on the same page" regarding expectations and rules when the lease begins. This, along with everyone being comfortable with one another, is key to establishing and maintaining a great working relationship between the landowner and the lessee. For landowners who live on their properties, compatibility with their hunters is paramount because season lease hunters are likely to be "underfoot" regularly. The hunting lease is a marriage of sorts between the landowner and the lessees, and if the parties rub each other the wrong way because of personalities, attitudes, disagreements on safety, land use ethics or any number of other things, the relationship will struggle and will generally lead to a counterproductive environment.

All things considered, in some areas, including Texas, leases are generally going to yield a higher net profit than other fee-based options. As mentioned earlier, offering lease hunts requires less overhead than other options, and there is a consistently robust market for hunting leases, so the landowner or proprietor is able to drive more cash to the bottom line.

Due to their diversity, you could write an entire book dedicated to the various features and "moving parts" associated with hunting leases. Instead, I have listed some features that are essential to most leases and included some comments for consideration. A few of these deal structure features are also covered in Chapter Two where I discussed key features between landowners and outfitters, which largely apply here as well.

OPPOSITE-TOP > Seasonal and year-round leases are common in Texas. Many feature hunting camps, like this one, which are established and maintained by the hunters. This camp in Webb County has been in place since 1994. Originally it included just the small brown trailer, but it has been upgraded and added onto several times over the years.

FEATURES THAT ARE ESSENTIAL TO MOST LEASE AGREEMENTS

AGREEMENT DOCUMENT

By conducting an internet search, you can find a tremendous amount of information on hunting leases, including some lease document templates that may be helpful. I am not a fan of long, complicated hunting leases that require an attorney to interpret confusing language. It is important to cover relevant matters in plain, simple English.

Texas A&M University Real Estate Center published *The Texas Deer Lease* written by Judon Fambrough. This is an excellent resource. It's not a bad idea to have an attorney review your lease document, but again, many of the attorney-generated leases I've reviewed over the years I find to be onerous and poorly constructed.

LEASE TERM

When enacting a lease with new tenants, I recommend that the initial arrangement is limited to one year. After a successful first year, if all parties are pleased with one another, I like the idea of a multi-year deal.

A long-term agreement incentivizes the hunters to be good stewards and wisely manage the wildlife resource that they will benefit from over time and provides the landowner with some stability for planning purposes. A three-year deal seems to be a good rule of thumb for many people's tastes and needs, and five years is often a bit more of a stretch. Anything beyond five years brings too much uncertainty into the picture because no one can accurately predict the future.

With that said, some landowners prefer a year-to-year lease agreement, even for longtime lessees. As I've previously stated, the integrity of the lease relationship between the landowners and the lessee will drive the longevity of the lease more so than the written term.

LEASE PRICING

Naturally, most lessors want to be paid as much for their hunting lease as possible. In discussing lease rates, I have found that many landowners and lessors focus on "keeping up with the Joneses" instead of recognizing the market's variable nature and how values of leases vary region to region and property to property. Facilities, livestock practices, equipment provisions, historic game management practices, quality and abundance of game, fishing opportunities, proximity to major cities, accessibility, limits on the number of hunters and/or harvest quotas, regional differences, and many other variables often shape the lease value and what someone may be willing to pay. Just because the landowners down the road receive ten dollars per acre for their hunting lease does not guarantee that everyone in the same area can command (or expect) that same rate.

One of the real wildcards is personal relationships and networks. Some landowners have unique connections to people who may be willing to pay a premium for the lease. For example, landowners who are involved professionally or personally with high-net-worth corporations or companies may be able to leverage those relationships and lease their property for a premium rate. Another lease pricing consideration is the quality of the lessees. Landowners and managers will attest that it can sometimes be challenging to find lessees who respect the ranch's rules, facilities, and wildlife resources. Once a group is in place who mirrors the ranch's stewardship ethic, you may want to consider whether attempting to maximize the lease rate at each renewal is worth the risk of losing good hunters. Peace of mind is worth something, and each time there is churn, the uncertainty of what is in the box can create sleepless nights for some.

If you price the existing lessees out of the picture, then you will be forced to find new hunters, which introduces a degree of uncertainty about the working relationship. Until they have signed a lease and begun using your property, it is impossible to know how well you will communicate with and relate to them and whether your goals and ethics truly align. The "costs" associated with a new group whose behavior is more problematic than the previous group may far exceed the increased revenue accrued from the change. There are real values associated with having a great tenant, but those values can sometimes be hard to measure. Of course, those intangible values may vary from one lessor to the next.

Lease payment schedules vary. It is common to require a 25—50 percent payment earlier in the year and require the remaining balance just prior to the start of hunting season. An early payment ensures the lessee's commitment and provides operating funds through the year.

HARVEST ALLOWANCES

Most hunting lease agreements have provisions that address harvest quotas or harvest parameters, especially on big game species and some upland bird species as well. It is common on leases that feature white-tailed deer to have a harvest allowance that is built into the lease agreement which defines how many quality bucks and cull bucks may be taken, but the doe harvest provision is often left open to be determined by a preseason survey.

Depending upon the management program's intensity, it is generally a good idea to include enough details to adequately define what constitutes a quality buck and a cull buck. With that said, I have seen plenty of examples where the details are too complicated or it is not a good fit for a particular program. So, while the agreement's language needs to clearly describe the harvest provisions' allowances and restrictions, these features cannot be cookie-cutter and taken from another ranch's lease agreement. Every program is different.

The cull buck harvest allowance on leases is one of the most likely areas for problems and infighting among lease members. Conflicts can easily arise when lease members are stretching cull buck harvest provisions; I have seen hunters get cross with their landowners when the landowner perceives the hunters are not reasonably honoring the cull buck criteria's parameters. I have also seen cull buck harvest provisions set many programs back because the harvest parameters are not a good fit for that specific deer herd or program. The bottom line is that in some hunting programs, cull buck allowances can be problematic if not properly structured and administered.

GUEST ALLOWANCES

This is another feature of a hunting lease that is prone to create problems if not managed properly. Guest allowance provisions are not unreasonable, but they need to be clearly defined. On leases that have fewer lease members than what the agreement will allow, it is common for guest allowances to be more lenient because the lease's capacity is already undersubscribed. On many leases, members can bring their immediate family, but those guests are often required to be with a lease member at all times while in the field. If guests are allowed to hunt, the guest's harvest typically is required to count against the lease member's harvest allotment.

It is necessary to ensure that everyone is on the same page when defining these guest allowances. For example, "immediate family members" can be loosely interpreted. Does it mean spouse/partner and children or does it also include the lessee's parents, siblings, and their children? The only way to avoid confusion is to define it in a manner appropriate for your specific operation.

Some lease members stretch the guest privileges, which can lead to conflict. With that said, I am an advocate of allowing guest privileges on hunting leases, as this not only creates a value-added component to the lease but can introduce new hunters to the tradition and cultivate their interest, thereby being a built-in hunter recruitment tool. Similarly, a hunting lease that does not allow kids on the property is shortsighted, from my perspective, regardless of the reasons for concern. We must get kids involved if hunting is going to have a sustainable, healthy future. Taking them to the lease is a great way to build their interest.

TERMINATION CLAUSES

Terminating a hunting lease while the term of the agreement is still in effect is not pleasant for either party. Most terminations result from the landowner selling the ranch, the landowner leasing to another third party, such as an oil and gas, wind energy or solar company that prevents hunting, or hunters who do not comply with the lease agreement. Building an "in case of sale clause" into the hunting lease document should be considered regardless of whether the landowner expresses an intent to sell. When a sales clause is triggered, lease money is generally refunded in its entirety or prorated depending upon the timing of the closing. Hunters have less "heartburn" when allowed to hunt through the current or upcoming season, but the buyer may not agree to such a provision.

In recent years, more wind farms have been built in locales that are popular hunting areas. Unlike the norm for oil and gas leases, the wind energy industry is not often open to having paid hunters on properties that are being developed for wind farms. In fact, landowners are generally paid an opportunity cost for not leasing those lands for hunting until the wind farm's construction phase is complete, which may require several years.

Although I have a difficult time buying into the wind energy companies' justification for staunchly prohibiting hunting, especially since the oil and gas industry has coexisted well with hunting programs for many decades, it seems to be the norm in many of these wind energy agreements. The prohibition can, at a minimum, temporarily halt hunting for a group of hunters on "their" lease for a few years. Like sale clauses, there is normally a prorated refund arrangement when such circumstances prevent hunting while the lease's term is in effect.

It is not uncommon for landowners or lessors to find themselves dealing with problems that escalate until lease termination becomes a viable consideration. Normally, problems can be resolved by addressing the concerns and having all parties agree to a reasonable resolution, preventing a full termination. I have found it best to try and manage matters effectively until the lease term ends unless infractions are severe or there are irreconcilable differences. If it is only a one-year deal, then simply do not renew the lease. If the recurring problems can be traced to a single hunter who is part of a group, then evicting the problematic individual may be the best option. This is especially true if the balance of the group is well-liked by the lessor.

When hunting leases are terminated, for whatever reason, it is vital that the departing hunters understand the importance of being responsible individuals during the exit process. Reprisals in any form can create additional problems. If the lessor suspects the exit process will trigger destructive or aggressive behavior, then it is a good idea to develop a plan that places limits on the hunters as they reenter the ranch to remove their property. Defining and limiting the time frame along with providing a degree of supervision can help prevent damage or any other type of problem.

ADVANTAGES OF LEASES

- Opportunity to develop deeper relationships with the hunters

- Low input costs and generally high bottom-line yields

- Hunters may feel more invested in the land and wildlife and consequently be more management minded

- Lower turnover rate

- Occasional ancillary assets benefit the landowner, such as hunters building permanent improvements or leaving behind blinds and game feeders

- Hunters generally pay for various practices that may benefit the wildlife resources, such as supplemental feeding, food plots, game surveys, etc.

- Strong market demand and relatively easy access to certain markets

DISADVANTAGES OF LEASES

- Heavy underfoot traffic

- Hunters tend to develop an ownership mentality, leading to pushy behavior

- Bad guys have a large and clear path to do bad things

- May deny or impede the landowner's ability to have quiet time and enjoy the use of their ranch as they may desire

- More difficult to pinpoint sources of problems, such as open gates or scattered trash, as the hunters will almost always deny being the problem's source

- Perhaps more added liability exposure, due to the protracted time that hunters may use the property without supervision? However, if landowners or lessors are providing fewer amenities and services than they would under an outfitted hunt, perhaps there is less risk of exposure and less room for gross negligence?

HUNTING CLUBS

Hunting clubs have existed in the U.S. since the late 1800s. When discussing fee-based hunting programs, the club concept remains popular in certain areas of the country. In the southeastern U.S., hunting clubs have been popular on TIMO (timber company) lands for decades, with some of these clubs being considered prestigious and highly acclaimed. Other clubs are found on individually owned private lands. Then there are some clubs that are member owned, which seems to be a bit more common in the Northeast. The structure of hunting clubs is similar to the constructs found in seasonal or year-round leases, so I am not going to go into as much detail here as I did in the lease section.

Some clubs have been in place for decades, steeped with a culture that reflects history and local nuances. Some of the more prestigious clubs have lengthy waiting lists and are priced accordingly. The governance of some clubs is strong and unbending. Other hunting clubs tend to be more pliable and often flex when circumstances call for reasonable change.

The hunting club concept tends to fit well with many of the game bird hunting programs, both put/take programs and those relying on native wild birds. The put/take bird hunting clubs often operate on a fee concept, based on annual dues with an additional assessment paid for the number of birds released or harvested. Guest allowances are the norm. Though the fee structure varies, hosting members are normally assessed a daily fee per guest. For native wild bird hunting clubs, the primary fees are normally tied to annual dues and occasional assessment fees. Other variable features (and expenses) for these clubs may include guides, boat rental, meals, and overnight lodging. Each club is different in terms of inclusions, annual overhead assessments, and extra fees.

Some clubs, especially the older and more prestigious clubs, restrict the number of members. Membership turnover is minimal in some clubs, so competition for available slots can be fierce and political. In other clubs, a departing member may sell their membership on a private treaty basis, and the new member will then be subject to the normal membership requirements.

Member-owned clubs rise to a higher level of financial commitment. These clubs generally have a hefty buy-in fee that gives the members undivided interests in certain features of the club property such as the land, lodging, and major equipment. Some of these clubs may allow the members to build and own a structure, such as a cabin, on the premises. Again, each club is unique.

Some hunting clubs have a significant organizational structure and are often run by an elected board. As previously mentioned, the internal politics of these hunting clubs can be sensitive and tricky to navigate. With member-owned clubs as well as those clubs with a higher dues structure, it is common to have at least one full-time employee who serves as a grounds manager or caretaker. Other clubs may have a larger staff, including chefs, housekeepers, biologists, and other support personnel.

OPPOSITE > Around the globe, much of the finest hunting takes place on privately owned lands. Although some hunters, especially those who live in places with deep public-lands hunting cultures, are offended by landowners charging access fees for hunting on their land, private landowners often hold the key to diverse wildlife habitat and sustainable wildlife populations.

ADVANTAGES OF HUNTING CLUBS

- Strong internal organizational management
- Low turnover in hunters
- Member-driven marketing and promotion
- High entertainment value for the members, leading to personal satisfaction for the proprietor or manager
- Depending upon club culture, board-driven decision-making may allow for greater adaptive operating procedures over time.
- Strong stability, allowing for enhanced visioning and planning

DISADVANTAGES OF HUNTING CLUBS

- Cultural entrenchment may make it more difficult to adapt and flex
- For clubs that are not member-owned, there may be significant underfoot traffic and high impacts on the land and its resources
- High demand on managing member-related affairs and interests
- Potential inability to manage the relationships between members, creating problems based on personality and conflicting interests
- With new clubs, it may require long, exhaustive front-end efforts to sell all memberships and to go through the "jelling" process to develop an efficient program

OUTFITTED HUNTS

Often referred to as package hunts, outfitted hunts generally emphasize service and amenities, although they are packaged in a variety of ways. Guides, meals, lodging, and game care are normally included as part of most outfitted hunts. More extensive packages may include airport shuttles, meat processing, hunting license procurement, and taxidermy arrangements. Of the four types of fee-based hunting programs covered in this chapter, outfitted hunts tend to be the most labor and cost intensive. They can also require the greatest expertise.

In some of the country's more remote areas, such as Alaska and portions of the Rocky Mountains, outfitted hunts have been popular hunting programs for many decades. The same thing could be said about international hunting destinations as well. Fundamentally, it is more difficult for hunters to be able to comfortably make "do-it-yourself" (DIY) hunts work when conditions are more demanding and access is more challenging. Furthermore, there are some species in locations like Alaska that require a licensed guide to be able to legally hunt those species.

In some areas of the U.S., the outfitting industry did not begin to fully mature until the 1980s and 1990s. Up until that point, leases, day hunts, and hunting clubs were the norm. Plus, fees generated from hunting did not represent a large revenue stream for many landowners prior to that time. However, the market for quality hunting opportunities grew immensely during the 1970s and 1980s, and landowners and hunting operators began to see an opportunity to monetize these game resources; as one might expect, business efforts formed around these increasing profit centers.

As competition grew within the outfitting and commercial hunting industry, hunting proprietors became more serious about offering amenities and services. Some outfitters still get by without improving their craft and business features, but as you find in so many other industries, increased competition has forced hunting proprietors to offer improved and value-added services to remain competitive.

Other chapters of this book will explore details regarding lodging considerations, food service, and customer service strategies, but let me point out that these features of the outfitting business have become even more important over the last ten to 20 years. Why? Primarily because of the industry's development and the competitive marketplace that has forced proprietors to up their game. That is not to say that marginal lodging, or bologna and cheese sandwiches will not cut the mustard in some cases, but with many types of hunts, when the consumer is provided with options and everything else is considered "equal," many consumers will opt for those operations that offer superlative amenities and services. Again, how does one develop or maintain a competitive edge?

There is still some allure that exists in the hunters' imaginations of traveling to the big unspoiled regions of the Rockies, being guided by mountain men who exude the persona of an earlier era, and riding horseback into remote wilderness to pursue big game. Outdoor columnists like Jack O'Connor, James (Jim) Zumbo, Jim Carmichael, and others helped fuel these dreams during the late 1960s, '70s, and into the '80s. Hunters pursuing those romantic adventures often found themselves staying in wall tents heated with a wood-burning stove, cooking game meat over an open fire and scratching out a living off the land for a few days. Those "rustic" hunts still exist, especially in areas like Alaska and in some of the remote wilderness areas of the western states, but most people today opt for more creature comforts when given the choice. Modern equipment, technology, increased access, and perhaps the softened brawn of modern culture has moved the outfitting industry away from its early rusticity to a more comfort-centric mindset.

Professionally, I have been involved with the entire gamut of fee-based hunting programs, including day

hunt operations, hunting clubs, lease programs, and outfitted hunts. Though I still dabble in each of these types of programs, over the last 25 years I have emphasized outfitted hunts. This type of hunting program is simply more fulfilling to me personally, but I will say that I have a love/hate relationship with the outfitting business.

Paradoxically, what I find most attractive about outfitted hunts is the necessity of becoming more deeply involved with the operations of these hunting programs, but at the same time, what I like the least are some of the same demands. Yeah, I know, perhaps that makes little sense to most people, but I suspect hunting industry veterans can relate. The time and energy invested in envisioning, planning, marketing, pre-hunt prepping, hosting

ABOVE > For busy hunters, booking outfitted hunts is an efficient way to enjoy a quality experience without investing a lot of time in planning and preparation.

the hunt, and the post-hunt duties of cleaning camp and shipping trophies places a huge demand on the outfitter. Pulling it all together can be stressful for even seasoned professionals. When all the efforts culminate in satisfied, smiling clients with their game, the profession is very rewarding.

Over the years, though, the business can take its toll. In addition to the pressures of producing good results and quality experiences, outfitters contend with long hours, extended absences from home and family, occasional unreasonable demands and unpleasant personalities, unexpected curve balls thrown by landowners/lessors/clients, and the unpredictable temperament of Mother Nature. These issues go with the territory. Sometimes the territory is good and sometimes it is not, but for me, it has largely been the former.

As our society becomes more urbanized, more people are disconnected from our outdoor world. With societal urbanization, fewer people understand how to function efficiently and safely in "wild" settings; therefore, the need for the assistance provided by an outfitter is growing. On the other hand, I am not so sure that the hunter receives as much satisfaction or inner connection to "the hunt" when so many of their needs are met by a third-party as opposed to DIY hunts. I also question whether hunters tend to cycle out of the hunting community faster or more prematurely if they are not more invested during the various stages of their hunting life.

As you can see, I identify both the pros and cons for hunters who principally rely on others to pull things together during their hunting trips. With that said, if providing outdoor assistance and brokering these hunting opportunities is what is required to get folks involved with hunting, then outfitting can nurture hunting participation, which is crucial for continued wildlife conservation funding. Further, this growing need for assistance benefits those outfitters who are relying on those consumers to support their businesses.

ADVANTAGES OF OUTFITTED/ PACKAGE HUNTS

- Greater supervision and control over the hunters

- Accurate accounting measures that identify what game resources are taken

- Enhanced selectivity over which game resources are potentially harvested

- Greater investment of time and resources from the proprietor, possibly increasing the proprietor's sense of satisfaction

- Allows proprietor to involve various people, such as family members or friends, to serve as guides or chefs or take on other supporting roles

- Increased control and safety protocols may help hedge against risks and liabilities inherent to hunting

DISADVANTAGES OF OUTFITTED/ PACKAGE HUNTS

- High financial overhead to administer the operation's demands and inputs

- Often not as profitable as other fee-based options, principally due to high overhead

- Increased pressures and emotional stress associated with producing successful outcomes for clients

- Exceedingly competitive markets, demanding increased efforts and higher costs associated with marketing

- The unpleasantness of dealing with unreasonable hunters, which is amplified because of the intimate and personal nature of outfitted hunting

- Greater expertise and specialized skills are required to service all areas of the operation

- Market strengths tend to fluctuate depending upon the state of the economies within the marketplaces as well as other influential market pressures

As discussed in this chapter, there are multiple fee-based hunting concepts that have merit and serve a purpose in the commercial hunting industry in the U.S. and elsewhere. Indeed, there are pros and cons for each commercial hunting concept; what makes the most sense for one operator or landowner may not for the next. The variables that dictate what may work best for each proprietor are diverse. They include the operation's goals, location, resource capabilities, game availability, species selection, and other variables. Occasionally, the local regulatory regime can shape or limit the type of program that is offered. Two examples of this include operating big game hunts in Alaska or offering outfitting services on government land. Though there are exceptions, the operations that demand the fewest inputs (especially cash intensive inputs) often yield the most profits. Therefore, it is best that proprietors consider a myriad of variables when contemplating the hunting program's business structure and then move forward in a measured, cautious manner as the program is being built and nurtured.

5 BASIC BUSINESS MANAGEMENT

ENTREPRENEURS IN MANY INDUSTRIES
RECOGNIZE THE IMPORTANCE OF
FOLLOWING BASIC PROCEDURES THAT
ARE TRADITIONALLY CONSIDERED PART AND
PARCEL OF CONCEIVING, FLEDGING, AND
DEVELOPING A BUSINESS.

ndividuals who have training or experience in business are better positioned to understand the fundamentals of the business world. Experienced businesspeople generally tackle their business-related endeavors with a level of knowledge and sophistication that allows them to better structure their business and operate it efficiently.

As previously mentioned, many people who get into the hunting business, especially those in the Lower 48, do not often come from business backgrounds. As a result, business acumen is often lacking in this industry. In my experience, people tend to get into the hunting business for the wrong reasons. Some people succumb to the allure of being a professional hunter. Others attempt to substitute their recreational passion for their vocation. Yet others chase professional dreams conjured up by reading Hemingway, O'Connor, or Boddington.

Regardless of the initial spark, these misguided reasons fuel a misplaced ambition that motivate some to become hunting outfitters without being properly prepared to be a responsible new business owner. Those proprietors who lack the necessary training or simply ignore sound business principles, often flounder operationally and are inadequately capitalized. Ultimately, they often end up failing.

Fortunately, it does not take a rocket scientist to develop some basic practices that follow traditional business models and allow the proprietor to integrate basic best practices and to develop a business style that provides for a greater probability of success. The remainder of this chapter provides a concise look at some business fundamentals that should be pondered by anyone who is considering starting a hunting enterprise. Much of the information can be applied to other types of businesses as well.

BUSINESS PLAN

Perhaps the most rudimentary component of early-stage business development is completing a written business plan. This should be a working document that is updated as needed, a road map for success, especially during the early stages of business development.

Furthermore, a business plan is often required for proprietors seeking funding through traditional lending institutions or private investors. Many business plan templates are readily available online, but for the hunting business, here is a basic structure that encompasses some primary considerations.

BASIC STRUCTURE OF A BUSINESS PLAN

EXECUTIVE SUMMARY

The executive summary should appear first in your business plan and briefly sum up what you expect your business to accomplish. In addition, it highlights what you intend to discuss in the rest of the plan. People disagree whether the executive summary should be written first or last. Personally, I prefer sketching out a rough executive summary first and then fine-tuning this section after I complete the rest of the plan. A good executive summary should be compelling. It contains the company's mission statement and a short description of its products and services. It might also be a good idea to briefly explain why you are starting your company and include details about your relevant experience.

COMPANY DESCRIPTION

The company description appears next, which includes key information about the business, its goals, and its targeted customers. It should also explain how the business will stand out from others in the industry and how the products and services that are being provided will be helpful to your target audience.

MARKET AND COMPETITION ANALYSIS

A market analysis should present information that addresses market trends regarding the demand for the services or products that are being offered. Such analysis should also identify customer segments that are relevant to the business, such as regional characteristics, income brackets, and other distinguishing features, like number of archers versus gun hunters and how this may play into any strategies for customer profiling. Also, there is a considerable amount to be gained by studying how competing businesses are packaging their services, products, pricing, and other pertinent information. If you have identified how you can develop a competitive advantage, then this should be outlined in this section.

MANAGEMENT AND ORGANIZATION STRUCTURE

This section should provide a concise biographical sketch of the owners, managers, and any staff who will be part of the business team. Relevant experience, strengths, and anticipated responsibilities should be listed. It should also indicate whether the business will operate as a partnership, a sole proprietorship, or a business with a different ownership structure.

BREAKDOWN OF PRODUCTS AND SERVICES

This section is a detailed summary of the hunt types offered by the company. The details should cover inclusions, exclusions, pricing, and any features that help define the hunting packages that are being offered to the marketplace. Any features that separate your products and services from most of the competition should be revisited in this section. Also, because most of your hunts will take place on a limited number of properties, outline the contingency plan to sustain the business if those properties are lost.

MARKETING PLAN

In a business plan, it is important to describe how you intend to get your products and services in front of potential clients. That is what marketing is all about. Along with describing the strategies you will take to promote your hunts, discuss the marketing budgets. These days, several different advertising mediums are available to hunting proprietors, so understand the pros and cons of each one before spending your money on marketing.

FINANCIAL DOCUMENTS AND PLANNING

To build accurate operational budgets, one must generate other financial documents to anticipate the various financial realities that will ultimately drive the business. Profit and loss statements, balance sheets, and cash flow projections are fundamental financial tools that should not be overlooked when developing a new business. In my experience, most new business owners tend to be a bit ambitious in their initial financial projections. It is important to temper expectations to avoid major financial pinches.

Every company is different, so functional business plans vary to some degree, but there are key components that should be part of every effective plan. It is always good to provide a clear and accurate summary of your business goals in your business plan. As previously mentioned, there is nothing wrong with treating a written business plan as a working document, subject to revisions as you—and the business—progress.

ENTITY FORMATION

One of the most important choices entrepreneurs make is the legal structure of their companies. This structure can impact how much you pay in taxes and it ,may affect the amount of paperwork that is required. The entity type may also affect your personal liability exposures.

The type of business entity chosen generally depends on three primary factors: liability, taxation, and record keeping. Here is a quick look at a few differences between the most common forms of business entities.

COMMON FORMS OF BUSINESS ENTITIES

SOLE PROPRIETORSHIP

This is the most common form of business organization. It is easy to form and offers complete managerial control for the owner. However, the owner is also personally liable for all financial obligations of the business.

PARTNERSHIP

A partnership involves two or more people who agree to share in the profits or losses of a business. The primary advantage is that it does not bear the tax burden of profits or the benefit of losses; profits or losses are "passed through" to partners to report on their individual income tax returns. A primary disadvantage is liability; each partner is personally liable for the business's financial obligations.

CORPORATION

A corporation is a legal business entity, separate from those who founded it. Like a person, the corporation can be taxed and can be held legally liable for its actions. The corporation can also make a profit. Corporate status shields the owners from personal liability, which is a key advantage. This is expensive to form and requires extensive record keeping. While double taxation is sometimes mentioned as a drawback to incorporation, the S corporation (or Subchapter corporation, a popular variation of the regular C corporation) avoids this problem by allowing income or losses to be passed through on individual tax returns, like a partnership.

LIMITED LIABILITY COMPANY (LLC)

A hybrid form of partnership, the LLC is gaining in popularity because it allows owners to take advantage of the benefits of both the corporation and partnership forms of business. An LLC can be advantageous because profits and losses can be passed through to owners without taxation of the business itself, while owners are shielded from personal liability.

When trying to determine what type of business structure best fits your situation, seek counsel from your accountant and corporate attorney.

OFFICE FRONT

In the hunting industry, an office front is not immediately necessary or important. Few hunting operations rely on walk-in traffic to create sales or to conduct normal business, so home offices are fine. Most start-up hunting outfitters work from a home office, which is sufficient and saves on overhead. Also, many hunting outfitters or proprietors are based in remote locations on ranches or rural properties, where existing ranch offices serve dual duty.

In my case, I operated from a home office for almost ten years. The primary downside of the home office, from my perspective, was my inability to "get away" from the business, which in the long run took a toll because I never had quiet time. Plus, home offices can place a strain on family life. Once we built a dedicated office, I was better able to find a balance in my life because I was finally able to separate my business and personal life. I do attribute part of my longevity in this industry to having a dedicated office outside our home.

OFFICE TOOLS

Fortunately, it is not necessary for hunting proprietors to spend a great deal on office equipment and supplies. The basic requirements include a computer with basic software tools, copy machine, printer, filing cabinets, desk, and miscellaneous office supplies. You can purchase the necessities for less than $3,000.

As you are setting up your office, do not underestimate the importance of well-organized business records. Although paper files are giving way to electronic files and digital record keeping, I still depend partially on hard copy filing systems, and we have several filing cabinets that house years of important records. We have been steadily transitioning to electronic record keeping, but my age and lack of knowledge in the tech world makes me a bit of a dinosaur when it comes to information storage. I still prefer to open a filing cabinet to retrieve a document of interest.

I have been fortunate to have "computer geeks" as part of our office team since the day I started the business, shortly after my college graduation. Their tech skills have offset my shortfalls. They have taught me how valuable a capable support team can be, both in the field and in the office, to a successful hunting enterprise.

CAPITAL

Capital, in most basic terms, is money, but more specifically it is the money required to produce goods and services. All businesses must have capital in order to maintain their operations. Business capital comes in two main forms: debt and equity. Debt refers to loans and other types of credit that must be repaid in the future, usually with interest. Equity, on the other hand, generally does not involve a direct obligation to repay the funds. Instead, equity investors receive an ownership position in the company, which usually takes the form of stock, thus the term "stock equity." Obviously, it requires cash to fledge and operate a business, regardless of the industry in question. In the hunting business, over the years, I have noticed two scenarios that tend to characterize most start-up hunting operations.

First, there are those who enter the industry on a shoestring budget and lack the financial capacity to comfortably take care of operating costs. The proprietor's inability to make ends meet is going to create its own fundamental problems which generally send the business into a tailspin. Furthermore, when a business is strapped for cash, its ability to seize growth opportunities is stymied, which is self-limiting. Many of these underfunded operations crash and burn within a few years, even with a sound business concept. Capital is comparable to fuel in the engine. No matter how functional the engine may be, it inevitably dies when it runs out of fuel.

The second scenario involves the new proprietor who comes with a source of wealth, often through family support. These people tend to spend money loosely in an unmeasured fashion. By being blissfully unaware of the bottom line, they create a money pit of an operation by buying lavish trucks, expensive pieces of equipment, and extravagant lodge furnishings. They generally invest in large marketing budgets and other cash-heavy expenses that create an upside-down profit and loss statement. In these cases, once the "romance" of being in the hunting business wears off, these proprietors tend to fade from the scene. They seek out an industry that yields a greater financial return with fewer headaches and less liability exposures.

At any rate, hunting proprietors may opt to fund through traditional options such as a conventional lending institution and/or investors. Both options have pros and cons. For small start-up companies, capital, whether it is debt or equity supported capital, is generally more expensive than it is for a larger, established company with a proven track record that creates less risk for the lenders or investors.

CASH FLOW

I have heard it said, "Cash is king," but I have also heard the saying, "Cash flow trumps cash." In the business world, both are important. Cash flow generally is an accurate indicator of business vibrancy, as long as the inflow of cash exceeds the outflow. That is a no brainer, correct? Cash inflow is the lifeblood of a business and comes from a variety of sources, such as payments from customers, loans, investors' monetary infusions, or interest on savings or investments. Cash is also important. When it comes time to pay for the things that are necessary to make your business run, such as lease payments, wages, marketing, insurance coverage, and other operating expenses, it takes money. Naturally, positive cash flow is preferred.

Positive cash flow means the business is running smoothly. High positive cash flow is even better because it will allow you to make new investments (hire employees, acquire more hunting land, etc.) and grow the business. Understanding and being able to project cash flow through the course of the year, and over time, allows the business owner to make smart financial decisions and operate the company without blindly running into a cash problem. Becoming comfortable and competent with cash flow issues is often a product of experience as well as historical financial trends. Both are integral to understanding and anticipating future cash positions for the company.

1 > Most hunting operations are not big enough to justify the expense of a dedicated office. However, in the long term, it is important that hunting proprietors separate their home lives and business lives to avoid burnout.

2 > During the start-up phase, it is vital to have enough funding to sustain the business until adequate cash flow provides financial stability. Small business loans are commonly used to help maintain businesses during frail, fledgling periods. Capital is also necessary to take advantage of growth opportunities. Under-capitalized businesses are often hamstrung when opportunities arise.

3 > Although most hunting operations do not require large capital investments in office equipment, it is critical to have basic office tools so the enterprise can function efficiently.

4 > For those business owners who struggle to understand basic financial documents, it is vital to have an office administrator or an accountant who can help with these business fundamentals.

5 > In today's era of technology and communication, on-the-fly and in-the-field administrative work is often key to staying caught up.

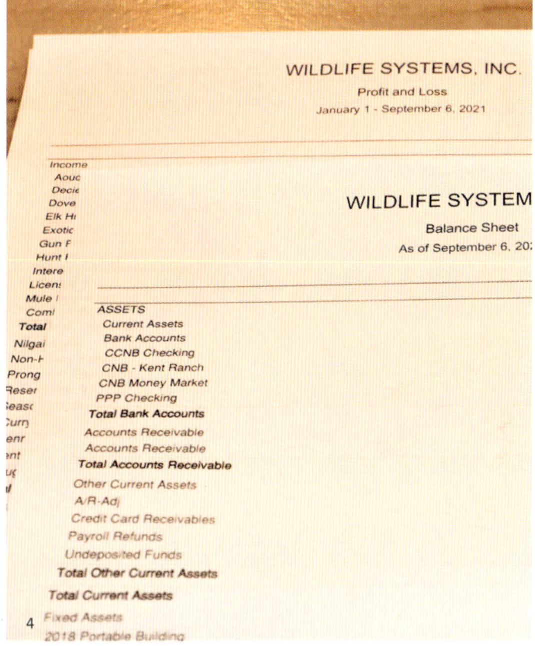

WILDLIFE SYSTEMS, INC.

Profit and Loss

January 1 - September 6, 2021

WILDLIFE SYSTEM

Balance Sheet

As of September 6, 20:

Income	
Aouc	
Decic	
Dove	
Elk H	
Exotic	
Gun F	
Hunt I	
Intere	
Licens	
Mule I	
Coml	
Total	
Nilgai	
Non-H	
Prong	
Reser	
Seasc	
Curry	
enr	
ant	
ug	
al	

ASSETS

Current Assets
  Bank Accounts
    CCNB Checking
    CNB - Kent Ranch
    CNB Money Market
    PPP Checking
  Total Bank Accounts
  Accounts Receivable
    Accounts Receivable
  Total Accounts Receivable
  Other Current Assets
    A/R-Adj
    Credit Card Receivables
  Payroll Refunds
  Undeposited Funds
  Total Other Current Assets
Total Current Assets
Fixed Assets
  2018 Portable Building

UNDERSTANDING COSTS

It is interesting to me that most small business owners, including those in the hunting industry, do not understand their true costs of doing business or the actual cost of delivering a particular product or service to their clients. In an ideal business world, the first step in establishing product or service prices is understanding your costs. Your price must be high enough to cover all the costs you incur and to make a profit. Period.

Business costs fall into three main categories: fixed costs, direct or variable costs, and capital costs. Depreciation, wear and tear on capital assets, is a fourth category.

BUSINESS COSTS

FIXED COSTS

Fixed costs are the costs that must be paid regardless of how much or how little is sold. For example, one of the fixed costs for a shop is the rent. This stays the same whether the shop sells one product or thousands. In the hunting business, the equivalent might be the lease fees that you pay to acquire the hunting rights on a property; it could be that the lessee pays the same sum of money to the landowner regardless of how many hunts the proprietor sells. Other fixed costs might include liability insurance, salaries for certain staff, marketing, utilities, telephone, vehicles, and perhaps professional fees.

DIRECT OR VARIABLE COSTS

Variable costs tend to change based on changes in sales. For businesses that simply sell a service, these costs tend to vary less. For those that sell products, the variable costs tend to fluctuate in a commensurate proportion to total sales. Variable costs in the hunting business might include contract fees for guides and cooks, food for hunting camps, mileage costs for travel, and depreciation on UTVs and work trucks. Also, lease fees or landowner fees, depending upon the deal structure, will often be a variable cost because the payments are based off the number of hunts sold. In some cases, the outfitter pays the landowner "x" amount per hunter or per animal, making it truly a variable cost, as opposed to paying a lump sum lease fee, which creates more financial risk to the outfitter.

CAPITAL COSTS

Capital costs are fixed costs that benefit your business for a long time. This includes items such as stands, feeders, lodges, various equipment, and company vehicles. Capital costs are also known as capital assets.

DEPRECIATION

Depreciation is the accounting term used to assign a value to the wear and tear on your capital assets. The value of things such as machinery, equipment, and vehicles fall as they are used or wear out. Depreciation means the cost of these assets are spread out, and they are written off against the profits of several years rather than just the year in which they are purchased.

In the hunting business, there is a tendency for some proprietors to not assign a cost value to certain people's time. For instance, if a landowner is in the ranching business and has a ranch hand who is on salary by the Ranch LLC but also fills feeders and guides for the Hunting LLC, landowners do not accurately apportion the overhead of the ranch hand to both enterprises. This oversight, intentionally or otherwise, creates some inaccuracies in the true costs associated with each enterprise.

Similarly, hunting company owners tend to overlook the cost value of their time if they are performing work for the company. In fact, there is an opportunity cost associated with their time. If they were not contributing their time to their company, they could be contributing their time to another employer and generating revenue from that time investment.

Once again, understanding all costs associated with the business is important in determining costs to produce products and services. Once those costs are determined and price points are established, they must fall within the range the market will bear. If the price is higher than what the market dictates, it becomes a fundamental problem in the business's financial metrics. In this case, the business owner may be forced to reevaluate their cost basis.

UNDERSTANDING PROFIT MARGINS

Profit margin is the amount of returns (or profit) a company generates as the result of its operational efforts. A basic formula for deriving this number is dividing the amount of generated profit (left after settling taxes) by the revenue. Calculating the margin is important for several reasons. The profit margin provides the company with a means of measuring its success; it makes it easier to determine how to allocate the profits in the upcoming year and identifies when profits must be increased to generate a more desirable margin in the upcoming fiscal year.

As a means of measuring the success of a company from year to year, the profit margin shows whether the company has gained or lost ground in comparison to past periods. These comparisons often provide some insight into how well a company has weathered a difficult economic period or managed to withstand new competition in the marketplace. If the company has managed to at least maintain the same margin of profit from one year to the next, despite adverse conditions, this indicates the company is performing well and is financially stable. Should the calculation reveal the company has lost ground, this can be the wakeup call that leads to reassessing the operation and trimming costs to improve the margin during the upcoming year.

Over the years, I have found it difficult to increase the margins of profit on the hunts that we sell for two primary reasons. First, I have never been able to increase the price of our hunts without triggering a subsequent increase in lease rates or landowner fees. It is not unusual for our landowner fees to get pushed up a year or two after we increase our hunt prices, effectively erasing the increased profit margin while concurrently increasing our cost basis. Second, some of our fixed costs and variable costs have increased over the years. Although my primary hunting business, Wildlife Systems, Inc., has remained profitable during most years, we have grown to accept that our end-of-year profits are generally tied more closely to total gross sales than improved margins of profit. Consequently, this places more pressure on increasing total sales over time even to "hold serve" on end-of-year profits.

PROPER BOOKKEEPING AND ACCOUNTING PRACTICES

Though it may be one of the least appealing aspects of owning and operating a business, your company will flounder without basic bookkeeping and accounting. You need to keep books in order so you can understand what is going on financially with the company as well as pay your taxes and remain in the good graces of the government agencies that regulate your business activities. Again, the hunting industry tends to lack the business sophistication that is found more widely in other industries. It is not uncommon for chaos to reign when tax season rolls around and the proprietor is scrambling trying to help the business's accountant to make sense of the books.

In addition to providing you with the tools to compile the information necessary to complete your tax returns and to perhaps apply for business loans, basic accounting and bookkeeping measures help you understand the business's financial performance. When you understand your company's financial workings, you are better able to keep your operations profitable and stay afloat. Accurate books allow you to see whether the company is financially efficient.

With the advent of electronic accounting programs such as QuickBooks, Peachtree, and others, bookkeeping and accounting prep work is much easier than it was in the days of the handwritten ledger. Also, a word to the wise: develop a good relationship with your accountant so that you are comfortable leaning on them for advice and direction.

When I moved to San Angelo in 1988, less than a year after starting the business, I was very fortunate to meet Jeffrey Bozeman right off the bat. In fact, Jeff, who was the second person I met upon my arrival, is still my accountant today and one of my best friends. As I have told Jeff before, one of the advantages of having him as my accountant and as a friend is that I can ask him dumb questions without worrying about feeling dumb!

PERSONNEL AND SUPPORT

During the year I started Wildlife Systems, Inc., shortly out of college, my Dad told me, "Your employees are to you, as ten is to one." He also mentioned this on several other occasions. For years I pondered his philosophy. Frankly, I used to think it was a somewhat elementary-level statement. But over time, I began to recognize the profound merit of my Dad's ideology that he was trying to instill in me. Through the eyes of his friends and coworkers, my dad was one of the most appreciated and respected men I have ever known. While he had many great traits that made him an effective leader, perhaps the most important characteristic came from his understanding that those around him represented 9/10 of the horsepower needed to get things done and make positive differences.

When people maintain that customers are a business's lifeblood, I respectfully disagree. Indeed, the customer base is important, but if it were not for the performance of the business's personnel, the customer base simply would not exist—and this would be a pointless discussion. In my opinion, the company's personnel are truly the company's lifeblood. In the hunting business, the support team who are "front and center" are the guides, cooks, and office personnel. I have found it most effective to seek out people with positive and friendly attitudes instead of worrying too much about locating the most experienced help. A bad attitude, even if it belongs to a skilled and experienced worker, can be cancerous and can create a counterproductive environment.

The hunting business is a service business. Camp staff often work long hours and sometimes deal with high-pressure circumstances, so one's ability to maintain a positive outlook and a pleasant demeanor is critical. As I have told our guides, "The most important thing you can wear to work is the smile on your face." To maximize the support team's productivity, I have found it is critical for everyone to "march in step." We often have several hunting camps running simultaneously, and it is not unusual for us to have 15 to 20 different guides and three to four cooks working from multiple camps at a given time; with that many moving parts, vibration in the wheel that's due to inadequate operating standards can result in costly problems.

We preach the importance of replicating a set of protocols and practices that work well. While our practices may not be the best for everyone in the industry, they work well for us, and we can replicate them with ease. Some of these protocols relate to how we perform our duties in the skinning shed, paperwork that is associated with each hunt, camp orientations, daily routines during the hunt, labeling of capes and antlers, as well as a myriad of other relevant matters. Repetition and replication are part of our strategy to create an efficient and effective program that can be applied cookie-cutter style among different camps. And along the way, we are always looking for ways to fine-tune and improve our operating culture.

To create this type of operating culture, there are four primary ingredients that we rely on to build this operational base.

OPERATIONAL BASE INGREDIENTS

- A company handbook that outlines an assortment of policies, protocols, and expectations
- Annual in-service meeting that involves in-person training
- Periodic emails that contain best practices recommendations and assessments
- Experienced leadership in each camp to help mentor newer guides and cooks and to help cultivate the operating culture that defines how we do things

Again, it is impossible to overemphasize the importance of the support team in developing a successful hunting business.

ORGANIZATION OF RESOURCES

A business is a composite of many parts. It is a single entity made from multiple interdependent units. Creating a single entity from multiple units is the result of organizing. Organizing is simply the process of bringing together diverse resources and putting them together in a way that makes the system work. Essentially, this is how natural resource ecology works. The overall ecological function is only as strong as the healthy functioning soils, plants, animals, and climatic features that are part of the same system. Of course, this analogy springs from the mind of a wildlife biologist who happens to be a business owner; that is how my feeble brain works.

Because the hunting business contends with many variables outside of the proprietor's control, it is paramount that a great deal of attention be given to the organization's details. There are many moving parts when it comes to hunting camps, including transporting clients to and from the field, dealing with harvested game, taking care of harvest photos and records, dealing with meat processing and taxidermy, adhering to ranch rules that are sometimes specific and unique to each individual property, pre-hunt and post-hunt communication with clients, ranch personnel, and camp staff, cataloging records and photos, dealing with flight delays, and the list goes on.

Bottom line? Dividends multiply for proprietors who have been diligent with their organizational efforts, which also helps cultivate an efficient, effective operational culture.

EVALUATE AND PLAN AHEAD

Whether it is a fledgling business or a long-tenured, well-established business, it is important for the proprietors and their support team to constantly evaluate performance and mechanics. Careful observation not only creates efficiency but helps identify "chinks in the armor" before they cause major problems, while also creating an environment where improvement and innovation thrive.

As part of the evaluation process, apply the lessons learned along the way and integrate the knowledge into the operational mix as you move forward. Improvement and progress are principally accomplished through appropriate planning. So, evaluate, plan, and implement over time, it will ensure improved results.

DIVERSIFY

As with wildlife habitat, diversity in the business world is good. A business that is one-dimensional cannot stand up to the seemingly endless host of pressures as well as a fully-formed, multi-faceted business. In the hunting business, the menu of hunts offered and the portfolio of hunting properties are two of the most obvious places for diversification. Case in point is the market for guided white-tailed deer hunt, which has softened over the last ten to 15 years. At one time, there was not another segment in the outfitting industry that rivaled the robust demand for quality whitetail hunts. However, in a matter of a few years, that market began to shrink and is currently a shell of what it used to be.

Wildlife Systems, Inc. was perhaps the largest whitetail outfitter in the country for several years. When the whitetail market began to constrict, the reduction placed a huge burden on our business to maintain gross sells. Fortunately, all our eggs were not in a single basket. We began adjusting and emphasizing other features of our business, including expanding to different game species and concentrating more effort on our wildlife-related consulting work.

Diversity in the hunting business should also be reflected in the ages and personalities of guides and cooks. Having a good mix of younger and older staffers not only allows you to match generational traits between clients and staff, but it also provides a potential pipeline of reinforcements should your older staffers decide to retire and/or pull back due to the toll that the work can take on veteran guides and cooks.

PROBLEM-SOLVING AND CONTINGENCIES

The business world is not always filled with green pastures, blue skies, and long runways. In fact, problems and problem-solving goes with the territory for business owners, managers, and the entire support team. Problems exist at all levels in the organizational chart, and it should be incumbent on all staff members to learn how to minimize these complications and to also know how to deal with challenges when they arise.

Though different people may have different styles as they address and work through challenges, there are some basic elements that are generally part of the problem-solving process.

PROBLEM-SOLVING PROCESS

DEFINE THE PROBLEM

Step one in finding a solution is diagnosing the problem—the context, background, and symptoms of the issue.

DETERMINE THE CAUSE(S)

It may take some digging to determine the underlying cause(s) of the emerging issue. The proprietor is often too distant from ground zero to assess the matter alone, so it is often necessary to gather input from the support team, or sometimes the best option may be allowing your support team to sort these matters out themselves. As they say, there are two (and sometimes three or four) sides to every story, so trying to sift through the rhetoric and distill the facts that define the problem's actual cause may be a greater challenge than one might expect.

DEVELOP ALTERNATIVE SOLUTIONS

When assessing possible solutions, it is helpful to identify the obvious alternatives as well as outside-of-the-box options. Exploring multiple options is often a good idea so the matter can be examined from the broadest perspective, which will hopefully lead to the best solution.

SELECT A SOLUTION

Selecting a solution generally boils down to two considerations: Which option makes the most sense and is most feasible? Which solution is the most preferred by those who are responsible for implementing it?

The approach outlined above provides a framework for solving problems that will be encountered.

EXAMPLES OF COMMON PROBLEMS IN THE HUNTING BUSINESS

- Incompatible personalities between guide and hunter
- Unexpected food allergies from clients in camp
- The client's poor shooting skills
- Inability of clients to meet the hunt's physical demands
- Lost luggage of clients who are traveling by air
- Faulty equipment that may impair the hunt, especially hunting vehicles
- Dealing with accidents and injuries of clients and guides
- Dealing with poachers
- Problems associated with wounded animals, including pushback from clients when wounded animal policies are enforced
- Loud snorers in bedrooms with other clients
- Inclement weather
- Illegal aliens walking through hunting areas and disrupting hunters, which has become increasingly more common along the Mexican border in recent years
- And a host of other potential problems that are always looming

Contingency plans are always valuable, especially when trying to stay ahead of possible problems and challenges. Backup guides and cooks, spare hunting vehicles, extra equipment and parts, alternative foods, and all-weather hunting blinds are a few elements of a well-rounded contingency plan that may help you solve problems expeditiously when they arise.

So think ahead, be prepared, count on people who are solid and reliable, and challenge your support team to think in the context of "what would I do if?"

TOP TIPS FOR BUSINESS ENTREPRENEURS

Over the years I have had an increasing number of people query me about my thoughts on key ingredients for business success. Successful businesspeople have different ideas, strategies, and platforms that led to their ability to enjoy positive results from their business ventures. And, different people have different ways that they might interpret and translate their own recipes for succeeding in the business world.

I think I would be remiss to not share some points that I feel represent fundamentals at succeeding as a business owner. These items below are not rocket science in complexity, as it's my opinion that the basics of business success are—should we say—basic.

BASICS OF BUSINESS SUCCESS

HAVE A BUSINESS PLAN

Creating a plan helps you process and visualize your thoughts more effectively—even if it is a handwritten document on a yellow notepad. If you would use a map to get yourself from Dallas to NYC, then why not use a map to get yourself from the start to the finish line with your business.

DO NOT BE UNDERCAPITALIZED

Projected cash flow during the fledgling stages is often overestimated. Be thrifty and resourceful but have access to enough start-up capital to make it through the lean times as well as having the necessary funds to ensure that basic operating needs are met. It is also important to budget enough start-up capital so you can leverage against good opportunities that require additional cash.

ESTABLISH A FRAMEWORK

Create operating practices that work well for your organization and have some degree of efficiency. Your entire team needs to understand the practices and march in step to create a successful operating culture. Predictability, replication, and repetition are key building blocks.

DO NOT BECOME TOO ENTRENCHED IN YOUR APPROACH

Though replication and repetition are important, adaptability is often the key in being able to see and accommodate emerging opportunities and to avoid boxing yourself into a failing corner.

SURROUND YOURSELF WITH GOOD PEOPLE

This rule of thumb is relevant to all phases and stages of life. However, as you enter the professional stages in life, seeking out and affiliating with people who exhibit integrity and good character will serve you well. As the late western novelist Elmer Kelton once said, "You are who you ride with."

ACQUIRE A MENTOR, OR SEVERAL

Do not be too timid or too proud to reach out to fellow professionals who may be able to provide resources, information, and/or guidance. Assuming a humble and honest demeanor is often key in establishing the type of trust and respect that creates a nurturing mentorship.

BE A PRO

Look the part, act the part, and be the part. Simple as that.

REINVEST IN YOUR BUSINESS

Rather than mine the profits of your business's success, leverage your growing resources in a fashion that helps establish stability, strength, and liquidity. With that said, never confuse the need to redeploy cash with the equally important need to become and remain cash healthy, so keep plenty of cash on hand.

REINVEST IN YOUR PROFESSION

Never underestimate the power of supporting your own industry. This can be accomplished through providing financial and technical assistance for those who are in the education or training stages of their careers, or it can be done by supporting trade groups and NGOs. It is a matter of giving back and/or paying it forward.

EDUCATION IS A LIFELONG PROCESS

Whether it is high-tech or high-touch, striving to improve yourself will serve you well. There is always room for improvement, whatever your craft may be, so avoid complacency at all costs; otherwise, the ever-changing world will leave you behind in a cloud of dust. Also, education is the willingness to learn from others, letting their failures serve as preventatives to you making the same or similar mistakes, and equally learning from their successes.

WRITE IN COMPLETE SENTENCES

Yes, you read that right. Our society regularly butchers the English language through shortcuts and sloppily written messages. Write it out, correctly and completely. When we become accustomed to taking shortcuts in life, these tendencies shape our broad operating culture and may cultivate other shortcuts that do not serve us or the business well. So, write in complete sentences, both from a literal and a metaphorical standpoint: try to finish the task de jour, properly and completely.

TREAT PEOPLE THE WAY YOU WISH TO BE TREATED

Be respectful, kind, and compassionate. And be nice! Being nice is free but generates immense returns on investment.

THERE'S NO REPLACEMENT FOR HARD WORK

There's something to be said for working smarter, not harder. But there are often no shortcuts for success, and long hours, 7-day work weeks, and tireless dedication is sometimes the difference between mediocrity and excellence.

TAKE TIME TO REFLECT

Self-introspection and evaluation are vital in absorbing and processing the lessons that have been self-generated through your journey as a person and business owner; lessons that may not reveal themselves until you put yourself into the right frame of mind. Matter of fact, reflection is important for all facets of life, professionally and personally. Some of my most fertile times for deep reflection are while cruising down the road listening to good music and allowing my mind to unwind and open.

DO NOT GIVE UP

In the words of the late Jim Valvano, college basketball player, coach, and broadcaster, during his famous ESPY (Excellence in Sports Performance Yearly) Awards speech, "Don't give up. Don't ever give up." You may also be familiar with astronaut Gene Kranz's observation, "Failure is not an option." Well, I am here to tell you that failure is indeed an option. The fear of failing is a huge motivator. But at the end of the day, the journey has less to do with whether you fail and more to do with learning from your failures and applying those hard-earned street smarts in a way that makes you a wiser person. Part of that self-acquired wisdom may be knowing when to say "enough is enough" and recognizing that perhaps it is time to try a new path in life. Failure can be an opportunity to simply start over, even if that means creating new dreams and revising old plans. So "Don't give up. Don't ever give up!"

6 PROFESSIONALISM

THE HUNTING BUSINESS, ESPECIALLY
IN PARTS OF THE U.S., IS STARVING FOR
BUSINESS OWNERS WHO ARE COMMITTED
TO OPERATING UNDER BUSINESS STANDARDS
THAT BETTER REFLECT THE PROFESSIONAL
IMAGES AND PROFESSIONAL CULTURES
OFTEN FOUND IN OTHER INDUSTRIES BUT
WHICH ARE LACKING IN THIS ONE.

OPPOSITE
Kent Yarbrough
2017 Mule Deer
Pecos County, Texas
Guide - Will Cantu

At times, I've had to challenge myself to feel proud about the career path I have taken, particularly when I step back and compare the professional norms in the hunting business to those found in other professions: sense of pride, sense of self-awareness, and lack of a collective appetite across the industry to self-govern a more refined behavioral pattern that creates enhanced optics regarding who we are and what we do as ambassadors for hunting.

About 15 years ago, I was speaking at a Texas Farm Bureau event in Fredericksburg, Texas. I was sharing the program with a good friend and colleague, Forrest Armke, who was the ranch manager of the historic Ford Ranch near Brady, Texas. Forrest's presentation preceded mine. When he finished, Forrest introduced me. Part of his introduction was, and this is verbatim as best I recall, "In some circles, outfitter is a four-letter word." And I must admit Forrest's observation was spot on. Indeed, the outfitting industry tends to lack integrity. The hunting business in general tends to lack professionalism, especially here in the U.S.

We discuss this every year at our annual company in-service meeting. I always share with our staff the same few thoughts on the importance of professionalism within our business. First, my mom did not clean houses to help pay for my college so that I could become some Bubba in the outfitting business. Second, the outfitting industry is indeed full of Bubbas. And third, it is not that difficult to separate yourself from the Bubbas of the world by simply applying some degree of professionalism in your approach to conducting business.

The Merriam-Webster dictionary defines professionalism as: "The conduct, aims, or qualities that characterize or mark a profession or a professional person." Cambridge defines professionalism as: "The combination of all the qualities that are connected with trained and skilled people." For me, professionalism runs much deeper and is more complex than what those definitions indicate. Professionalism embodies behavior that is shaped by discipline and character, resulting in high ethical and moral standards. Professionalism is often easy to recognize when you see it. The greatest professionals exhibit exemplary behavior when there is no gallery to observe them. Lack of professionalism does not reflect well on the industry.

This topic of professionalism is broad and somewhat complex. Entire books are written on this subject. Although I will not take a deep dive on this topic in this book, this part of the hunting industry is too important for me not to examine more closely, so I'll explore some personal thoughts on what it requires to be a true professional in this field.

MIXING BUSINESS WITH PLEASURE

Many people get into the hunting business because of their love for hunting, and that is no surprise. Thus, it is not uncommon for hunting proprietors to personally hunt on the same properties that they offer paid hunts to clients. This is a delicate matter and essentially boils down to balance and situational discretion. In my opinion, these "opposing" activities can exist mutually with little or no conflict if there are clear lines drawn to avoid problems.

By hunting on their outfitted lands, outfitters and guides can open themselves up to justified scrutiny from not only the hunting clients, but from their landlords as well. Outfitters and guides hunting on the properties that their clients are hunting on may create the perception, especially in the clients' minds, that the outfitting group has its hands in the collective cookie jar. From a landlord's perspective, personal hunting by the outfitting group may foster some degree of distrust or concern. I tell our guides each year that we do not want our landowners concerning themselves with what we are doing on their properties; our role is to provide a service on those places, not recreating or self serving, or goofing off. In my opinion, discretion, open communication, and reasonable judgment can ensure that acceptable practices do not cross the line into something more conflicting.

PROFESSIONALS VERSUS TRADESMEN

There is something to be said about people who undertake their jobs with pride. Regardless of their professions, they are deeply committed students of their trade and take their jobs to a higher level through passion and performance. These people stand in stark contrast to those who simply go through the required motions to earn a paycheck, simply performing job-related tasks with little emotional investment.

In the U.S., we tend to hold professions that require a high level of education, training, and experience in higher regard than those professions that require skill or trade alone. In our professional caste system, both white-collar professionals and blue-collar skilled workers are valued more than unskilled laborers. This distinction is interesting but arbitrary because every single segment is essential to our economy. With that said, it exists and got me to thinking about where outfitters and hunting guides fit in this hierarchy? While the answer is debatable, I would say that American society often puts our profession on the bottom of the pyramid. If we were outfitting in Africa, the situation would be reversed because the professional hunting trade is often viewed much differently. Professional hunters (PHs) are generally revered in African society, viewed with greater esteem than here in the U.S.

Let me say here, what society thinks about a profession is a lot less important than how individuals view their professions. Some people, regardless of job titles and skill sets, are consummate professionals, while others with the same jobs and responsibilities are merely paycheck grubbers. Who would you rather do business with? In the American hunting business, it is entirely possible—and preferable—to be a professional. How? Challenge yourself, take pride in every aspect of your work, and strive to improve your skills and service. Treat your day-to-day occupation as an opportunity to do something you love instead of a drudgery-filled job. Legendary NBA star Julius Irving summed it up well when he said, "Being a professional is doing the things you love to do on the days you don't feel like doing them." This desire comes natural to some while it is developed over time with others.

COMPETENCY

Knowledge is power. More knowledge maximizes your capacity to excel professionally. As a hunting guide, are you content to simply put your client in a position to fill their tag? Or do you also strive to be an interpreter for your client, pointing out the various plant and animal species while explaining the ecology of how those species interact? As an outfitter, are you satisfied to simply plod along doing things the same way you have in the past as a matter of convenience, or are you willing to explore for innovative use of the newer tools, techniques, and technologies that continue to evolve?

Henry Ford once said, "Anyone who stops learning is old, whether at 20 or 80. Anyone who keeps learning stays young." Ford's observation not only identifies how to stay mentally fresh but how to develop the mental edge that professionalism requires. Today we live a life of convenience, where information is available at our fingertips. Google and other search engines have made it possible for us to find self-help resources and acquire the information we need in mere seconds. Whether it is equipment-related, something to do with wildlife diseases, general first aid information, or endless other topics, the internet is a treasure trove for those who thirst for knowledge. But, and it is a big but, do not forget to combine that "book knowledge" with the practical applications that are only gained through trial and error and hands-on learning in the field.

From a competency standpoint, I have always been amazed at the disparity between African PHs and U.S. hunting guides. Granted, there are exceptions, but generally the difference between the levels of professional competency between the two is a stark contrast. One reason for the difference is the rigorous training and certification process that is required in many African countries to obtain a professional hunter's license. On top of the training, the professional culture of the hunting business defines itself a bit differently than that of the same culture in the U.S. Regardless, until someone has seen the difference firsthand, it is difficult to appreciate the chasm separating the two. Seeing African hunting professionals in action can be a bit humbling for an American hunting professional.

I was fortunate that my mentor, Dick Laros, invited me to accompany him and his wife Norma as an observer on a safari in Zimbabwe about five years after I started WSI. By then, I knew just enough about wildlife and the hunting business to be a young, arrogant professional. Spending 14 days in the African bush with a couple of seasoned African PHs knocked me down several notches and highlighted my deficiencies in several key areas. Since then, I have traveled to Africa many times as well as other destinations around the globe. Each of these trips has provided a great opportunity to advance my own skills by learning from others.

COMMUNICATION AND INTERACTION

Good communication skills and productive interactions with other people are essential to achieving professionalism in the hunting business. Despite its outdoor setting, hunting is a service-oriented business where there is a personal interface between the professional and the client, not to mention the many hazards that can pose safety and health risks to all involved if communication breaks down.

If you are entering the hunting business, it is paramount that you become comfortable and capable of communicating and interacting well with others. Interestingly, some introverts are attracted to hunting and wildlife due to the solitude that the outdoors offers. When introverts, individuals who get their energy from being alone, gravitate into the hunting business, they sometimes must overcome inherent barriers to effectively work in this space. Introverts who fail to adapt to this people-oriented and service-oriented business environment may perform poorly, or at worst, may inadvertently place the client in jeopardy by not properly communicating.

There are many options for people to improve their communication abilities. Toastmasters has been around for many years and is a great way to become more comfortable speaking in front of people and improving communication skills. Online tutorials are also available to assist people with communication training. In the Lone Star State, Texas Brigades is an exceptional youth conservation leadership program that includes communication skills as part of its curriculum. The program gently, but persistently, pushes introverted kids out of their comfort zones, sometimes transforming them in amazing ways. It is not uncommon for kids who enter Brigades camps as shy individuals to leave the camp with a newfound confidence in their improved interpersonal skills.

Again, part of professional development in the hunting business should be to focus on achieving effective communication skills. In today's world where kids are growing up with cellular phones with more computing power than the original space shuttle, they generally communicate by text or typing instead of talking. Our dependence on smart phones and other technology has diminished our desire to communicate verbally and use correct grammar. Furthermore, because texting is a shortcut communication technique, people have become accustomed to using abbreviated words, acronyms and emojis and littering modern writing with plenty of crapola.

In recent years, I have given several presentations to college students focusing on becoming successful professionals. One of my tips is to always use complete sentences and correct grammar, even if it is simply a text. In my opinion, when we butcher our writing skills through texting, the butchery carries over into our other communication. It is a turnoff for me to see smart, capable people bastardizing language and thereby disrupting communication.

APPEARANCE AND DEMEANOR

Every year at our company in-service meeting, I tell our guides and cooks, "The most important thing you can wear to work is the smile on your face." I also tell them to dress for the occasion. Part of being a professional is looking like a pro. An individual's appearance and the image they project is hugely influential. Your overall image is reflected through your clothing, facial expressions, and body language.

A hunting guide should look the part. If you are going to be a guide, do not show up for work looking like a mechanic or an accountant. Camouflage clothing is not a must, but shirts and jackets reflecting the styles of traditional field apparel should be considered. Jeans, khakis, and camo pants are good choices for bottoms. An appropriate hat is also a must, perhaps sporting the logo of the outfitting company, indicating you ride for the brand, because you do—and should. Avoid wearing bloody, soiled clothing in camp when possible. In public locations such as airports, bloody hunting clothes are an absolute no-no because of the image it creates regarding hunters and hunting.

In addition to clothing, facial expressions and body language are equally important in terms of projecting a professional and positive image. As mentioned before, a smile signals a person that is open, friendly, warm, and ready to take care of business, which shapes other people's perception and interactions. First impressions are terribly important, so be courteous, offer up a firm handshake and perhaps a big hug—and the relationship will immediately be off to a good start. The hunting business could use an industry-wide facelift. So, look the part, act the part, and be a pro!

ETHICS

The Merriam-Webster dictionary defines ethics as: "(1) the discipline dealing with what is good and bad and with moral duty and obligation; (2b) of the principles of conduct governing an individual or a group; (2c) a guiding philosophy; (2d) a consciousness of moral importance." My simple interpretation of ethics is, "doing the right thing for the right reason." The fundamental premise is relatively easy to understand, albeit still somewhat ambiguous.

The term "hunting ethics" is tossed around loosely these days. Slob hunters and those who exhibit poor morals through their hunting practices certainly project a poor image to a watchful, extremely critical society. The topics of animal welfare and guns, both of which are related to hunting, can be hot button issues today in mainstream America. A hunter's behavior does not go unnoticed by the masses. When we recognize that most people already view hunting and guns through a negative lens, the hunting community should be on high alert. We, who enjoy the tradition, should not only conduct ourselves in a way that is above reproach but hold other hunters to the same high standard. Unfortunately, we do not.

In many cases, we are our own worst enemy. We post disturbing images and messages on social media. We have hunting shows on TV that have too much rah-rah and too little respect for the harvested animals. We make poor choices in how we respond to our critics when we are put on the spot. And we even have game management laws that allow us to "manage" our game resources in an intensive fashion that is largely indefensible. Our hunting community has not yet learned how to play the public image game as smart and as hard as we should.

While on the subject of hunting ethics, I would be remiss if I did not touch on Aldo Leopold's philosophy in his essay "The Land Ethic." Leopold, considered by many to be the father of wildlife ecology and

management, spent a lot of time and effort exploring the values of what he referred to as a "land ethic." A land ethic is a philosophy or theoretical framework about how, ethically, humans should regard the land. In *A Sand County Almanac*, a classic text of the environmental movement, Leopold argues that there is a critical need for a "new ethic," an "ethic dealing with human's relation to land and to the animals and plants which grow upon it." He raised that concern in his writings as early as 1949.

Clearly, Leopold recognized a need to improve our relationship with the land (and its animals), some 70-plus years ago. Leopold's land ethic philosophy is a little too nuanced and multifaceted for me to dive into deeply in this book, but we cannot discuss the importance of hunting ethics without considering Leopold's land ethic because they are intertwined. In my opinion, our hunting community has done a poor job of seizing the moment and controlling the narrative regarding a hunter's role and relationship with the land and the game resources tied to the land. Now do not get me wrong, hunters unequivocally are—and have been—the pioneers and champions of U.S. wildlife conservation since the early 1900s. With that said, we have fallen short in understanding our relationship with those resources and communicating our complicated but essential relationship to the public in an effective and clear way. I think it is past due for us to reformat the narrative of selling the merits of hunting to the public, and I'll expand on that later in this book.

I am not sure that our game laws have kept pace with the tools and technologies that are commonplace management practices for managing, raising, and growing some game animals. (I will also take a closer look at some of these concerns in a later chapter.) I have heard many people say, "You can't legislate ethics." Often, these comments have been used as a convenient crutch during policy battles over deer breeding when reform is being considered at the Texas Legislature. I say "baloney!" When you look at game laws across the U.S., you will find many regulations and statutes that are based more on ethics than they are on biology. For example, some game animals can be legally hunted at night while others cannot; there is no scientific basis for this difference. And the list continues. You can hunt female deer during their mating season but not female turkeys, but there is no science that explains this difference. You can hunt upland birds without a plug in your shotgun but not migratory birds; again, no science. In some states you can use game calls for certain species as long as they are not delivered from an electronic device, but there is no science that suggests that electronic calls may compromise the population health of those game animals and non-electronic calls will not. You can use a centerfire caliber on big game animals, but rimfire is outlawed in some states. Archery hunters often get a head start over gun hunters for big game animals in many states. Using drones is forbidden in certain states for some hunting purposes, but is there any science that shows that the use of drones is not good for the sustainable population health of those game species? Hunting over bait is banned in some states, as is hunting from a vehicle, while these practices are lawful in other states, and the list goes on and on.

These game laws often have less to do with compromising the resource's population and more to do with ethics and social pressures. Societal pressures change over time. The tools and technologies we use to grow and hunt game animals have evolved drastically over time. Have our game laws kept pace with these changes? I do not think so. Frankly, the question of whether ethics can or should be legislated is a farce, providing some stakeholder groups with a convenient argument to suit their needs. For more than 100 years, we have used ethics to help shape our game laws. We should continue to use ethics in tandem with sound science to shape future game laws. In my opinion, a combination of sound biological, ecological social science and reasonable ethics provide a strong recipe for good decision-making in our natural resource policy world, and this includes promulgating the rules and regulations related to hunting.

Okay, I will admit I wandered a bit afield over the last few paragraphs, but circling back to the fundamental topic: If you want to be a professional in the hunting business, ethics must be part of the process and should be a constant focal point that helps shape your practices and behavior. Doing the right things for the right reasons will serve you well.

ACCOUNTABILITY

Accountability is another component of professionalism. Owning your actions, whether they are good, bad, or indifferent, is a fundamental trait of responsible people. These days, it seems that many people do not want to be accountable for their own actions and it is a shame. Why? When mistakes are made or when performance falls short, owning up to what went wrong and why it went wrong is the best way to learn. These lessons allow us to grow and make better decisions in the future.

Because it is often easier or more convenient, defaulting to an "it is not my problem" mentality is tempting. Eventually, that type of attitude contributes to a counterproductive behavioral culture that can poison a work environment. Eat your humble pie, remember what it tastes like, and allow that experience to linger to avoid making those mistakes again. Holding yourself accountable is part of being a pro.

GIVING BACK

Some of the most successful and happy people are those who consciously give back to society. The benevolent, philanthropic fiber of our country inspires people; it nurtures noble causes; it speaks to humanity—and good deeds generally find their way to those generous people who make meaningful contributions to our society. Nurturing professional associations, conservation organizations, and other nonprofits through

advocacy and goodwill can be accomplished by giving time, money, or material goods.

There are plenty of hunting and conservation advocacy groups that can benefit from your donations. These groups rely on volunteer support for strength and sustainability. The Boone and Crockett Club, Rocky Mountain Elk Foundation, and Dallas Safari Club are a few of these groups that serve as the voices and advocates for hunting and wildlife. Without people who give back through such organizations, hunting would be a shell of what it is today and so would our wildlife resources.

I am fortunate that I became involved with the Texas Wildlife Association (TWA) shortly after I started Wildlife Systems, Inc. (WSI). Early on, I struggled with the idea that I was "just" a wildlife biologist, or "just" a guide, or "just" an outfitter. My self-induced inferiority complex stemmed from my realization that many people did not particularly value my chosen field. From my vantage point, it seemed as if my profession was not as meaningful, in the eyes of family and friends, as that of an architect, engineer, or doctor.

Getting involved with TWA allowed me to have a platform where my contributions could make a difference. Volunteering

ABOVE > One aspect of professionalism in the hunting business is reinvesting in the industry. Mentoring young and beginning hunters is one of the best ways to give back.

ABOVE > The hunting industry's level of professionalism would rise if all participants used social media more carefully and thoughtfully. Social media is the lens the public uses to peer into the hunting world.

inspired me to be a better professional. It also allowed me to meet successful people who shared similar interests, and our affiliation enabled me to learn from them. Plus, my volunteer contributions have been reciprocated in many ways, which reinforces the adage of "what goes around comes around."

Whether it is education, law enforcement, energy development, medicine, or plumbing, your chosen field needs your support so that your profession has a voice and advocates. Advocacy groups require volunteers to support their existence. As long as groups such as Ducks Unlimited (DU), TWA, Dallas Safari Club, and The Wildlife Society remain strong, hunting and wildlife have a fighting chance in the future. Be a pro and give back.

SOCIAL MEDIA

In this day and age, we cannot have a conversation about professionalism without discussing social media. Whether it is hunting or anything else, our society does not do a good job of self-policing social media content.

These media tools could be our most convenient and effective means of being responsible ambassadors for hunting, but we fail ourselves time and again. It is not that hunters are failing to use these tools, but rather we use these tools poorly by posting crapola. Distasteful photos, poorly written content laced with crude comments, poor grammar as well as a tendency to avoid the extra effort required to share an image and tell a story that is wholesome and tasteful, does our industry and our hunting heritage a disservice. At a minimum, when our hunting community uses social media irresponsibly, we come across as a bunch of uneducated country bumpkins. At worst, we portray ourselves as ruthless, bloodthirsty savages who have no regard for the animals we hunt.

We live in value-driven societies. When we perceive things as being good—good for us, our families, our friends, or our communities—we tend to take care of those things, whatever they may be. We will likely advocate for whatever "good" may be. However, when we perceive things as being bad—bad for us, our family, our friends, or our community—we tend to try to abolish those things. Societal values shape mainstream America, and whatever does not fit well within mainstream America's perception of good generally gets squeezed out of our lives. When the majority of the public becomes averse to certain practices, they will react either by changing the law or by applying peer pressure.

Ultimately, the disfavored practice disappears, either because of law or social intolerance.

Widespread public perception is a powerful force. The optics created through social media are most effective at changing societal opinions. Forces that can be generated through the influence of social media are beyond what anyone could have realistically imagined some ten years ago. As we move forward, the hunting community must become better stewards of our communication efforts, which includes self-policing in order to appeal—or at least not alienate—mainstream America. The responsible use of social media tools is the best way to accomplish this. In the "Game Harvest Photography" chapter, I offer tips for using harvest and hunting images wisely to help address these concerns.

In my opinion, hunting professionals have an increased obligation to effectively advocate for responsible social media use. In the context of the hunting world, social media offers us the greatest opportunity to promote professionalism within our own ranks, and part of the good news is that it does not take a rocket scientist to successfully master social media. Good photos combined with well-written content is the key to advancing our communication efforts—and our cherished tradition.

As I mentioned in the opening paragraph of this chapter, our industry is starving for improved professionalism. Outfitters, guides, and others who work in this field should consider themselves ambassadors for hunting and as advocates for our important hunting heritage. So, be a pro!

7 MARKETING

IN A COMPETITIVE BUSINESS ENVIRONMENT,
GAINING MARKET SHARE THROUGH SALES
IS OFTEN WHAT SEPARATES YOU FROM
COMPETING PRODUCTS OR SERVICES.

G aining a certain market threshold will ultimately be one of the factors that determines whether a business is financially sound enough to stay afloat. Considering that more than 50 percent of businesses go under within five years of their inception, it does not take a rocket scientist to recognize that most businesses simply do not gain enough market share to be sustainable.

Sales are a function of various factors, but from a fundamental standpoint, sales of services and products partially stem from successful marketing. While marketing can be broadly defined, it essentially refers to activities undertaken by a company to promote product or services. Marketing generates the strategies that sales techniques, business communication, and business development are built upon. In the hunting business, proprietors bundle features of various service packages that are tailored to meet the demands of a specific base of potential customers. Proprietors then strategically place that product in front of a market segment, hoping to generate sales or book hunts. In simplified terms, this is how revenue is generated. However, the marketing process is multifaceted, and several components require closer examination.

KNOW YOUR PRODUCT

Knowing your product seems like an easy proposition, does it not? Like so many situations, there is much more here than meets the eye. Ideally, a product should fulfill a certain consumer demand or be so compelling that consumers believe they need it. The hunting business is highly competitive, which ultimately creates a saturation effect that can make high sales performance challenging.

This fierce competition begs the question—how can one company outcompete another? Obviously, one proprietor may be able to offer something unique that separates that company's offerings from most of the competition. This observation begs an additional question—is that product unique compared to the competing products, or is the salesperson able to showcase the features of that product better than the competition? It could be some of both. "Knowing your product" goes much deeper than the product concept itself and speaks to the importance of the proprietor or the salesperson intimately understanding the product. Knowing your product makes you a better salesperson and allows you and your support team to deliver that product more effectively.

In the hunting business, the product is made up of many components and subcomponents. I will sketch an outline, using a bobwhite quail hunt package as an example, to help illustrate this point.

A FEW COMPONENTS OF THE HUNTING PRODUCT

HUNT DURATION

- If you begin the hunt on the afternoon of the arrival day, does the start time compress things too much, especially if clients deal with travel problems such as flight delays?

- If you end the hunt with a morning outing, does this cause the departure, which includes time for the clients to come back to camp, clean up, eat, and catch a flight back home at a reasonable hour, to be too harried and hurried?

- What is the sweet spot regarding duration of hunt? It should reflect the demands of the marketplace, being long enough so clients do not feel terribly rushed but not so long that it consumes more time than clients can comfortably carve from their schedules.

- Furthermore, the longer the duration of the hunt, the greater the overhead likely accrued in servicing your clients. Can these costs be passed along to the clients without overpricing the package?

- Are your guides and cooks part-time contractors? If so, do they have the flexibility to do a four-day program, as opposed to a two-and-a-half-day program?

- Do you have enough good bird dogs to offer a four-day bird hunt and keep dogs rested and ready to go, or does the availability of dogs limit hunting opportunities to two or three days?

MEALS

- How difficult might it be to find a good chef?

- Will your budget allow you to hire a trained, professional chef, or will you be restricted to a self-taught cook who has a more limited culinary repertoire? And even if you can afford a professional chef, how difficult might it be to find a Culinary Arts graduate from Johnson & Wales University who is content living in a remote setting and working out of your kitchen setup?

- If it is a Texas-based operation, do you want to offer Tex-Mex cuisine as part of the meal lineup? If so, and your clients are from up north, will they enjoy the unfamiliar flavors, especially if items are spiced up a bit?

- Do you want to integrate game meats into the mix to make things interesting for your clients? If so, does your cook have experience preparing game meats, and do you have a ready supply of those meats?

- How will you know about possible food allergies or dietary restrictions prior to the start of the hunt? Do you have the capacity to address specific needs such as peanut, shellfish, or MSG allergies; diabetes, lactose intolerance, or gluten intolerance; or any religious or other health-related dietary restriction without compromising the meal plan for the other clients who have no dietary limits?

- Will you serve wine with the evening meal? If so, does your budget allow you to offer quality wines? If not, will a cheap wine diminish the mealtime experience?

- On steak night, will your budget allow serving 1.5" thick, prime ribeyes, as opposed to 1" choice sirloins? If you go with the cheaper steaks, will the lower quality of beef reduce the mealtime experience so much that the client is dissatisfied?

- If you are going to send a sack lunch to be eaten in the field, will it be served off the messy tailgate of a truck, or will it be served off a tablecloth cover portable with nice dishes and quality servingware? These two dining experiences are vastly different. Which is best for you? Which is best for your clients?

GUIDES AND DOGS

- Will you raise your own bird dogs and hire your own guides to run those dogs? Or will you strictly rely on third-party dogs and handlers?

- Will your budget allow you to hire top-shelf handlers with dogs and nice hunting rigs? If so, do you have access to those people?

- Are your kennels adequate for the number of dogs that you need to support your hunt volume and equipped for all types of weather/seasons?

- What about traps or snares that may be on neighboring properties as well as grass burs and snakes that are seemingly everywhere? How might you best deal with those dog-related concerns?

- Are your kennels located far enough away from your lodging to ensure that barking dogs do not disturb the peace and quiet around the lodge area?

- What if your third-party bird dog contractor becomes ill or has vehicle problems? What is your Plan B or even your Plan C?

BIRDS

- What if you have a poor quail hatch for a year or two and run low on birds? Do you apologize and send some refunds and reduce your number of hunters, or do you perhaps offer no hunts that year?

- During lean quail years, do you mitigate the shortfall of wild birds with pen-raised birds? If so, will your clients be satisfied with this arrangement if they anticipated a wild quail hunt? Do you have a source for pen-raised birds if you get into a pinch?

- If you run low on birds, are you capable of leasing additional country that might help mitigate your shortfall, and if so, will your budget allow you to invest in that additional country that may carry a hefty lease price?

These are just four components of a possible hunting package, including some of the subcomponents to consider. Of course, there are many other possible components to contemplate. I hope you can see my point—knowing your product and knowing it well—is more complex than many people realize.

Why is it important that you intimately understand your product? First, when someone calls you and begins asking you a thousand questions about your hunts, your ability to intelligently answer their questions without too much uncertainty makes you a better salesperson. Second, when you and your people understand your product offerings well, it allows your team to deliver the total service package with greater ease, greater efficiency, and greater performance outcomes. And third, a deeper understanding of your product allows you to make smarter decisions as you move forward, tinkering with operations so that you can maximize both your service and your bottom-line.

A final, but important, point that I will make about "knowing your product" is to also understand the shelf life that some products have in the hunting business. In my case, where I lease the lands that we outfit, the hunts that I offer essentially have a shelf life of less than one year. For example, if I contract with a landowner to have the right to conduct ten whitetail hunts on their property, and I guarantee the payments on those ten spots, they are only valid through the end of the upcoming whitetail season. If I pay for ten and only sell six of those spots, I am typically not allowed to roll those unsold spots over into the next season. So, the shelf life of those hunts are similar to bananas at the grocery store; the grocer either sells the bananas before they spoil, or the grocer has a sunk cost in a perishable product. This relatively short shelf life creates an extra layer of financial risk for the hunting proprietor. In most retail businesses, the product has a much longer, often undefined, and perhaps unrestricted shelf life, which provides the business proprietor the luxury of more time to move their merchandise, effectively reducing the financial risk by some degree. I currently spend roughly $1.5 million per year on landowner fees, so that creates pressure to perform well.

When catastrophic events take place, like the terrorist attacks on September 11, 2001, hunting markets can crash instantly. Or, when the price of crude drops from 140 dollars to 40 dollars, and the stock market crashes like it did in late 2008 and early 2009, it can seriously affect the hunting markets' strength—and it did. Or when COVID-19 paralyzed our world in 2020, hunting operations in some areas of the globe lost a full year's worth of revenue. When you consider those uncontrollable variables and couple them with the limited shelf life for hunts that need to be sold by the next season as part of the deal structure with landowners, this creates a delicate relationship between risk and reward features of the business model for many outfitters. This need to hit certain sales thresholds under such business models places tremendous pressure on marketing success; otherwise the proprietor can lose their shirttail in short order. The nature of such financial risk should give pause to anyone who thinks that the outfitting business is all fun and games!

ABOVE > Some outfitters have created market niches by catering to archers. Although they are not as robust as archery markets, those who hunt with blackpowder rifles, handguns, and crossbows represent other potential market segments for outfitters who want to cultivate niches.

PRICE CONSIDERATIONS

Similar to knowing your product, knowing how to price your product is more complex than simply picking out a random number you feel is a fair and good price. In the "Basic Business Management" chapter, we explored the importance of understanding costs and margins, both of which come to bear in establishing price points. From my perspective, when it comes to establishing price points, one of the most fundamental considerations is this: what is the highest price I can charge for my product or service without the risk of overpricing and losing sales that yield diminishing returns at the end of the day? I do not want to leave money on the table, but I do not want to lose too many sales opportunities because my product is overpriced relative to comparable products. Furthermore, I want to ensure my hunts are affordable enough that sales do not crater if there is an economic downturn and the hunting markets contract. Again, it is a delicate balance when considering today's hunting market while also anticipating future market fluctuations.

The internet is a huge tool when it comes to evaluating price strategies. In a competitive marketplace, your competition cannot be ignored. How are they packaging their products, and how are they pricing those products? Those similar hunting packages and their prices are what I consider to be the comparables or "comps." Again, in a competitive marketplace where consumers have many options for similar products and services, price comparisons may determine who makes the sale and who does not. Researching online comps is an easy way to help get an idea about what constitutes competitive pricing. Granted, there are some hunting operations that do not post their prices on their websites, while others do a tremendous amount of deal making or negotiating, which in turn creates false price points. All things considered, evaluating comps should be part of the process as you establish your prices. Over time, if your business practices are sound and if you are offering a solid hunting product, your client base and the marketplace will reveal whether you are overpriced. Then, it is a matter of trying to make pricing adjustments based on that awareness.

From a proprietor's standpoint, it is obviously easier to adjust price points up rather than down, as long as the market will accommodate those increased adjustments. However, when a proprietor is forced to lower prices due to market pressures, then a deep dive into analyzing costs and margins must be conducted if adequate profit margins are going to be maintained. It is simple math, and good math does not lie. Reducing prices often results in a classic ripple effect because fixed and/or variable costs must be reduced. This may require renegotiating deals with vendors or perhaps landowners, and perhaps making decisions that impact support staff. And for the sake of short-term and even long-term financial health, these cost adjustments should not have much lag time; otherwise, the financial impact on the proprietor can be painful.

PROMOTIONAL MESSAGING

Promotional messaging is the art of creating content that is delivered to the consumer (hunter) and presented in a way that compels the consumer to take the next step toward purchasing the product. Content generally includes written information, photos and/or videos, and perhaps other graphics.

With written material, unless you are a good writer, do yourself a favor and pay someone to write your content. Written content will likely be used for brochures, websites, and e-blasts. Correct grammar, as in style and substance, is essential to a successful marketing campaign. You will likely need to describe your hunting packages and tell your story by giving background information for your company. The consumer should be able to easily and completely understand your product quickly enough that they do not lose interest before acting. Today, more than ever, brevity is extremely important because most people read quickly or skim over information and shop impatiently.

Most people in the hunting business are not seasoned writers, so again, either have someone write your content or, at a minimum, edit the material that you write. In my opinion, a poorly written promotional message that butchers the English language and disregards the rules of grammar is a cardinal sin.

PHOTOS

Photos are another piece of the promotional platform. They are incredibly important in the hunting business. Photos of game animals, especially harvest photos, stimulate hunters' interest. When I entered the professional hunting industry in the 1980s, most harvest photos taken by hunters were low-quality, distasteful images. Fortunately, we have made great strides over the last decade in improving the general quality of the hunting photos floating around. Some of this improvement can be attributed to technologically advanced, high-quality cameras that are affordable, but much of the progress can be traced to hunters refining their photography skills in a conscious effort to take quality photos. (Harvest photos are so important I have dedicated an entire chapter to them.)

In addition to harvest photos, you will likely need images of lodging, staff, equipment (in some cases), and perhaps some scenic shots. Live wildlife photos are occasionally effective in some types of promotional platforms as well. However, harvest photos and lodging photos tend to be the most compelling to hunters. Video clips are often used on websites, social media, and other marketing mediums. Smart phone videos, in my book, are typically not high quality enough to use as bona fide marketing tools, especially if they are shot and edited by a novice. Depending on your time constraints, skill level, and budget, you can either purchase decent HD video equipment or hire a videographer to capture and edit the material. Reasonably priced programs such as Adobe Creative Suite, which has recently been replaced by Adobe Creative Cloud, allow users to create graphic designs and edit photos and videos. It is better to use a graphic designer, if your marketing budget will permit, to create your presentation materials so they are as eye-appealing and professional as possible.

As a recap, promotional messaging is better with well-written text and eye-catching images to create a compelling "story" about your products and services. In my experience, the photos pique hunting consumers' interest, while the text allows them to weed out options that may not fit their needs.

ADVERTISING MEDIUMS

When I began WSI in 1987, the hunting business relied on magazine and newspaper ads, along with direct mail, to advertise. Hunting trade shows featuring exhibitors were just emerging. Very few hunting programs were on television, and it was difficult to make a trade that included an appearance on one of those shows. The World Wide Web did not come onto the scene until 1992, so internet marketing was not an option.

Frankly, things were much simpler back then. Competition within the hunting industry was limited. In my opinion, with little effort, a hunting outfitter offering a decent product could easily gain enough market share to make a go of the business. In some ways, those were the good old days in the hunting business. Today, it is very different. These days, a hunting proprietor has a myriad of advertising options. In some ways, the range of choices has added convenience, but the seemingly limitless assortment of ad options has split the market pie into a zillion little slices. Furthermore, there are no magic formulas or silver bullets that guarantee hunting proprietors will get their hunts sold.

Let's take a closer look at the primary advertising mediums that are available in the outfitting industry.

ADVERTISING MEDIUMS

PRINT ADS

At one time, this was a highly effective option for outfitters looking to book their hunts. I can remember running a one-inch ad in *Petersen's Hunting* magazine and getting flooded with letters in the mail requesting a brochure. Back in the 1980s, the primary hunting magazines that had national circulation were *Field & Steam*, *Petersen's Hunting*, *Outdoor Life*, and *Sports Afield*. Sure, there were others, but these were the most popular and far-reaching ones. Although print magazines are giving way to online publications, an endless number of hunting titles continue to populate the newsstand and circulate around the country. Also, at one time, certain newspapers, such as the *Dallas Morning News* and *Houston Chronicle*, were effective options for selling hunts. As our society moves toward digital platforms, print ads in all industries do not wield the influence they once did.

One disadvantage to magazine ads is the often long production time required to get the ad in front of consumers. A magazine released in April requires an ad space reservation in late January, which precludes last-minute marketing efforts. I find print ads to be of little value today in our efforts to sell hunts. However, I do value using print ads as part of our efforts to brand our business.

HUNTING INDUSTRY TRADE SHOWS

Over the past 40 years, trade shows in the hunting industry have undergone an interesting progression. Back in the 1980s, the Safari Club International Convention, The Great American Outdoor Show (also known as the Harrisburg [Pennsylvania] show), a couple of Hunters Extravaganza events sponsored by the Texas Trophy Hunters Association, the World Fishing & Outdoor Expo in Suffern, New York, and a few others filled the roster of well-attended shows where people spent big money freely.

The Harrisburg show, which attracted about a half million people during its 12-day run, was an absolute target-rich environment for selling hunts. The Lehigh Valley Outdoor Expo Sports Show in Allentown, Pennsylvania, was a small show, but I exhibited there from 1989 until it shut down in 2003. (It was revived in 2013.) The early years were phenomenal for booking hunts and meeting great people. From about 1995 to 2010, outdoor shows popped up all over the country. Like print ads, this proliferation created some convenience, but it sliced the pie into many tiny pieces.

Today, I generally do not exhibit at shows because I do not find them to be highly effective for selling hunts. Plus, our staff is extremely busy from late August through late May, and many of the better shows take place during January and February. Frankly, it is hard for us to dedicate the time to participate in those shows. With all of this said, many hunting operations do well at the shows. They are particularly effective for international operations that rely on these shows to advertise to American consumers. The most successful exhibitors generate new business while cultivating repeat business.

TELEVISION SHOWS

The first television show centering around hunting, at least that I recall, was *The American Sportsman* that ran on the ABC network from 1965 to 1986. The hosts were Joe Foss, Grits Gresham, and Curt Gowdy. I was a kid during the early years of that show, and I recall living vicariously through their televised adventures. Few outfitters had an opportunity to serve as a host on *The American Sportsman* hunts, so TV shows were not a true advertising option back then.

During the early 1990s, The Nashville Network's Sunday evening outdoor block became part of the media mix with *Remington Country*, *North American Hunter*, *Realtree Outdoors*, and *Buckmasters*. Outfitters lucky enough to host a hunt on one of those shows during that era were deluged with phone calls. Some years later, from about 2005 to 2015, a huge number of hunting shows emerged through the cable and satellite networks. Suddenly, it was possible to watch hunting on television 24/7, which certainly changed the dynamic of using TV shows to sell hunts.

Today, I find hunting shows have little value for marketing hunts, but like print ads, I see value in the national exposure to create brand recognition for WSI.

RIGHT > Since the 1980s, exhibiting at conventions and hunter extravaganzas has been a popular way for hunting outfitters to get their names out in fertile markets. As the number of events increased, their effectiveness was diluted, and it became more difficult for some operations to continue to find as much success through this marketing outlet.

DIRECT POSTAL MAIL

From about 1990 to 2000, I experienced an exceptionally good response rate to direct mail. Building a sizable mailing list took several years, but when we sent out a brochure or newsletter, we received a great response.

Design, postage, and printing costs make direct mail advertising expensive. At one time, though, it was arguably the best marketing tool available. Just as with print ads, the current trend is away from direct mail because of its relatively short shelf life, increasing print and postage costs, and our society's growing sensitivity to excessively using timber products such as paper.

Today, direct postal mail has given way to direct digital mail.

DIRECT DIGITAL MAIL

Digital media is an inexpensive and convenient method of getting marketing information to people expediently. We use e-blasts to distribute three marketing tools: WSI ENews, WSI Photo Play by Play, and stand-alone promotional pieces. These tools affordably and effectively sell hunts, and the process's overall expediency is highly attractive.

On the downside, many hunting operations do not have a large database of email addresses to populate their distribution list. Accumulating this information can take years of effort, plus a fair amount of work in keeping the list current. We have about 32,000 contacts on our list, and it has taken a tremendous effort to accrue them. While there are companies that sell this data, the integrity of the contacts is questionable. There is no guarantee on how current the list is or whether the list is composed of largely qualified buyers for what you are offering.

SOCIAL MEDIA

Social media platforms have made it affordable for almost any hunting proprietors to get their information in front of people. However, I have mixed emotions about these digital platforms. For one, from a selfish standpoint, I resent the fact that now all potential competitors can afford relatively effective marketing outlets through these social media platforms. It was not always that way. As an old school practitioner, I am envious that these "Johnny-come-latelies" are not required to have a significant marketing budget to enter the marketplace. Although I know it is not a fair characterization (and I apologize), I consider those outfitters who rely solely on social media to find their new clients to be bottom-feeders.

Our digital world is rapidly changing, and some of the digital platforms that are currently being used for marketing include Facebook, Instagram, LinkedIn, YouTube, TikTok, and Snapchat, among others. Currently, Facebook and Instagram are the primary platforms used for marketing hunts. To access large markets through these digital platforms, it is important to build your community of "friends" and "likes," which can be accomplished by directly soliciting or inviting people. When posts are well received, they are sometimes shared, which increases the post's reach. This sometimes generates friend requests from other people's networks. Posts that go viral may reach a huge number of people in mere hours. More ambitious social media users can pay to "boost" specific posts. As part of the cost of boosting, you have access to filters that allow you to have some degree of control over the demographic and psychographic profiles of the boosted post's recipients.

As discussed in the "Professionalism" chapter, social media has become a soft underbelly for our hunting community. Thanks to the laxity and low-quality content that is the standard of many hunters, guides, and outfitters, our adversaries have access to plenty of damaging material. I will not elaborate much on that concerning matter, except to say: WE ALL NEED TO BE GOOD STEWARDS WHILE POSTING CONTENT FOR THE OUTSIDE WORLD TO SEE, EVER MINDFUL OF OUR POTENTIAL TO IMPACT THIS TRADITION.

ABOVE > In the early 1990s, the internet provided outfitters with a new and convenient way to reach large markets and websites became mainstream marketing platforms and remain effective today.

WEBSITES

When the World Wide Web became widely available in the early 90s, I am not sure anyone had a clue how much that technology would change our world. I will admit, I have always been a bit of a dinosaur when it comes to computers, but I fortunately had a few key people, such as my wife Deborah, who were computer geeks. We created a website long before many of our competitors and learned just enough about search engine optimization (SEO) that we were, perhaps, the most visible hunting outfitter on the internet at that time. Virtually all our relevant search terms landed us on the first page, often in the top three matches. Our website became our most effective marketing tool.

Then in 2011, Google made some significant algorithm changes. After that change, the search engines used different features to recognize websites' relevance and value. Over an 18-month period, our WSI website went from being highly visible to being an "also ran." By then I was exceptionally busy as a TWA officer, and I treated my real job more like a part-time job. I simply did not have the time to devote to certain "nonessential" aspects of our business, which included keeping up with SEO changes.

Beginning in 2014, WSI began an honest effort to discover why our website lost its strong, visible position and tried to address the problems. Since then, we have spent tens of thousands of dollars on SEO work. While we have regained much of our organic internet presence over the last few years, it is not what it once was. It will likely never be that strong of a presence again because of the many changes that have taken place, including the emergence of millions of sites with relevant language that dilutes the impact of any single site.

Regarding websites, I cannot imagine in this day and age a business vying for market share in a competitive industry without a website. Websites have largely replaced brochures as the primary sources of information on products, services, or companies. The key to leveraging the website's strength is the consumers' ability to find the site. This does not happen by accident. Ideally, consumers find your website organically via keyword submission through search engines. For example, if someone is interested in booking a whitetail hunt in Texas and they search for "Texas deer hunting," then you want your site to be a match. Even more importantly, you want your website to show up on the first two to three pages of search results. If your website is buried more deeply than that, the consumer will likely not find it.

I just Googled "Texas deer hunts." That single phrase elicited 20,600,000 matches. Yes, you read that correctly—more than 20 million. This, more than anything, illustrates my point on the industry's competitive nature and the dilution effect prevalent on the internet these days.

Website ranking is accomplished through two methods: organically through keyword submission and search engine optimization (SEO), and through sponsored listings (Ad Words) or Pay Per Click (PPC). To achieve organic presence, your website must be optimized properly to help search engines such as Google understand and present websites properly. Achieving SEO dominance can take several years and can be relatively expensive if you are paying a firm to manage that process. On the other hand, PPC provides instant visibility. You bid on certain key phrases, and those rates vary depending on the level of competition for those phrases. When you do a keyword search, you will see at the top and bottom of the page websites that are designated as "Ad" listings, which is part of the PPC process. When someone clicks on your page through PPC, you are charged a fee based on the rate for that search phrase, hence the name "Pay Per Click."

Even if your website is not highly visible through search engines, your site is still valuable as an information resource. In modern marketing, an updated, well-designed website has replaced brochures as a company's go-to information source.

WRITERS

Over the years, I have utilized outdoor writers to create exposure through print publications. Like so many other advertising mediums, the effectiveness of this type of exposure has changed over the last few decades. There was a time when articles written on your hunting operation by outdoor journalists such as Craig Boddington, John Wootters, Larry Weishuhn, Hal Swiggett, Russell Tinsley, and many others would generate considerable attention, especially if you had an ad in that same issue. Like other print-based advertising strategies, this type of publicity does not carry as much weight as it once did for sales, but for long-term branding, this exposure can be effective.

A word to the wise: it is generally a safer bet to work with staff writers at high-profile publications as opposed to freelance writers. Freelancers query editors with the hope they can get their manuscripts published. When a hunt is provided to a writer, generally there is no guarantee that it will result in "getting some ink." Some of the uncertainty is removed by collaborating with a staff writer. Additionally, some writers have larger followings than others, so the amount of attention generated from any given story can vary.

BOOKING AGENTS

Similar to travel agents, who arrange various travel details for their clients, the hunting industry has booking agents, industry professionals who have access to the marketplace and consumers. Some have an active and loyal client base who depend on the agent to assist with their hunting trips. While booking agents in the hunting industry have proliferated over time, there are many agents who are reliable and have a relatively strong client list. The advantage of establishing a relationship with a trusted agent who can produce business is that you can rely on them to go through the time-consuming and expensive process of marketing the hunts, allowing you to focus on the other aspects of your operation.

However, using an agent has several potential downsides. First, you will be paying a commission to the agent for their referrals, which is typically 10—15 percent on big game hunts and 15—20 percent on bird hunts. Can you afford to carve off that percentage of your hunt fees for someone else? A second potential downside is the possibility of the agent misrepresenting your hunts. If the agent overpromises, you and your support team will be closest to the heat when clients express their outrage over misrepresentation. And last, some agents promise the outfitter the moon simply to gain an opportunity to have some quality hunts to market. Then, they fail to generate the amount of business you counted on, leaving you holding the bag to either hurriedly sell the hunts or absorb the loss.

Personally, I have used agents sparingly over the years, principally because marketing is part of our business plan and offerings. Also, the profit margins on most of our hunt packages cannot absorb a 10—15 percent commission because our margins are sometimes not much more than that.

International operations tend to find booking agents to be an attractive and viable option. Hunting operations in Africa, New Zealand, Europe, Argentina, and other destinations are obviously far removed from the strong American hunting marketplace. Plus, there may be language barriers, time differences, and other issues that make structuring their budgets to make room for an agent feasible and practical.

And finally, established booking agents are reluctant to represent someone they do not know, especially if the outfitter has little to no track record. As a new hunting proprietor, you might get the cold shoulder if you contact a successful agent, like the understandable stiff-arm I received from Jim McCarthy, of Jim McCarthy Adventures, when I cold called him back in 1988.

BRANDING

Branding, in the business world, is the process of creating a unique name and image for a product or company in consumers' minds, mainly through advertising campaigns with a consistent theme. Branding aims to establish a significant and differentiated presence in the market that attracts and retains loyal customers.

When you look at Yeti coolers, you will see one of the most successful examples of branding in the outdoor industry, or any other industry for that matter. With their competitors selling coolers for 20 dollars, brothers Roy and Ryan Seiders turned $300 coolers into a $450 million cult brand in a matter of a few years. How did Roy and Ryan Seiders pull off such a feat? Well, they created and offered a high-quality product that does a great job of keeping cold stuff cold, but more importantly, they created a branding campaign that took the country by storm. From 2006 when the company was launched until 2011 when sales hit $29 million, Yeti became the "gotta have" brand and continues to be a market leader today.

The Seiders not only created an image in the consumer's mind based on their slogan "Wildly Stronger! Keep Ice Longer!" but by building their community following and their operating philosophy around their passionate commitment to the outdoors. Knockoffs have come along, but none with Yeti's success, which is a testimony to the Yeti branding. Successful branding often takes years to achieve because it requires repetition to fully develop an image in consumers' minds. Few outfitters have been highly successful in this facet of marketing.

At one time, Ric Martin achieved it briefly, as did George Taulman with United States Outfitters; both have faded from the outdoor scene. In the booking agency business, Jack Atcheson & Sons, Inc. became a household name in hunting circles, and the company has done a great job of holding onto its visibility over the years since its founding in 1955. Jim Shockey, a Canadian outdoor writer, professional big game outfitter, and television producer/host for several hunting shows, has done a remarkable job with his branding efforts, but much of his name recognition is tied to his television shows, product endorsements, and speaking engagements as opposed to his hunting packages. Orvis has developed a strong brand in the wing shooting and fishing industries, more so as a booking agent than as an outfitter. Many others have developed strong brand recognition in the marketplace, especially some of the African operations.

Successful branding strategies generally have multiple features, including purpose, consistency, and emotional impact. Purpose essentially explains why you are in the business and the specific customer needs that you fulfill. Effective branding gives you purpose, and without purpose, a business cannot stand out from its competition. Consistency requires generating a theme that reflects your products and services and then creating repetition so consumers see that theme time and time again. Emotional impact touches the consumer in a way that is not simply tied to the product or service but has an ancillary feature as well. The Seiders established an emotional connection through their passionate commitment to the outdoors and its health. Also, satisfied clients who are repeat customers and serve as brand ambassadors for you are integral as well.

To do branding right takes time, often a great deal of marketing capital, and clientele loyalty. Successful branding also requires some durability to remain in the industry long enough so things can "marinate and mature." For perspective, WSI has been around for more than 34 years, and we have spent millions of dollars on marketing, and yet, we have barely scratched the surface when it comes to developing a significant hunting industry brand. In fact, thinking about it makes me want to have a stiff drink and reevaluate a few things!

CLIENT RETENTION

When generating sales, it is easier and less expensive to retain existing business than acquire new business, plain and simple. Client retention is the lifeblood for most successful businesses. In the hunting business, if you have a lot of churn or client turnover, it is not only expensive to try to replace dropped clients, but high churn signals unhappy clients, which can prompt more churn. Unhappy clients tend to voice their opinions to other potential consumers. Negative chatter can tarnish a business's reputation in the industry. A poor industry reputation is its own form of cancer. Therefore, reasonable client retention in the hunting business is paramount, and a high retention rate is gold!

What does it take to retain clients in the hunting business? Fundamentally, it hinges on the satisfaction level of clients who are passing through your camps. However, once you have a happy client, there are strategies for generating rebookings.

ABOVE > Now known as swag, these promotional items are not only gifts for clients but essential components of a company's branding strategy.

RETENTION STRATEGIES

REBOOKING POLICY

Back in 2002, in the aftermath of the 9/11 terrorist attacks, we integrated a standardized rebooking policy into our program. If hunters passing through our camps express an interest in rebooking that same hunt the following year, we require them to pay $300 within 30 days of their hunt's completion to hold their spot. Once we know the dates, prices, and details for that hunt for the next season, we request the remainder of their deposit accompanied by the booking agreement. Should the price of the hunt increase by more than 10 percent, they have the option of bowing out and receiving a $300 refund. We only charge a $300 rebooking fee because we want to make it easy for them to commit. In my opinion, once people are invested with some amount of cash, and perhaps even more importantly, when they are mentally invested, developing "buyer's remorse" is less likely. The rebooking fee is designed to "strike while the iron is hot," while also giving us a better sense of the number of repeat clients going into the next year so we can plan accordingly. If our retention is high, we may explore new growth opportunities, but if it is low, we may consider retracting in some areas.

STANDARD FOLLOW-UPS

Although it requires some time and effort, especially if your operation deals with several 100 clients each year, it is always a good idea to follow-up with your hunters within four to six weeks of their hunt's completion. A follow-up phone call or email allows you to interact with them while they (hopefully) are still "feeling the love" of the hunt. Relationships are more easily cultivated when people are in this mood. And just like our rebooking policy is designed to "strike while the iron is hot," following-up while the experiences of their hunt are still fresh in their minds increases the likelihood of converting their happiness into repeat business. While either an email or phone call is effective, the former is more time efficient, and the latter is warmer and more personal.

INFORMAL FOLLOW-UPS

From time to time, one of our staffers will contact clients who have hunted with us previously. The follow-up's intent is to let them know that we are thinking of them and checking to see how they are doing, with the hope that the conversation may lead to a discussion about available hunting opportunities. From a fundamental standpoint, the communication boils down to the importance of relationship building, which is central to client retention.

UNEXPECTED DIRECT COMMUNICATION

We used to send out birthday cards to our clients and we continued to do that after they hunted with us. Over many years, we accrued a few thousand names and birthdates which made it very difficult for us to maintain this form of communication, so we eventually discontinued it. In retrospect, we probably should have continued with this type of relationship-building customer communication. Thank you cards can be another unexpected form of direct client communication. We generally send out a WSI customized "thank you" card shortly after our clients have booked their hunts to personalize things a bit. While there may be more merit to sending these cards after the hunt, it fits our program better to send them out prior to the hunt.

MEDIA TOOLS

Current technology makes it easy to create appealing newsletters and other digital-based tools. It makes good sense to periodically release newsletters to your customer list. This communication helps recreate fond memories of previous hunts that clients have had with our operation. As Robert Ruark wrote in *The Old Man and the Boy*, "the best part of hunting and fishing was the thinking about going and the talking about it after you got back." This is all part of the romance of the hunting experience. The more romantic you can make it to clients, even long after the hunt, the more fertile the ground is for retention.

PHOTOS

When discussing client retention strategies, the topic would not be complete without mentioning the impact that quality photos may have on relationship building. Most hunters like seeing harvest photos, especially of themselves. We make it a point to capture photos of almost all our harvested game and make these photos available to our clients.

Many of these photos are made available through the photo gallery page of our website, many are built into our WSI Photo Play by Play and e-blasts, and some are provided directly to clients who request them. (Harvest photos are so important in the hunting business that I have devoted an entire chapter to this subject.)

WORD OF MOUTH

It is commonly said, "The best form of advertising is word of mouth," and this is true. I tell our staff every year, we want to transform happy clients into ambassadors for our company. We want them to share the gospel with their friends, family, colleagues, acquaintances, and random strangers. We want them to be unpaid salesmen for our company. And ultimately, we want our clients to feel as though they are cheating on us if they choose to hunt with a competitor.

People have a ladder of emotional connection with vendors and service providers. The further up the ladder that you can push your clients, the stronger the relationship becomes. Some of the strategies that are discussed in this retention section represent core methods of trying to push your clients up that ladder. Developing ambassadors through your client base may happen by accident in some cases, but it can also be cultivated through active, strategic steps.

Though customer retention is a separate matter than marketing, retention strength unequivocally interacts with marketing strategies, and greater retention generally equals less burden on marketing success. Customer retention cannot be overemphasized or overlooked. There are certain thresholds of retention that, if not met, will doom a business to failure. As they say, and as my experience has proven, it is less expensive to keep a client than it is to replace a client.

ABOVE > A business owner should never underestimate the importance of client retention, which results from providing quality goods and services as well as relationship building.

8 # LODGING
AND FACILITIES

I HAVE BEEN FORTUNATE TO HUNT AROUND THE WORLD, STAYING IN AN ASSORTMENT OF HOTELS, FIVE-STAR LODGES, SIMPLE RANCH HOUSES, CAMPERS, CONVERTED HORSE TRAILERS, TENTS, AND UNDER THE OPEN SKIES. EACH CAMP OFFERED SOMETHING SPECIAL.

OPPOSITE
Clint Updike
2008 White-tailed Deer
Runnels County, Texas
Guide - Todd Lee

Similarly, through my business, we have hosted hunts on properties with facilities that span the entire spectrum of luxury and have enjoyed at least some degree of success with each type of lodging. However, since the mid-1980s, expectations have changed, with an increasing percentage of hunters being pickier about lodging and sleeping arrangements.

Competition has driven a lot of the change. Through the years, operations with enough capital have invested in high-end camps as a way to outpace other outfitters. Another factor is social norms. Today, people are more accustomed to the creature comforts of home, plush amenities, and lavish lodging when they travel.

Lodging is an integral part of a hunting operation. It often dictates realistic price points for hunting packages and shapes the type of client suited for any given hunting program. Lodging may have a bearing on sales and retention, and ultimately may weigh heavily on the operation's long-term viability. A proprietor should consider many variables and features when establishing and evaluating this part of a hunting program.

LODGES AND CABINS

In the Lower 48, the most common type of hunting camp uses permanent structures, such as lodges or cabins. Early on, private hunting ranches simply took advantage of existing facilities, usually older ranch houses. Often the houses were slightly modified to better accommodate hunting guests. Generally, king and queen beds were replaced with twin-size bunk beds, and the facade and decor were updated so that the previous family home would now look more like a hunting camp. The "ranch house" cabin's floor plan generally spanned 1,400 to 1,800 square feet and included three bedrooms, one or two bathrooms, a modest living and dining area, and a kitchen. Over the years, these camps have functioned well and, in some cases, still do.

As hunting values escalated and recreation, not agriculture production, began driving ranch sales, bigger and better-appointed lodges began appearing on the scene. This shift occurred around 1995. Most of the lodges built over the last few decades are relatively modest, but very comfortable facilities. However, some are known for their opulent lodging.

The emergence of luxury facilities represents an industry-wide paradigm shift prompted by increased competition and increased financial economies. If one hunting operation has a four or five-star lodge and the other offers a basic ranch house, and all other things are considered equal, who gains more market share? Widespread improvement in lodging quality has forced many operations to either buck up and make some upgrades or run the very real risk of being left behind. Some operations that were unable to keep up have faded from the scene.

Because there are so many variables, including costs, that influence hunting lodge design and construction, it is impossible to sketch out the perfect facility. With that said, there are some general features that are worth considering in terms of functionality.

FUNCTIONAL FEATURES

BEDROOMS

Over the last two decades, people seemingly have become more sensitive about their sleep environment. In the past, four to six people, often sleeping in bunk beds, shared a bedroom. We currently receive more requests for private sleeping quarters. In fact, some hunters refuse to share a bedroom with anyone other than their spouse, period.

Privacy and sleeping space dictate a hunting facility's size more than any other aspect of the building. Very few hunting operations have a lodge that can accommodate large groups and offer private bedrooms; there are more today than 20 years ago, but these facilities are the exceptions. To make the most of the available space, twin-size beds are the norm in most hunting camps. However, if space is not a limiting factor and you anticipate that your group sizes will run on the smaller side, it is beneficial to have a room or two outfitted with a queen or king-size bed for couples and individuals who prefer the extra bed space.

Bunk beds are not as commonly used as they once were. Again, I think this reflects on our society's evolving expectations and marketplace competition. With that said, the top bunk creates an additional storage space for gun cases, duffel bags, and equipment, which reduces floor clutter. We do have a few camps with bunk beds that are full-size on the bottom and twin-size on top. While they offer more sleeping space and are off the floor, they do necessitate multiple sizes of bedding, which complicates things to some degree.

Over the years, WSI has drifted toward a double occupancy sleeping arrangement. We do have some camps where private bedrooms are an option sometimes, and we do occasionally have large groups, our dove hunts for example, where we may assign as many as four clients to each bedroom. Double occupancy is our norm, and that seems to be in line with most hunting programs. Beyond privacy, not many hunters are too particular about other bedroom features, such as high thread count linens, in-room coffee machines, or reading lights. Some upscale lodges do provide those extra amenities.

ABOVE > For those who are planning to construct or remodel a hunting facility, never underestimate the importance of having ample bathroom space. I suggest no more than two to three people per bathroom. Some clients will demand a private bedroom and bathroom.

BATHROOMS

In many hunting facilities, bathrooms are a bottleneck. First thing in the morning, upon return from the afternoon hunt, and just prior to bedtime, there will be a point when people will want to use the bathroom at the same time. If you are building a recreational guest facility, do not let bathrooms be an afterthought. As a rule of thumb, having more than three people use a single bathroom will create issues and possible client-pushback.

Ideally, each bedroom should have its own private bathroom. Depending on the facility's layout, a common bathroom located near the living area or great room is generally beneficial. Using a five-bedroom lodge as an example, the ideal facility will have a minimum of five bathrooms and perhaps a sixth one associated with the common area, which may be a half bathroom. And for planning purposes, stand-up showers are far superior to bathtubs, which are almost obsolete in the world of hunting camps.

Bathrooms should be cleaned daily, even if it means assigning the cook or one of the guides the responsibility of a quick scrub. While clean bathrooms may seem like a small detail in the overall scheme of a successful hunt, I cannot emphasize how important it is, especially in shared bathrooms.

Provide an adequate number of bath and hand towels. Generally, I figure on a minimum of two for each hunter. Plus, having a paper towel holder in each bathroom has proven to be a good idea. Some hunters arrive back at camp with bloody hands, and paper towels can help keep regular towels clean and stain-free. To keep wet towels off the floor and encourage clients to use them multiple times, install an ample number of towel hangers. Body wash, shampoo, hand soap, and air freshener should all be in the bathroom, as well as plenty of toilet paper.

KITCHEN

The kitchen and its functionality are extremely important. Again, depending upon budgets, space limitations, and average group size, a commercial-style kitchen may be necessary to comfortably meet the operation's food service needs. Most operations can make do with a more modest, homestyle kitchen. If I were going to create a hybrid between a homestyle and commercial-style kitchen, I would invest in a commercial stove and oven, as well as a commercial refrigerator and freezer. Walk-in coolers and freezers are handy, but unless you are catering to large groups on a regular basis, these features are expensive, and maintenance and electricity costs can be high. Again, depending upon average group sizes, you may or may not need other commercial-grade equipment like mixers, heat lamps, dishwashers, etc. I discuss this further in the "Culinary Considerations" chapter.

SERVING MEALS

When it comes to serving the meal, there are generally three main options. Most functionally is an arrangement that is buffet style, where the clients and staff serve themselves and then take a seat at the dining table. Under this type of arrangement, the layout for the buffet can be an important consideration. There are great advantages for the cook to go directly from the kitchen area to the buffet serving area without having to transport food very far. A serving island that separates the kitchen from the dining area is efficient and highly functional, and your cooks will greatly appreciate this effective layout. I prefer the buffet style option for its ease and functionality. Post-COVID, buffets have become less common due to heightened human health and safety concerns. Consequently, encouraging or requiring hand-sanitizing at the front of the buffet line may be a good safety measure. I was initially seeing, and we were for a period of time requiring, that our people also mask-up while they went through the line, but we have now discontinued that requirement in our camps.

A second option is what some refer to as family style, where the items are placed on large platters and located on the dining table, and your guests serve themselves while seated at the table. I find this dining style to be awkward, forcing people to pass or reach over one another, and some guests are reluctant to ask someone at the opposite end of the table to pass the jelly, etc. This is my least favorite serving style of these three.

And the third option is a more formal restaurant style serving arrangement where you have a waiter that delivers the plated meals, but this requires additional labor and may be cumbersome. For those nicer lodges that have plenty of space and are catering to a more affluent market, offering a separate, formal dining room with nice plates is appealing. Labor capacity, client expectations, and facility details will all play a role in whether this style of serving is a good fit.

Some camps offer full, properly arranged place settings to accommodate starters, salads, entrées, and desserts as well as coffee, iced tea, and wine. Not only does this add to the initial cost of properly equipping a facility, but it also can add to the amount and cost of labor necessary to provide this amenity, including the time it takes to clean and the space it takes to store these items. For affluent groups or high-end corporate events, these niceties may go a long way in leaving a lasting positive impression, but again, there are variables that will shape whether this part of the food service is practical and/or necessary.

GREAT ROOM AND DINING ROOM/AREA

Depending on the floor space and design, a combined great room and dining area can be highly functional. If a more formal setting is desired, a separate dining room may be necessary. These days, open floorplans, where the great room is simply an extension of the dining room, are considered the norm. The dining tables and chairs are situated alongside an adjoining gathering space where comfortable sofas, recliners, end tables, a television, and other furnishings are arranged to facilitate conversation and relaxation. When clients are not hunting or sleeping, they will likely congregate in the great room, so make sure there is plenty of comfortable seating.

Should you have enough space in the great room, you may want to go heavy on the recliners, as those will be the most popular seating option, and you will find that your clients enjoy a comfy spot to either take a midday siesta or to kick back and relax before calling it a night. Sofas are nice, but with large groups there tends to be wasted space. Men often reject the idea of sharing space on a three-person sofa with two other men, so you may want to consider that when selecting furniture.

End tables provide convenient spots where clients can set their drinks, but they do take up space, which can sometimes be at a premium. However, if space allows, you will find that end tables and coffee tables will be used often to hold drinking glasses and other small items. They are also a handy way to keep books and magazines within easy reach.

In the Lower 48, a television (like it or not) with satellite is a necessity because many people have become so accustomed to watching sporting events and news daily. You would think that part of the beauty of a hunting trip is to get away from some of these modern features of our lives, and for some it is, but not for everyone. I have had clients cancel their trip when they found out that a certain sporting event would not be available on TV at a particular camp; that pretty much sums up how important this amenity is to some people. So, I recommend that you consider a nice flat screen with satellite coverage, as I think that you will find that it will be frequently used.

Some of the nicer lodges provide an office and/or media room outfitted with some basic office equipment, such as computer, printer, scanner, desk, phone, and other office necessities. Internet service, and perhaps Wi-Fi, has become a focal point for many clients these days. Our society depends so heavily on internet access that it can be a disadvantage when this amenity is not available, especially if there is no cellular service. In rural areas where we have camps with no internet service, it is common for clients, if they have their own vehicles, to drive until they can reach cellular service so they can check emails and make phone calls. Obviously, this is not an option in some areas of the world, but this characterizes how Americans are addicted to their technology and ever-present communication.

TENTS AND CAMPERS

Back around 2005, a good friend of mine, Jeffrey Bozeman, and I went on a black bear hunt on Vancouver Island. Our camp was located alongside a creek. The outfitter and guide had done a wonderful job creating a temporary, but basic camp. It included a makeshift shower with running water that was pumped from the stream, a wall tent that served as the cooking and dining area, and some other basic features. We slept in a converted horse trailer with a very comfortable bunk room in the front section. The back end of the trailer had been repurposed for equipment storage. Using their creativity, this outfit had designed a simple, comfortable remote camp that was also easily portable.

Many African operations excel at transforming a tent camp into something nicer than most permanent camps in other areas of the world. I have been amazed at the plush accommodations of some African bush camps. The operations in Alaska often rely on tents. If they are fly camps, small, lightweight micro tents are common. Alaskan wall tent base camps vary from well-appointed, functional, and aesthetically pleasing to "roughing it."

Tents and campers can work fine, but the market appeal of these options depends on the alternatives available from competitors operating in the same area. As I have already mentioned, competition can have a strong influence on what appeals to the market and what does not. Over the years, we have only conducted a few hunts from tents and campers. Quite frankly, we are not setup to handle this type of hunt well.

Steve Jones, with Backcountry Hunts, has been offering a teepee-style tent hunt for many years and seems to have carved out a niche for himself with his unique camp setups. He has set his operation apart by being creative. While novel options may have market appeal, remember, they require personnel who are craftsmen and have the skills to support these camps efficiently and effectively.

HOTELS

We have relied on hotels on various occasions over the years. Some worked. Some did not.

We used to offer some pronghorn hunts near Raton, New Mexico, and would house our hunters and staff in a hotel that had an indoor swimming pool. The pronghorn season in northern New Mexico falls during late August, when temperatures can still be hot. Our clients seemed to really enjoy that arrangement because they could cool off in the pool, lounge around, and relax in a comfortable setting. We have successfully offered hotel-based turkey hunts in Oklahoma as well. However, it seems like our whitetail hunts that we have conducted from hotels in Texas never went over very well.

Again, it boils down to what alternatives exist for the marketplace; all other things being equal, an operation that offers comfortable lodging on the ranch or in the field will generally outcompete those who are offering similar hunts from a hotel. Given the choice, most hunters want to "get off of the concrete" when they are vacationing by hunting.

STAFF

As you are planning, do not forget you will need ample sleeping space for guides and cooks. Over the years, we have often needed to improvise to have enough sleeping space for the staff. Back in the early days of my career, we purchased and used a portable Morgan building to serve as a staff bedroom on a property north of San Angelo, Texas. This tiny building had no windows, a large shop-type door, three sets of bunks and very little open space. The guides "affectionately" referred to that building as "the coffin," but we made do. On some occasions, the facilities allow our guides and cook to enjoy the same high-quality lodging as our clients do.

Bottom line, make sure that you have plenty of space for your support team. The fresher and more well-rested your people are, the more likely they will be able to consistently perform at a high standard.

OPPOSITE > Though not as popular as they once were, tent camps are still common in remote hunting areas where permanent lodging is not an option. Offering comfortable accommodations in tent camps requires a great deal of work and skill, but there are some amazing examples of extraordinary tent camps that feature plush amenities.

OUTDOOR AREA

A hunting camp or lodge is not complete without an outdoor lounging area. This may be as simple as a fire ring with chairs or can be more highly improved with tables, lighting, decorative and aesthetic features, and perhaps a covered area. An evening outdoor fire is generally the centerpiece for gathering after the evening meal and before bedtime. A fire is spiritual and is part of the cultural ambiance when hunters gather at the end of the day. When the weather is nice, this aspect of the camp-life may very well be the most pleasing element of the hunt for some people, allowing them to unwind, reflect on the day's events, share stories of the past, and connect with others in camp, or perhaps allow a person to connect with their inner-self.

On many of the international hunts that I've attended, when weather permits, the midday lunch is often served at an outdoor dining facility. This type of dining arrangement can be more difficult on the kitchen staff. With labor rates being much less in some international locales, as opposed to the U.S., proprietors often have a full camp staff with chefs and waiters, which allows for greater reach regarding the ability to transport food from the kitchen area to an outdoor dining area and to be able to clean up after the meal. A solo kitchen person with no assistance will find this type of dining arrangement to generally be impractical.

ABOVE > In some cases, an outdoor fire pit serves as the centerpiece for evening activities, with clients and guides enjoying the outdoor atmosphere and absorbing the spiritual ambiance that campfires offer.

OPPOSITE-TOP > Five-star lodging, like this at Vermejo, can create new opportunities for corporate clients, as well as individuals who simply demand and can afford high-end facilities.

CLEANLINESS AND ORGANIZATION

There is merit in doing the best with what you have. A luxurious lodge may not be an option for you. Perhaps a modest ranch house is the only option. Regardless of the facility, you can control its cleanliness and organization. I will admit when I was younger, we did not always pay as much attention to this crucial detail as we should have. I was young, naive, and trying to pinch pennies, so I did not generally hire a house cleaner, thinking I could press hunting guides into that role. (For the record, hunting guides generally do not make very good house cleaners). The hunting business is fraught with circumstances and variables that are largely outside of the proprietor's control, but maintaining a clean and organized facility is completely within your control. This seemingly small detail (and others like it) can make a sizable difference at the end of the day.

Suffice it to say, the style, quality, and scale of hunting facilities are endless. Competition and pricing will often dictate what's acceptable within the marketplace. When all other variables are considered equal, including pricing, hunters will be prone to choose an option that offers comfortable facilities, so proprietors who offer a bit more in this area will have a competitive edge. People being people, some are accustomed to and prefer nice, upscale amenities, and this "demand" seems to be more common these days than 25-plus years ago. The best rule of thumb is making the most with what you have available and leveraging your operating budget as best you can. And another rule of thumb, even when hunting is good, don't underestimate the importance of a functional, comfortable hunting facility if you are serious about getting into and staying in the hunting business.

9 CULINARY CONSIDERATIONS

WHILE HUMANS MUST EAT TO SURVIVE, MEALTIME IS OFTEN AN OCCASION. OUR TEAM STRIVES TO DELIVER MEMORABLE, WELL-PREPARED MEALS THAT KEEP OUR CLIENTS SATISFIED.

OPPOSITE
Justin Trail
2007 Mule Deer
Brewster County, Texas
Guide - Brent Charlesworth

am one of that growing group of people who spends a considerable amount of time planning and preparing meals, researching the best restaurants when traveling, and shaping their lifestyle, or at least part of it, through dining experiences. Participants in this emerging food-centric trend are dubbed "foodies." Foodies have spurred the development of foodie culture, which reflects a variety of different influences, including ethnicity, health consciousness, age, and regional preferences.

An influential group of foodies, particularly in the hunting industry, are the locavores, people who seek out locally grown or produced food that is often organic. Locavores have driven the popularity of urban micro-farming, where ingenious people construct gardens in backyards, on rooftops, and other previously unutilized micro areas. Because locavores are intrigued by the age-old process of harvesting and processing their own wild, organic meats, they have become the fastest growing source of new hunters.

Food is an important part, arguably one the most important parts, of the hunting experience. Even with do-it-yourself hunts, there is something almost spiritual about cooking foods over an open campfire, and the camaraderie enjoyed at mealtime is often the camp experience's centerpiece. Even some backcountry hunters with limited equipment and supplies make the most of their meals. Food is central to life and is fundamental to a well-balanced hunting trip experience.

From a commercial hunting standpoint, providing quality meals and enjoyable dining experiences should be a proprietor's top priority. The hunting business can be frustrating because there are so many variables outside of the proprietor's control, but food is not one of them. High-quality food can sometimes transform a marginal hunt into a great experience for your hunting clients. Conversely, poor-quality food can reduce a positive experience into something unsatisfactory. Do not underestimate the service portfolio's culinary side.

BUDGETS

Although I do not think it is wise for a commercial hunting program to cut corners when it comes to food quality, a realistic budget is required to control costs. Generally, as the hunt's price rises, so do clients' expectations, so it is not unreasonable for the food budget to reflect the hunt's price point as long as certain "thresholds" are met.

In hunting camp, quantity is important. Make sure your chef understands that it is a cardinal sin to run short of food for both clients and staff during a meal. Some chefs are good money managers, and some are not. Those chefs who understand how to shop wisely, use their supplies efficiently, and re-purpose certain leftovers can often save as much as 25 percent on total grocery costs without impacting meal quality.

MATCHING FOOD WITH CLIENTS

When possible, let at least some portion of the meal plan reflect the clients' ethnicity, home, or preferred tastes. With that said, if you are hosting a group of Italian hunters and plan on serving Italian food at any meal, your chef should be accomplished in that cuisine because the clients will likely have high standards. If your chef is not comfortable preparing homemade Italian food at that quality level, then offer other types of meals. Under no circumstances is frozen lasagna or jarred spaghetti sauce an acceptable substitute.

Here in Texas, we are accustomed to spicy foods that pack some heat—and often carry hot sauce when we travel to ensure our favorite taste profile is represented on the table. I have found that clients from Texas, the Southwest, and the Deep South are generally fine with a kick of heat in their food, but clients from the northern and eastern parts of the country prefer blander food and may not enjoy the spiciness. As a result, I have learned to proceed with caution and take culinary clues from our clients' home regions. I also try to build some regional and local favorites into the meal plan. Again, here in Texas, Mexican food is popular, and generally clients appreciate at least one Tex-Mex meal.

ABOVE > Although food and its quality is more important to some clients than others, meals are often the most central activity in a hunting camp. Poor food can greatly diminish an otherwise great hunting experience.

Along the coast, fresh seafood is a fitting option, but possible seafood allergies should be sorted out ahead of time. In the southern U.S., some dishes, often referred to as "down home" or "low country" cooking, such as biscuits and gravy, collard greens, fried chicken, red beans, grits, and cornbread, that reflect the Old South are fitting. Since Texas is known for its high-quality beef, we typically have a steak night on each of our hunts where we serve a nice ribeye with a baked potato and fresh green beans.

When possible, allow your clients to have some input on certain aspects of the meal plan. Email, phone calls, and questionnaires are all ways to gather client information. While client input is ideal, this type of interaction does not fit into most hunting operations because it requires more planning, places greater demands on the chef's talent, and can also create purchasing challenges on groceries. Flex where you can, but recognize that a pragmatic approach to meal planning is okay as well.

MEATS

For the "centerpiece" dinner on each hunt, we either serve beef or seafood. When it comes to steaks, I suggest splurging on prime grade. When you look at many of the other beef options such as ground beef, chili meat, and stew meat, there is not a noticeable difference in quality between grades, but with steaks, it is worth the additional cost to serve quality, prime meats. I prefer ribeyes because they have less waste than T-bones and are generally less expensive than tenderloin. Strip steak and sirloins are fine, but with steaks as a centerpiece meal, I suggest stepping it up, and lower grade strips and sirloins always fall below a passing grade for quality food service in camps and lodges.

Although 1.5" thick steaks are considered man-sized cuts, there will be a considerable amount of waste, so I suggest cutting the steaks to 1"—1.25". With some outlets, the butcher will custom cut your steaks. While it will take additional time, there are advantages of buying a whole rib roll and cutting the steaks yourself. Rather than wrapping in bulk, wrapping and freezing steaks individually or in pairs provides more flexibility when it comes to feeding groups of different sizes. Steaks do not benefit from being thawed and then refrozen.

Seafood is a bit of a wild card. If you have a trusted source where you can buy fresh seafood, then this becomes a more accessible option. Fish fillets, as well as shellfish, are popular table fare for many people, but be mindful of seafood allergies, especially with shellfish. Again, a simple questionnaire is one way to identify these possible health matters.

In the south, fish fries are popular and can be a festive occasion, as can seafood boils. Because some seafood choices are pricey, they may exceed the budget. Freshwater fish, such as catfish, are economical, but I have found that some people from northern states are not big catfish fans, so again, knowing a client's preference may be helpful. However, I find catfish that is properly fried to be outstanding, especially when paired with a good homemade cocktail or tartar sauce.

OPPOSITE-TOP > Guides who make the extra effort to provide a nice meal in the field deserve an extra star. A small fire and hot meal beat a cold sandwich every time.

OPPOSITE-BOTTOM > When possible, there should always be fresh vegetables included with at least one meal each day. Canned and frozen veggies are okay but should not be a substitute for fresh vegetables and fruits if they are available.

FRESH VEGGIES AND FRUITS

One of my culinary pet peeves is chefs who heavily rely on canned goods, especially vegetables. Yes, fresh, quality vegetables take up more shopping cart and storage space, but they can make a huge difference in the overall integrity of the meals. This is true for both green and starchy vegetables. From both a nutrition and taste standpoint, fresh produce cannot be overrated.

Frozen vegetables are superior to canned vegetables. However, when push comes to shove and it is necessary to serve canned vegetables, spruce them up. Canned green beans can be elevated by adding minced onion, fresh garlic, and bacon fat. A dollop of real butter can do the same for canned corn. And never serve boxed potatoes. They are poor substitutes for the real thing—and a sure sign that your chef is being a bit lazy.

Fresh fruit is always a nice addition to the dining room. Bananas, oranges, apples, grapes, and other options are often popular during breakfast, as midday snacks, and sometimes as a dessert. Again, while fresh fruits take up room in the shopping cart and in the storage room, they add a little to the overall meal costs but can make a significant difference.

APPETIZERS

Appetizers should be provided with each of the evening meals, and perhaps with some of the lunches as well. Most hunters are not prepared to immediately jump into a big meal after arriving back to camp from the afternoon or evening hunt but prefer to wash up, enjoy a cool beverage, and have a tasty snack as they relax and share some stories about the day's outing.

Appetizers can be simple snacks such as mixed nuts, chips and dip, and nachos, or they can be more elaborate such as BBQ chicken wings and drumettes, crudité platters, smoked sausage and cheese, jalapeño poppers, and an assortment of other substantial choices.

DESSERTS

Desserts are, shall we say, icing on the cake when it comes to meals in hunting lodges. In my experience, homemade desserts are the Achilles' heel for many accomplished chefs, which is interesting because there are many great dessert options that do not require exceptional baking skills.

Desserts during the lunch meal can be something simple, such as store-bought cookies, ice cream, or other purchased sweets. Fruit makes a nice dessert with the lunch meal as well. I think the evening meal should include a well-prepared dessert. While there are some good store-bought desserts that are convenient, I think that chefs who are worth their salt should produce homemade items. Yes, it adds some extra work to a busy daily routine, but that is what the chef is paid to do. Plus, a delicious dessert literally ends the day on a sweet note. And by all means, if a store-bought pie is served, take it out of the box before setting it out so that it is not so stinking obvious that it was store-bought. There are a few tricks to make store-bought desserts appear to be homemade, and there are also simple ways to enhance store-bought desserts, but the homemade versions are generally the preferred route. Going the extra mile and paying attention to little details can be a difference maker for the chef—and the hunt.

GAME MEATS

As mentioned earlier, interest, new or renewed, in game meats is growing. Some of this interest is likely driven through our emerging locavore culture, while other people may have simply grown to appreciate the great flavors of properly processed and prepared game meats. Most hunters enjoy having game served during their hunting excursions. Many hunters find it especially rewarding when the chef prepares the "catch of the day" game that was taken during that hunt.

If game preparation is not one of your chef's strong points, it might be safer to incorporate game into soup, chili, spaghetti meat sauce, or other dishes that include ground and cubed meat. Smoked sausage that uses venison is often a good choice, as are roasts cooked in slow cookers. The same thing applies to wild fowl; items such as dove poppers, fried quail, fried turkey "fingers," pan-seared duck breast, and baked pheasant are all examples of relatively easy dishes that incorporate game birds. Though it may be considered cheating by some, there is a bit of convenience associated with purchasing farm-raised game meats such as bison, exotic deer, quail, pheasant, and rabbit. These farm-raised options are not cost-cutters like field harvested game, but they are a convenient way to build these nice treats into your meals.

FOOD SAFETY

Food safety for your clients and staff should be a constant priority, not an afterthought. Nutritious food is not only part of the customer service mix, but also the overall risk management program. Ultimately, it is the proprietor's responsibility to have a process in place that mitigates any risks associated with food safety, but chefs should be aware that understanding the basics of food safety and integrating practices into their regular routine is part of their job description.

For simplicity, addressing food safety can be broken into three categories: personal hygiene, time and temperature control of foods, and cross-contamination.

ABOVE-LEFT/RIGHT > Incorporating game meat into the meal plan is generally a good way to add a special culinary feature while saving on food costs. Here, I am preparing a mule deer loin taken from a Texas state record mule deer I harvested in 2019.

FOOD SAFETY GUIDELINES

PERSONAL HYGIENE

Chefs must observe the highest possible standards of personal hygiene to help ensure that food is not contaminated by pathogenic microorganisms, physical or chemical hazards. In addition to protecting food, high personal hygiene standards also play an important part in creating a good image in the clients' eyes.

From a business perspective, handwashing, fingernail length and hygiene, food worker illness policy, hair length and coverings, uniforms, glove use, jewelry, personal cleanliness, or practices such as eating, drinking, or using tobacco while preparing food are all elements of defining personal hygiene standards for the chef and any kitchen helpers. Because poor handwashing is one of the leading causes of foodborne illness, hand hygiene practices should be a focal point of the standard operating procedure (SOP) for the kitchen. Post-COVID has quickly created a paradigm of which hand-sanitizing is a must, and sanitizing dispensers should be scattered about in the kitchen, dining area, and other locations as well.

TIME AND TEMPERATURE CONTROL OF FOODS

Potentially hazardous bacterial growth in susceptible foods can be reduced by limiting the time food is in the "danger zone" (41°F–135°F) during any steps of the food flow, from shopping and transporting to serving. The Food and Drug Administration (FDA) Food Code recommends no more than a cumulative six hours in the danger zone. Use a thermometer to chart time and temperature based upon your menu for cold holding (41°F), hot holding (140°F), cooking (based on the food), reheating (165°F), and cooling. Rapid cooling of leftover hot foods or foods cooked several hours in advance of serving is a special challenge. To keep your clients healthy, I suggest researching food safety protocols, especially those relating to temperature controls. A simple Google search is all it takes.

CROSS-CONTAMINATION PREVENTION

Cross-contamination is the transfer of harmful microorganisms or substances to food and can be caused by a multitude of food handling errors in all stages of food flow. The three routes of cross-contamination include food to food, hands to food, and equipment to food. Cross-contamination can occur at any time. Ready-to-eat foods are most likely to be contaminated through mishandling and must receive special attention to avoid potential problems. Avoid touching raw meats and then touching ready-to-eat foods such as lettuce, fruits, and other items that will not be cooked. The same prohibition applies to using utensils on raw meats. After working with raw food, thoroughly wash your hands, utensils, and countertops with hot, soapy water, which helps prevent possible cross-contamination. These easy, no-brainer SOPs should become second nature to your kitchen staff.

FOOD ALLERGIES

A food allergy is an immune system response, which can range from mild to life threatening, from consuming certain foods or food additives. For those who are sensitive, a reaction can occur within minutes or hours. If someone has a serious food allergy, even trace amounts can trigger a response; therefore, it is important to know in advance if kitchen staff must contend with a food allergy or other special dietary needs. It is best to have all camp attendees complete a questionnaire prior to their visit allowing for adequate preparation.

The eight leading causes of food allergies are: milk, eggs, fish, shellfish, tree nuts, peanuts, wheat, and soybeans. The U.S. Department of Agriculture's Food Safety and Inspection Service (FSIS) and the FDA both have laws requiring that all the ingredients in a food product be listed on the food label. People with a known food allergy who begin experiencing symptoms while or after eating a food should initiate treatment immediately and go to a nearby emergency facility if symptoms progress. Promptly administering epinephrine by an autoinjector (EpiPen) during the early symptoms of Anaphylaxis may help prevent serious consequences. To be safe, store an EpiPen, along with other first aid supplies, in a designated, easy-to-find location and make sure the entire camp staff is familiar with this location. It's also not a bad idea to point this location out during the client orientation. Risk management at all levels involves staying ahead of possible threats while being prepared when incidents occur.

Diabetes, lactose intolerance, and gluten intolerance are the special dietary considerations we encounter most regularly at WSI. We are contending with them much more often now than we were 30 years ago. According to health experts, the occurrence of diabetes has skyrocketed in the U.S., and conditions such as gluten and lactose intolerance are much more widely recognized now.

Bottom line, food safety is more than making your facility look clean. Real mistakes that can threaten people's health and impact the hunt's success can happen at any step in the flow of food through your facility, from receiving, storage, preparation, and cooking, to holding, cooling, reheating, or serving. It is better to be safe than sorry at every step. Pay attention to your kitchen staff's training, ensuring that they are practicing the SOPs that keep guests and staff healthy during the hunt.

LEFT > Food allergies can be a serious consideration when crafting a meal plan for the hunt. Simple questionnaires that are filled out and submitted by clients, well before the hunt, allow kitchen staff to plan accordingly. Do not forget to include the guides' special food needs as well.

KITCHENS, COOKING EQUIPMENT AND SERVING WARE

Even the most talented chef will be handicapped by an inadequate kitchen. Hunting lodges and camps have kitchens that vary from basic domestic-grade arrangements to large commercial-style facilities. While it is nice to have plenty of floor, freezer, refrigerator, oven, and grill space as well as a full assembly of equipment and utensils, many hunting facilities will likely have a modest kitchen arrangement.

From an appliance standpoint, the necessities include a refrigerator, freezer, stove/oven, and microwave. Floor space, capital expenditure budget, and capacity requirements will dictate whether you can get by with residential appliances or whether you must upgrade to commercial appliances. There is a broad list of other small appliances, including mixers, warmers, fryers, dishwashers, and other items that may, or may not, be categorized as a necessity by chefs. Of course, kitchens also need water, hand utensils, storage containers, cutlery, and other miscellaneous items that make up the standard array of kitchen basics. Refrigerator and oven space are common pinch points in some modest kitchens. Though the lack of adequate provisions can present challenges for the kitchen staff, good chefs generally can improvise and make do when notified in advance so they can plan how to overcome the shortfalls.

Depending upon the price points of hunts, clients' expectations, and the operation's culinary service goals, all meals may be presented on fine serving ware, or they may all be served on paper plates, but it will likely be somewhere in-between. In most of our camps, I am fine with using paper plates during lunch but prefer that the evening meal be served on "real" plates. Even on hunts where most of the meals are served at a permanent lodge or cabin, I applaud those guides who are willing to take the extra step in being able to provide a proper field lunch. Basic sack lunches generally will suffice, but having a small portable stove or building a small cooking fire and providing a hot lunch in the field can be a real client pleaser.

Most of the kitchens that we have worked with over the years are not properly set up for formal dining. Again, the standards of adequacy will typically be directed by client expectations, which can easily be tempered by how the hunt is promoted. The last thing the camp staff wants are clients with unrealistic expectations, which then places the staff in the unenviable position of realigning expectations or disappointing the client.

The kitchen is the chef's domain and workspace. The kitchen also seems to be a magnet for clients and guides who tend to drift toward the aromas that are whetting their appetites. Before you know it, folks are in the middle of the kitchen telling hunting stories and unintentionally getting right in the middle of the chef's business during the frenzy that comes with an approaching mealtime. It is important to try and manage these impromptu gatherings to avoid interrupting the chef's production process and to avoid annoying your kitchen personnel. Similarly, do not allow your clients or guides to use the kitchen sink to wash up their bloody, dirty hands, which is not simply a cross-contamination concern, but these practices are a surefire way to raise the hackles of the kitchen staff. That is what the sink in the bathroom is for. The hunting camp's operating culture should respect these boundaries to ensure that the kitchen operations are efficient and relatively drama-free.

Whether it is simply warming up soup or throwing a ribeye and vegetables on a piece of expanded metal over an open fire, these culinary field pleasures can be difference makers on some hunts. Food-related services boil down to learning how to apply a few basic techniques while being willing to dedicate the extra time to elevating your overall skills as a dedicated chef or as a guide who is multi-tasking as a cook.

CHEFS

Over the last 30-plus years, I have had many different individuals who have helped in our hunting camps' kitchens. Most, but not all, prefer the term *cook* not *chef*, but I favor the title *chef* for those who oversee our meal preparation.

While some of our chefs have been formally trained, most have been self-taught. Several of the chefs have been exceptionally skilled, and others barely got by. But most of our chefs over the years have fallen somewhere in-between. Whether someone is a Johnson & Wales trained chef or a self-taught professional does not matter much to me. What does matter is our chefs' desire to refine their skills and broaden their cooking repertoire. Kitchen excellence comes more from dedication and desire than from a diploma, similar to other crafts. When people have developed their cooking skills and have a pleasant, accommodating personality, then as an outfitter, you have a true winner.

I have often said that the chef is more important than the individual guides. A guide's work generally affects one or two clients at a time while the chef touches all clients and all other staffers. Chefs are central to the entire camp, and their performance will unequivocally leave an impression on everyone. Food quality is obviously important when it comes to camp chefs, but their ability to be good hosts and to be "Johnny-on-the-spot" is key, as well.

Strangely, some chefs want to run the entire show and get in the middle of everyone's business, including the guides. This type of meddling will often result in some conflict. It is important for your chefs to understand their role land respect the field staff's boundaries, just as the field staff must respect the kitchen staff's boundaries, while proactively trying to serve everyone to the best of their abilities.

Attention to detail is central to the chefs' abilities to do their job well, as this trait will affect food safety, the organization and cleanliness of the kitchen and dining areas, the punctuality and efficiency of meal service, the customer service approach, and the meal's quality. The attention to detail will also, hopefully, bleed over into the effort on purchasing groceries, which can impact budget performance and product quality. Focusing on detail, detail, detail should be the camp chef's overarching goal.

Days are often long for camp chefs, so stamina is another important feature of well-rounded kitchen professionals. Their ability to work efficiently and to sneak in a nap each day can go a long way in helping them to stay fresh and sharp, both mentally and physically, which will affect their performance along the way. And let's face it, the older we get, the more our body typically feels the rigors of a long day, but age also has a way of creating wisdom, which in turn can allow us to work smarter.

Taking care of everyone's food needs can create a lot of pressure, and the more tired we are, the less we are able to cope with stress well. So, by design, getting adequate daily rest is important. If chefs are not well organized, they may be forced to spend unnecessary time going into town each day to fetch overlooked groceries when they could have been getting some needed rest. Again, attention to detail, proper planning, and good organizational skills go a long way.

I cannot overstate the importance of quality food service in a hunting operation. All people depend upon food for nutrition to support their health, and most people enjoy and appreciate delicious, high-quality food as part of their lifestyle. When you combine a pleasing culinary experience with a strong, hospitable support team in a hunting camp, you are advancing the ball in the right direction to help ensure your hunting program is successful. Hire talented people, provide them with sound direction, equip them with satisfactory tools and facilities, make sure they purchase quality food products in adequate quantities—and you will have plenty of smiles to go around.

OPPOSITE-TOP > Hunting proprietors should never underestimate the importance of capable chefs. Finding qualified chefs is often more difficult than finding qualified guides.

10 GUIDES

WHILE A SUCCESSFUL HUNTING OPERATION INCLUDES MANY KEY COMPONENTS, NONE ARE MORE CENTRAL TO THE BUSINESS THAN THE GUIDES. WORKING AS A HUNTING GUIDE IS A ROMANTIC NOTION FOR A LARGE PERCENTAGE OF OUTDOORSMEN, ESPECIALLY YOUNGER FOLKS.

OPPOSITE
Jay Dreibelbis
2021 Pronghorn
Brewster County, Texas
Guide - Don Richardson

For kids who grow up hunting and fishing, it is not surprising that many dream about being a professional hunting guide and getting paid to participate in an activity that is fun and exciting. While working as a hunting guide delivers many rewards, pay is not normally one of them. Sure, guides can and often do make modest financial returns for their efforts, especially when you figure in gratuities, but as I have told my guides on many occasions, there is an easier way to make a buck.

Due to the hunting business's seasonal nature, few operations have a large staff of full-time guides. Thus, most hunting guides in the U.S. are either part-time or seasonal. Some international operations have larger full-time staffs, but this is more likely due to the disparity in labor costs around the world. An outfitter's inability to keep guides busy through the course of the year with most U.S. operations makes it preventative for most of those operations to have a heavy staff of full-time guides. Consequently, most guides are part-time and many of them have other jobs that keep them busy when they are not tending to hunting clients.

SOURCING PROSPECTIVE GUIDES

Locating quality guides is not easy. We currently rely on about 30 to 35 guides to fulfill our needs throughout the year. The talent and depth of our guide roster reflects a 35-year effort to construct a pipeline of quality people. Over the years, word-of-mouth has proven to be the most effective and reliable method of finding dependable guides. Many of the new guides that have been added to our roster over time have been acquaintances of our existing guides or referred to us by friends. Referrals are the most common way that proprietors find support staff, and they are the most probable way for aspiring guides to find work.

Guide schools have come and gone in the U.S. over the years. I guess there are still a few guide schools in operation, but the ones that I'm familiar with in years past were programs that not only offered technical training for their students, but also assisted with job placement for their graduates. One of our busiest part-time guides, Jackie Murphy, who is a former CPA, completed a guide program in Colorado about 18 years ago. One of his instructors introduced Jackie to us, and Jackie, a world-class guide, proved to be a great "get." In fact, the person who referred him was the head of that school and was already part of our network, having previously guided for WSI around 1990. With the future health and vibrancy of the guide and outfitting business being somewhat in question, I suspect that hunting guide schools are not likely to be strong sources in locating guides in the future.

In some countries, including many in Africa, the registration requirements to become a professional hunter (guide) can be more involved and complex, requiring several years of formal education and training as well as a prescribed amount of practical field work. These programs are great options for hunting operators who are searching for help in those countries.

Many part-time guides are retired from another occupation and are looking for something to keep them busy. In my experience, these retirees generally make good guides. They are typically mature and settled into a stage of life that has fewer distractions than those of younger people. Also, as retirees, they generally consider the money they make as "additive," so the relatively modest compensation earned from guiding is acceptable.

For outfitters who are looking for young guides who have wildlife-related degrees, the Texas A&M University Wildlife Job Board is a great platform for finding prospective guides. We have had success in recruiting motivated, young talent using this resource, which is the world's largest digital platform dedicated to natural resource jobs. There is a ton of traffic on that site.

ABOVE > Backcountry hunts often require guides who know how to break down animals in the field and who are physically capable of packing these animals out, piece by piece. Master guide, Jackie Murphy, is seen here packing an aoudad ram off a West Texas mountain.

QUALITIES AND TRAITS

A preexisting profile for the perfect guide does not exist. Personally, when it comes to adding new guides, I would rather have people who are open-minded and adaptable instead of those who are completely set in their ways. While there are certainly exceptions, younger people seem to be more ready to embrace new approaches. "Old crusties" certainly bring valuable skills and years of experience to the table, but if they are unwilling to adapt to our way of doing things, then they do not have a place on our team. With that said, young, green guides may not have fully mastered the necessary skill set, and clients will often recognize their lack of experience. Ideally, our guide roster includes a blend of young talent and veteran guides. The latter can mentor the up-and-comers.

I think it goes without saying that an aspiring hunting guide must come from a hunting background. I love younger guides who grew up hunting and have had an opportunity to travel on various hunts in different regions. However, some of the young guides who have a lot of travel experience can come across as cocky, and they tend to overcompensate for their youth and lack of skills with bravado instead of humility and respect. It tends to backfire and can be a turnoff, especially to older, veteran guides. Our young guides hear my sermons on the value of patience, humility, and earned respect. I also tell our young guides their best, most immediate pathway to success is working harder than everyone else and making themselves available to everyone—both clients and staff—in the camp.

Over the years, some of our younger guides have found their way to us through internships and seasonal tech positions offered by various university natural resource programs. This has been a great source for seasonal help. Many of these college students are highly motivated and eager to learn. Some fit in as behind-the-scenes labor while others are integrated into our guiding mix, depending on their hunting experience and maturity level. We have employed 40 to 50 of these interns and techs over the years. Of these younger hires, about 25 percent have proven to be highly capable workers, roughly 50 percent have been good steady workers, and the remainder have not fit well into our program. This segment of our support team has been integral to our success.

Currently, all our guides are men. While I would like to integrate some women guides into our professional mix, most of our camps do not have sufficient sleeping space for us to provide the separate accommodations and privacy for a mixed roster of men and women guides. Unfortunately, women are often disadvantaged in the guiding industry. In my experience, many hunters are narrow-minded and do not want women guiding them. Again, it is unfortunate, but this industry is built on tradition and has been slow to change. For years I have been thinking of expanding WSI's services to include hunting options exclusively for women, perhaps hosting some women-only hunts. That would be a great platform to engage women guides.

Most of our Texas hunts are not physically demanding, so it is not necessary for our guides to be triathletes. However, there are many hunts in the U.S. and around the globe that are physically demanding. In those cases, guides must be in good shape to adequately perform their tasks and to avoid placing their clients at risk.

Personality is extremely important in the guiding business. As far as I am concerned, an outstanding guide must have, at a minimum, "decent" people skills. Now that does not mean that a guide must have an outgoing and gregarious personality, but it does mean that negative, grumpy guides do not have a place on our team. It is okay to be quiet. As they say, "still waters run deep," and that can indeed be the case with guides who are more reserved. Bottom line, a willingness to accommodate clients, patience, a positive attitude, and loyalty to the proprietor are essential qualities that I look for when vetting new guides. I am too old to put up with drama.

Any behavior that can—or does—create drama will be squashed one-way or another.

Guides who are adept at skinning, quartering, and fully caping animals for taxidermy are a plus. It is not unusual for us to have new guides who can gut and skin but are inexperienced when it comes to caping and even quartering carcasses. As long as they are good with a knife and willing to learn, it does not take long for them to master how we process animals, including skinning the animals so the capes are ready for the taxidermist.

In the early days, I was as much as a guide as I was an outfitter. So, I greatly appreciate the important role of a guide, and I'm sensitive to the inherent challenges that guides face on a recurring basis, sometimes daily. I greatly admire those guides who are constantly working on their craft, whether it be their skills with harvest photos, scouting and understanding game patterns, deepening their intellect of animal and plant taxonomy, honing their proficiency in caping heads and quartering carcasses, on the endless array of other details that go into that craft.

LICENSING AND/OR REGISTRATION REQUIREMENTS

When it comes to guiding, the licensing or registration requirements vary immensely by state and country. In Texas, there are no licensing requirements for guides. While I have mixed emotions about this, it would be difficult to create a mandatory guiding certification in Texas where 96 percent of the land is privately owned. Many people, other than professional hunting guides, host hunts on private land that are not commercial ventures. On top of that, changing the long-established culture of commercial hunting in Texas would face tremendous resistance and potentially create chaos.

In many western states where there is a large percentage of public lands, guide and outfitting licensing and/or registration is common. I have always found it interesting that many states require licensing whether the guiding and outfitting takes place on public land or private land. Although I have been shaped and biased, by growing up in a private lands state, it feels like an overreach for individual states to require licensing for guiding or outfitting on private lands. I can see the need for such credentials on public lands, but I think licensing should be optional on private lands, at least in the Lower 48. However, I would favor an accredited program that allows those guides and outfitters to leverage their accreditation in promoting their services. Even then, I am not a huge fan of requiring such credentials on private lands.

I am opposed to the regulations that some states, such as New Mexico, have imposed that make it more difficult, or even impossible, for nonresident guides and outfitters to work on private lands. To me, this practice is discriminatory. In my opinion, landowners should decide who they want to guide or outfit on their property. If they elect to work with a nonresident professional, the nonresident contractor should not face greater obstacles than a resident contractor. Nonetheless, whatever licensing or registration requirements are in place in the state or country in question obviously will influence the pool of prospective guides available to a hunting proprietor.

PAY SCHEDULES

As previously mentioned, there are easier ways to make money than by guiding hunters. I will also say that while a person working as a hunting guide will not be wealthy, according to most financial standards, the work can be immensely gratifying. The wealth, measured in relationships, memories, and time outdoors, is not directly tied to a bank account.

Most hunting guides are paid a daily fee that can vary considerably. For instance, waterfowl outfitters who are providing well-trained dogs will be paid a bit more than a typical deer guide because there is considerable value and overhead associated with sporting dogs. Furthermore, quail guides who provide a team of bird dogs and a quail rig (outfitted truck and trailer) will fetch an even higher rate than a typical waterfowl guide. Pack guides with horses will be paid for their horse(s) as well as the gear necessary to hunt from horses. For these and a variety of other reasons, guiding rates can range widely. As with most industries, labor rates found across the hunting industry generally create the "normal" compensation rate for guides.

On occasion, full-time and seasonal guides earn monthly salaries. Once again, these monthly rates vary because of the aforementioned variables as well as the geographic location of the hunting operation. If the hunts are guided from trucks or utility terrain vehicles (UTVs), some guides provide their own vehicles. Less frequently, the proprietor will provide vehicles for on-property use. All our part-time guides and seasonal guides provide their own vehicles. For vehicle and fuel compensation, WSI pays them one rate for the commute to and from the property and a second higher rate while they are on the ranch working the hunt. Some of our guides travel several 100 miles one-way, so we must have a way to keep commuting costs in check. To manage mileage-related costs, we try to schedule multiple hunts back-to-back on a single property or on nearby properties, bundling these assigned hunts and avoiding long-distance deadheading for a single hunt.

OTHER SUPPORT NEEDS

In addition to guides and chefs, most hunting operations will require additional field support staff who are responsible for prepping equipment, filling feeders, caring for dogs and horses, repairing stands, and various other "behind-the-scenes" activities. We generally rely on either our seasonal or full-time employees to take care of these tasks.

As Roger Staubach, the legendary former quarterback for the Dallas Cowboys, used to say, "Spectacular achievement is always preceded by unspectacular preparation." Indeed, repairing equipment, filling feeders, and feeding horses are not glamorous tasks, but they are essential for the rest of the hunting operation to function. This behind-the-scenes work also helps the guides successfully serve the company's clients, so guides should show their appreciation to these other team members to ensure good staff-team relations.

Every single job contributes to the operation's efficiency, effectiveness, and overall performance. Never underestimate the importance of the unsung heroes who make everyone in camp look good when the clients roll in.

1 > Having a blend of older and younger guides provides several benefits to outfitting businesses, including creating a support staff pipeline that contributes to long-term business stability while also allowing veterans to groom rookies.

2> Hunting guides are often expected to perform other not-so-glamorous work that is integral to the success of the operation. Behind-the-scenes work is part of the cog assembly that helps ensure the operation works like a finely tuned machine.

3> Continuing education through technical training ensures that guides are well-versed in a broad range of responsibilities. The late Dr. Bob Dittmar is shown here training WSI guides on how to pull samples for CWD testing.

MARCHING IN STEP

As a proprietor, I am very fortunate to have a strong team of guides, cooks, and other support personnel. The crew's quality and depth make my life easier and more peaceful. As a business owner, nothing is more liberating than knowing that I do not have to be in the middle of everything to ensure good performance. In fact, when the right people with the right training are in place, business performance is often better than when the owner or general manager is looking over everyone's shoulders.

For the camp staff, namely the guides and kitchen staff, to perform optimally, everyone must be marching in step. Believe me, this does not happen by accident. As I have already covered, the entire support team must be well-trained. Fortunately, proper training is not rocket science. To maximize the guides' productivity, you should develop and implement sound, standardized practices that define your operating culture. All camp staffers should understand and be part of these best management practices. In-service training, handbooks, occasional emails, and mentoring by seasoned veterans are all components for developing a successful operating culture.

As I tell our support team, our practices may not be the "best practices," but they work well for us and are simple enough to replicate without too much additional effort or unnecessary complication. As we move forward, we are always looking for ways to fine-tune our process, increase our capacity, and improve our performance.

NONCOMPETE AND CLIENT PROTECTION CONSIDERATIONS

For business owners, one of the greatest frustrations is to train employees, only to see them become direct competitors. The frustration is magnified if a former employee poaches valuable clients. In the hunting business, relationships are often stronger between clients and their respective guides than they are between the clients and the proprietor. The guides and clients essentially live together for several days, which creates a better opportunity to bond. Those bonds endure, and it is not unusual for clients to follow third-party guides if they start their own business or begin working with another outfitter. It has happened to me many times. While it is frustrating, it is the nature of the game. Frankly, I don't worry about these things as much as I used to, which I guess reflects my jaded style and my now worrying more about other pressing needs. Plus, I think what comes around often goes around, so I'm content in allowing things to take their own natural course and not becoming drawn into the temptation of seeking reprisal.

Although I do have WSI's full-time employees sign a noncompete and/or client protection agreement, I do not have our part-time and seasonal third-party guides sign any type of protection document. I have struggled with this issue. When it comes to third-party contractors, I do not know that a signed agreement would tip the legal scales in WSI's favor. If the document's legal value is questionable, then it may be better to simply lay out clear expectations ahead of time to the part-time guides and any third-party contractors about what is expected of them regarding boundaries and concerns.

In the past, I have relied on our company handbook, in-service meetings, and occasional memos to address this matter. I would like to think that mutual trust and respect provides ample safeguards against client poaching, but I have been horribly disappointed at times with various guides, chefs, and clients who deliberately carried business away from WSI. In some instances, this behavior was not intended to undermine me or my business, but nonetheless it creates a "damned if you do and damned if you don't" situation. If the poaching is not dealt with properly, it can create its own problems. If you as the outfitter react too aggressively to the new "competition," it may alienate other support personnel, but if you do nothing, it may send the wrong message to your loyal guides and chefs, or at worst, encourage others to attempt the same thievery.

At the time of this writing, I am 58 years old and have committed 35 years of my life to building WSI. My response to this disrespectful breach of trust varies from situation to situation. There are times where I do not tolerate it at all, and then there are times where I ignore the situation because I refuse to be confrontational and would rather avoid the drama that such "fights" can and will create. At the end of the day, the business owner must protect the company's interests, which also protects the support team's interest. The business owner pays for marketing, assumes most of the liability, and incurs the full spectrum of overhead costs associated with running a business, so there must be some safeguards in place to protect those investments. Unfortunately, enforcing boundaries and standing up for the company's long-term interests means sometimes stepping on toes. But, as previously stated, I don't get wound up as easily as I used to about these and other nagging type issues.

As the Miles Law states, "Where you stand [on an issue] generally depends upon where you sit." Third-party and part-time support will likely be viewing any unfolding situation through a different lens than the business owner. In the end, it boils down to open communication and faith. As a business owner, I believe that if you treat your people right, then the vast majority of them will reciprocate your honesty, fairness, loyalty, and respect.

As I pointed out earlier in this chapter, there is a certain degree of romance associated with the idea of professionally guiding hunters. For some guides, that romance lingers throughout the guiding career; for others, the romance wains when the long hours and various other demands of the job set in. For those guides who are in this field for the right reason and are willing to patiently work through the formative stages of developing their craft, the rewards of their work can be immensely gratifying, especially when they reach that stage when their well-rounded capabilities allow them to perform their tasks with excellence and confidence, even during the most challenging of times. Like any other job, guiding is a job, and some days are more enjoyable than others. Maintaining appropriate perspective is a key ingredient for any hunting guides to find longevity in this industry. And for the proprietors, who are fortunate to accrue a cadre of guides who have sorted out the requisites for making things work well in this space, those proprietors should consider themselves fortunate—I am one of those and I am thankful.

11 EQUIPMENT AND GEAR

THE BASIC EQUIPMENT AND GEAR NECESSARY FOR A HUNTING OPERATION TO FUNCTION EFFICIENTLY VARIES DEPENDING ON THE SITUATION.

The list of essential equipment and gear is influenced by variables, including the species being hunted, the property's location and its remoteness/terrain, and the "opulence" of the overall hunting experience.

What's already available and being supplied by the ranch or landowner and what the outfitter may already have on hand will likely dictate how large a capital investment will be required to get things up to speed to meet the required infrastructure that's necessary to begin catering to paying hunters. Some hunting proprietors may have the cash to go "all in" on equipment and gear, while others may have to make more modest choices. I assure you, one can spend as much as the heart desires when supplying a hunting property and hunting operation with equipment and gear. I've seen ranches spend an absolute fortune outfitting the property with lavish improvements, but these properties are often owned by folks who have made their fortune in a different industry, and the driving forces that shape these investments can be altogether different than that of a proprietor who does not come from those means and has much different motives with the business venture.

Guides must also have access to some basic equipment to be successful in the field. Many hunting businesses, including WSI, require their guides to provide most, or all, of their own needed tools and equipment. Regardless, in every situation there is some basic equipment that is considered essential. This chapter principally addresses those essentials.

VEHICLES

Transportation that is suitable to the terrain is integral to every hunting operation. In many areas, automobiles and UTVs are the most common means of transportation. Outfitters and guides should not be underserved here. An unreliable vehicle can leave clients and guides stranded in remote areas, which will likely cost the client valuable hunting time that they have paid for.

In some cases, the outfitter provides company vehicles that all guides can use, while other operations require that third-party guides provide their own vehicles. As mentioned previously, I generally require the guides to provide their own transportation. When guides provide their own vehicles, they are typically compensated in some form, often based on mileage or perhaps a daily fee. Variables apply here, such as access to fuel that's on the property, provided by the proprietor, versus the guide refueling their vehicle in town at their own expense and how this may interact with mileage reimbursement rates.

Once again, sound reliability of ground transportation of clients is a necessity. Furthermore, guides should keep the vehicles clean and free of trash and clutter. Trashy, cluttered vehicles are a pet peeve of mine. I would advise that guides be required to spend a few minutes each day policing their vehicles, which could mean disposing of any accumulated trash, wiping down surfaces, and cleaning windows.

In areas with extreme conditions, such as rugged terrain or exceptionally wet environments, guides may need to use UTVs or even semiaquatic vehicles. Argo vehicles are amphibious vehicles that are used commonly in parts of Canada and Alaska where wet tundra is inaccessible with any other type of vehicle. Argos are also occasionally used by waterfowl operations in flooded areas and wetlands. Snowmobiles are occasionally used in areas that have deep snowpack conditions. In coastal areas and in locations that involve lakes, rivers, bays, and inlets, shallow water boats are commonly used for transporting clients to and from hunting areas. Sleds pulled by dogs may be used in areas where polar bear and muskox are hunted. Mountain hunts may involve horses and mules for transportation. The bottom line is that the terrain and remoteness of the hunting area will dictate what type of transportation is feasible and necessary. Will the outfitter provide these transportation means, will it be the guides, or will there be a hybrid arrangement?

Because the ability to transport hunters to and from hunting areas is essential, it is wise to prepare for the unexpected. For instance, four-wheel drive trucks are often the vehicle of choice for guides in most areas of Texas. However, during the fall of 2018, we experienced record rainfall in some areas of the state. The pastures in those locations became so saturated over a two-month period that UTVs were the only way to get our hunters in and out of the field. After scrambling around for several days trying to avoid investing $15,000—$20,000 per machine to amass a fleet of UTVs, we were able to find a rental company that provided the necessary vehicles. These were late-in-the game adjustments that literally were bumping against start-timing of hunts; to say these were anxious challenges is putting it lightly, but we made it work despite some unbudgeted expenses.

With the exception of packing out a few elk when WSI ran elk hunts in Colorado, we have not used horses within our hunting operation. Some remote, mountain type hunts require horses, but frankly, placing clients on horses in rough terrain can represent a huge liability. On top of that, raising and caring for horses is a major commitment requiring specialized expertise and appropriate facilities. Most operations, including ours, are simply not set up to incorporate horses into their program. Although some hunters without any equestrian experience may think it is romantic to be part of a pack string that ventures into remote wild areas, most hunters are not capable of riding horses in rugged terrain. Over the years, I have known several hunters who have been involved with "train wrecks" that ended badly. My advice is to avoid placing clients on horseback, if possible.

BLINDS OR STANDS

Depending upon the species being hunted, hunting blinds can be a critical part of field operations. For example, white-tailed deer and waterfowl often require blinds. Because WSI leases the hunting rights on various properties, our company tries to avoid spending an excessive amount on these improvements because it can be challenging to move this equipment if we lose the lease. We encourage the landowners to provide the blinds or to shoulder the capital expenditures required for these infrastructure investments, which may mean them paying for the blinds and us providing the labor to get them in-place on the property.

These days, some blinds are extremely posh, and a single deer blind can cost more than $5,000. The same thing holds true for waterfowl blinds. I have seen blinds equipped with solar-powered TVs, urinals, cots, electric coffee pots, and heaters. Obviously, these extra amenities are niceties, not necessities, but even well-built

ABOVE > Tractors and other types of heavy equipment are often necessary to move and set up large, heavy items. For operations that do not own heavy equipment, rentals or third-party services may be necessary.

conventional commercial blinds can carry a hefty price tag. Because supplying any property requires multiple blinds, the cost rapidly multiplies and the investment can be significant. Since blinds are a major investment, they should be anchored sufficiently to avoid wind damage, and they should be maintained annually to help extend their lifespan.

Through the years, we have built many homemade blinds which have served their purpose well. While building a blind can provide some savings, construction requires skilled labor plus adequate shop space and tools. Lightweight pop-up blinds have become common in recent years. These are very handy for temporary setups for whitetail and turkey hunting. Make sure the blinds are adequately sized. Even though two people can squeeze into a 4'x4' blind, this size blind should be considered a single blind and is best suited for a solo hunter. I find 4'x6' and 5'x6' blinds to be better suited for one to two hunters plus a guide. Waterfowl blinds are generally much larger. At a minimum, they should be designed to accommodate at least four clients plus a guide, and perhaps an outside platform for a dog.

Like horses, hunting blinds can be a liability for the proprietor. The highest risk associated with elevated blinds is the chance that clients may fall as they enter or exit. Some years ago, during a single white-tailed deer season in Texas, there were two separate incidents where hunters accidentally dropped loaded rifles while climbing into an elevated deer blind. When the guns hit the ground, they discharged and both hunters were killed. A year later, a hunter fell from his elevated blind and landed on a T-post that had been used to secure the blind. The impaled hunter died, and his young son witnessed the fatal accident.

Hunting proprietors should implement measures to reduce risks associated with blinds. Choosing blinds with stairs and handrails instead of ladders can help mitigate the risks. In recent years, I have seen a trend toward using ground blinds and short towers instead of tall tower blinds, which reduces the risk. Other best practices should include requiring all guns to be unloaded while people are climbing in and out of blinds. Guides should also hold the clients' guns as they enter the blind and hand the clients their firearms once they are securely inside. When it is time to exit, the process is reversed. Guides exit first, and clients pass their empty guns down to the guide who holds them as the clients climb down.

Repair faulty steps, exterminate insects, including bees and spiders, and use common sense approaches to address any problem areas.

FEEDERS

Feeding and baiting laws vary between countries and states. Here in the U.S., baiting is strictly prohibited in migratory bird hunting, but in some states like Texas, hunting deer and turkeys over feed is a legal and common practice. Depending upon the location and game species, using feeders may or may not be a consideration. In our Texas whitetail hunting operations, feeders are considered required equipment. The proprietor can spend a considerable amount of money acquiring feeders. They commonly cost $500 —$1,000 each depending upon the style, capacity, and brand. Most feeders used for hunting will hold 300 to 500 pounds of feed, but some of the jumbo feeders may hold one thousand to two thousand pounds. The larger feeders are often more expensive, but once they are filled, they can end up saving time because they do not have to be refilled as often.

We have used a variety of different brands and styles of timer mechanisms. While some are better than others, none are foolproof. In fact, feeders seem to be the bane of my existence at times. No matter how often they are checked and tested, they seem to malfunction at the most inopportune time—when hunters are present. Nonetheless, if you are going to rely on automatic feeders, you must make the extra effort to try and ensure that they are functioning properly.

In recent years, ground-fill feeders have become popular. This feeder can be filled while standing on the ground or from the back of a truck as opposed to the top of a ladder. I highly recommend this style of feeder. Ground-fill feeders not only reduce labor but also the risk of falling from a ladder and the liability incurred by such an accident. My father-in-law took a spill while filling a deer feeder in 2000, resulting in a compound fracture to his lower leg and somewhat permanently impairing him for life, so this obviously left an impression on me.

Depending on the hunting program, supplemental feeders may be a consideration. These are designed to deliver enough protein-based feed to increase performance, such as antler growth or reproductive success, and tend to have larger hoppers and more capacity. Most hold somewhere between one thousand to two thousand pounds. Generally, these free-flowing feeders are delivering "free-choice" feed. Once again, the proprietor can spend a considerable amount of money purchasing supplemental feeders. I have had relatively good luck finding used feeders at discounted prices. Most of these used feeders have been acquired from hunters who recently left a lease or sometimes from landowners who recently purchased a new property and are liquidating items they do not need.

LOANER OR RENTAL GUNS

From time to time, clients need a loaner or rental gun. Common situations include someone traveling from an international location, an invitee of a corporate group, or someone traveling by plane whose gun did not make it with the hunter to the destination airport. On other occasions, a client's gun malfunctions or shoots inaccurately. Most operations have guns available for rent when unforeseen circumstances arise. When setting the rental rate, always add an additional amount to cover the unpredictable cost of ammunition. When clients are test-shooting the rental gun off the bench or even missing multiple shots, clients can burn through a significant amount of ammo.

As of July of 2022, at the time of my final round of edits to this book, ammunition around the U.S. has been scarce for over a year and costs have risen astronomically. Under these circumstances, I do not consider charging clients for ammo as "nickel-and-diming" them, as this variable cost can add up. Some gun manufactures offer discount programs for outfitters. The companies can benefit from the exposure they receive when outfitting operations make those brands available to their clients. For proprietors considering gun purchases for their businesses, the discount programs are worth checking out, but again, until ammo shortages straighten out, discounted supplies may be unlikely.

Another option is making arrangements for your guides to provide rental guns. Since WSI hunts on so many different properties from many different camps, we often rely on this arrangement. We encourage our guides to have a spare gun during the hunt and to predetermine a rental rate so the clients will know what to expect if they need the gun. As an operational note, even when our guides furnish the rental guns, WSI collects those fees and then pays the guide. By doing this, we are trying to ensure that the client does not "blend" the gun rental fee with the guide's tip, which could potentially "rob" the guide of the rental monies.

GUIDE'S EQUIPMENT

As with any trade, the tradesman, in this case the guide, must be properly equipped. The guides' hunting vehicles often serve as the "storeroom" for their tools and equipment.

When it comes to necessary equipment, especially in remote locations, it is better to be overstocked than understocked. In my experience, international guides and professional hunters are often better equipped and prepared than typical American guides. Some of their preparedness can be attributed to the need to be self-sufficient in extremely remote locations, and some of it can be ascribed to a higher degree of professionalism that is found in some of these other countries, such as in Africa.

ITEMS THAT MIGHT BE INCLUDED IN A BASIC CHECKLIST FOR GUIDE EQUIPMENT

- optics (binoculars and spotting scope)
- knives and sharpener
- first aid kit
- daypack and possibly a pack frame
- lighter (for starting fires)
- flashlight with extra batteries
- small head lamp
- duct tape and small rope
- red surveyor's tape
- hand tools
- spare tire or two
- tow rope and/or chain
- ratchet straps and bungee cords
- shooting sticks
- various specialty items, such as decoys, etc.
- tire plug kit and electric pump
- tarp
- trash bags
- zip ties
- pry or cheater bar
- ax and/or cordless Sawzall
- water container
- cell phone or two-way radios

ABOVE > Guides should have a broad assembly of tools and equipment that stays in their hunting vehicles, allowing them to deal with various challenges that may arise in camp or in the field.

Guides should, no, make that must, purchase high-quality equipment that is reliable. For instance, high-quality optics are expensive, but binoculars and spotting scopes can make a huge difference in a guide's ability to locate animals and make sound decisions when advising about shooting a particular animal. For guides who are just acquiring their equipment, there may be some areas where they may temporarily cut corners, such as with hand saws instead of cordless electric saws, while there is other equipment, such as binoculars, that should be the highest quality they can afford.

Again, having guides that are appropriately equipped for the field is essential. Guides who short themselves of necessary equipment will eventually pay the price, and that price may be costly for the proprietor as well. It is just a matter of time before failed or lacking equipment will cost their clients valuable hunting time, or worse, put someone at risk. Plus, the guide's preparedness reflects on the operation and ultimately plays a part in the proprietor's success. Again, make sure your guides and staff members have all the tools that may be required to perform necessary functions.

12 CUSTOMER SERVICE STRATEGIES

THE HUNTING BUSINESS, LIKE NO OTHER, OFFERS PROPRIETORS AN OPPORTUNITY TO CREATIVELY EMPLOY CUSTOMER SERVICE STRATEGIES AS A CENTRAL PART OF THEIR BUSINESS MODEL'S SUCCESS.

The ground is fertile and the need is strong for actively developing an operating culture that capitalizes on the unique features described in Chapter One, where I claim "there is no business like the hunting business."

Indeed, the hunting business is a strange and difficult business in many ways. One of the unique aspects of this business is that the camp staff is essentially living with the clients for several days. In fact, on some of the Alaskan, Canadian, and African safaris, they may be living with clients for ten to 21 days. I assure you, when you are spending that amount of close and intimate time with a person, even if it is three or four days, you have an exceptionally fertile opportunity to develop a relationship with that person. Discussions and topics often will range across the spectrum, from business details to family, sports, personal issues, and perhaps even religion and politics. The camp staff will leave a distinct impression on the client. It will likely be good or bad because generally, there is no in-between. In my opinion, there is no other industry where the circumstances for measurable success, in this case game harvest, are so unpredictable, which makes customer service so imperative for the perceived success of the overall adventure. As mentioned previously, there are aspects of this business that are outside of the proprietor's control, but customer service strategies are squarely within reach.

Back in 2002, I was hunting Cape buffalo with Ronnie Sparrow in the Luangwa Valley in Zambia. At one point in our hunt discussion, we began comparing notes about difficult clients. After a prolonged discussion, Ronnie looked at me with a big smile on his face and said, "You American guides are a bunch of pussies. You only have to live with your clients for a few days at a time, where we are often living with our clients for ten to 21 days!" He went on to explain that he preferred the difficult clients because they kept his routine from becoming stale. According to him, "I treat it as a game. It is them against me. If their difficult personality gets the best of me, then they win. If I suck it up and continue to have a smile on my face and maintain a steady service delivery, then I win." Bingo. Ronnie summed up well the fundamental premise that should prevail in any industry through holding steady with even the most challenging of client interactions.

Each year I share this story with our WSI staff at our annual in-service meeting. It really boils down to maintaining appropriate perspective, self-discipline, focus, and emotional control. When you can convert the tough customers into loyal clients, you can certainly do the same with less difficult people. In fact, I have found that when you win over difficult customers, they often possess personality traits that make them the most loyal of all clients.

OPERATING CULTURE

Superlative, strategic customer service across a company comes largely from developing an operating culture. Our people understand that while it is important that they each express their own unique personalities, it is paramount that we embrace the company's protocols and practices so we can deliver top-notch service consistently across all of our camps. These practices must be replicable and ingrained in our support team so that they can perform them reliably with "their eyes closed." When a group works in tandem, performing the tasks with excellence, the service appears to be effortless and seamless.

Once these practices become deeply integrated into the routines and are perpetuated through standard operating procedures (SOPs) and through mentoring, then you eventually establish an operating culture that will ultimately define that sector of the business, and perhaps define the business itself. It is extremely important to recognize that while operating cultures can be shaped through excellence, they can also be shaped through poor performance—and if it is the latter, the company is doomed.

Developing a successful operating culture does not happen overnight, and the more "reprogramming" a proprietor or the manager must do to correct poor practices, the longer it takes to create a sound operating culture. Incorporate SOPs from the very beginning so you do not have to waste time and energy correcting improper practices and bad habits that developed in the absence of clear expectations.

Again, SOPs will vary from operation to operation, but successfully creating an individual operating culture boils down to the entire support team understanding their respective roles and marching in step toward the common goal of delivering a positive experience for every guest. The staff, regardless of their job title and role, must be on the same page in their level of understanding, buy-in, and commitment to delivering superlative service. One bad apple can be disruptive and likely will undermine or compromise the sectors of the business where they serve.

From a customer service standpoint, the success of your operating culture depends on everyone's ability to keep their eyes on the big picture without overlooking the details, down to the tiniest facet. It takes both layers to maximize customer service production—big picture and granular.

BEFORE THE HUNT

Customer service in the hunting business begins well before the hunters arrive in camp. Never underestimate the importance of the people who answer the office phone, as they often serve as the initial point of contact and a primary company voice through the process. The person who answers the phone MUST be pleasant and patient. It is rule #1 and #2 and #3. Be pleasant and patient. I'll repeat, be pleasant and patient. And be responsive!

I will admit, as I have gotten older, maintaining a pleasant tone with some people over the phone has become more difficult. I catch myself being intolerant and impatient, which is not good for customer service, sales, or for client retention; therefore, having an office administrator who can communicate with reliable patience, courtesy, and good humor has become even more important to me and the company. I find myself spending less time casually and intentionally visiting with clients over the phone, often opting to rely on my office assistant or on email. Maybe this is a reflection of how business cultures have evolved, but I do think this has become a fault of mine, and I'm not sure that I have an appetite to dedicate the time and effort required to interact with such a vast clientele on a regular basis, which is all the more reason to involve my assistant. Yes, it's a personal flaw, I'll admit.

As they say, "You never get a second chance to make a first impression." The people answering the phone are on the front line in many ways. If negative energy or complications are created through their tone of voice and attitude or by omitting important information, then their poor performance will ripple through the operation and cause complications for other support staff.

Phone etiquette is just one facet of good office administrators. They will likely be the primary source for the information that helps clients be well-prepared for the trip, on many levels. Our office administrator provides clients with essential information such as directions to the venue, equipment needs, license requirements, contact numbers, start and end times of the hunt, payment details, and many other miscellaneous details that are part of the booking and preparatory process and that help ensure a good experience; because a well-prepared client is generally a happier client.

While our office administrator talks clients through the process, we have found it is essential to provide a collection of resources that the client can reference as they prepare for their hunt. We have found a pre-hunt packet is the best way to accomplish this.

TOP-LEFT > Customer service in the hunting business often begins with a friendly, accommodating voice on the phone. This person also serves as the face of the business.

TOP-RIGHT > Because first impressions are lasting impressions, the support team needs to deliver quality, attentive service from the time they meet the clients at the airport. A smooth transition into the hunt establishes a positive tone, making it easier to build success throughout the hunt.

PRE-HUNT PACKET COMPONENTS

- Checklist of items to bring
- Normal weather conditions
- Suggested clothing and garments
- Gun or caliber restrictions
- Tips for flying with firearms
- Directions to property
- Contact numbers
- Shipping of meat and trophies
- Taxidermy options
- Miscellaneous policies and camp rules
- Payment and cancellation policies
- Client profile form or questionnaire
- Hunting license requirements
- Suggestions on gratuities

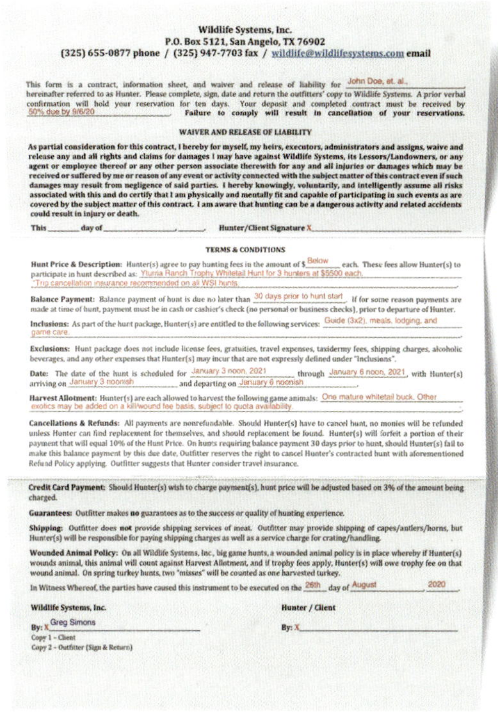

Wildlife Systems, Inc.
P.O. Box 5121, San Angelo, TX 76902
(325) 655-0877 phone / (325) 947-7703 fax / wildlife@wildlifesystems.com email

This form is a contract, information sheet, and waiver and release of liability for John Doe, et. al., hereinafter referred to as Hunter. Please complete, sign, date and return the outfitters' copy to Wildlife Systems. A prior verbal confirmation will hold your reservation for ten days. Your deposit and completed contract must be received by 50% due by 9/6/20. **Failure to comply will result in cancellation of your reservations.**

WAIVER AND RELEASE OF LIABILITY

As partial consideration for this contract, I hereby for myself, my heirs, executors, administrators and assigns, waive and release any and all rights and claims for damages I may have against Wildlife Systems, its Lessors/Landowners, or any agent or employee thereof or any other person associate therewith for any and all injuries or damages which may be received or suffered by me or reason of any event or activity connected with the subject matter of this contract even if such damages may result from negligence of said parties. I hereby knowingly, voluntarily, and intelligently assume all risks associated with this and do certify that I am physically and mentally fit and capable of participating in such events as are covered by the subject matter of this contract. I am aware that hunting can be a dangerous activity and related accidents could result in injury or death.

This _____ day of ________, ____. Hunter/Client Signature X__________

TERMS & CONDITIONS

Hunt Price & Description: Hunter(s) agree to pay hunting fees in the amount of $Below each. These fees allow Hunter(s) to participate in hunt described as: Yturria Ranch Trophy Whitetail Hunt for 3 hunters at $5500 each. *Trip cancellation insurance recommended on all WSI hunts.

Balance Payment: Balance payment of hunt is due no later than 30 days prior to hunt start. If for some reason payments are made at time of hunt, payment must be in cash or cashier's check (no personal or business checks), prior to departure of Hunter.

Inclusions: As part of the hunt package, Hunter(s) are entitled to the following services: Guide (3x2), meals, lodging, and game care.

Exclusions: Hunt package does not include license fees, gratuities, travel expenses, taxidermy fees, shipping charges, alcoholic beverages, and any other expenses that Hunter(s) may incur that are not expressly defined under "Inclusions".

Date: The date of the hunt is scheduled for January 3 noon, 2021 through January 6 noon, 2021, with Hunter(s) arriving on January 3 noonish and departing on January 6 noonish.

Harvest Allotment: Hunter(s) are each allowed to harvest the following game animals: One mature whitetail buck. Other exotics may be added on a kill/wound fee basis, subject to quota availability.

Cancellations & Refunds: All payments are nonrefundable. Should Hunter(s) have to cancel hunt, no monies will be refunded unless Hunter can find replacement for themselves, and should replacement be found. Hunter(s) will forfeit a portion of their payment that will equal 10% of the Hunt Price. On hunts requiring balance payment 30 days prior to hunt, should Hunter(s) fail to make this balance payment by this due date, Outfitter reserves the right to cancel Hunter's contracted hunt with aforementioned Refund Policy applying. Outfitter suggests that Hunter consider travel insurance.

Credit Card Payment: Should Hunter(s) wish to charge payment(s), hunt price will be adjusted based on 3% of the amount being charged.

Guarantees: Outfitter makes no guarantees as to the success or quality of hunting experience.

Shipping: Outfitter does not provide shipping services of meat. Outfitter may provide shipping of capes/antlers/horns, but Hunter(s) will be responsible for paying shipping charges as well as a service charge for crating/handling.

Wounded Animal Policy: On all Wildlife Systems, Inc., big game hunts, a wounded animal policy is in place whereby if Hunter(s) wounds animal, this animal will count against Harvest Allotment, and if trophy fees apply, Hunter(s) will owe trophy fee on that wound animal. On spring turkey hunts, two "misses" will be counted as one harvested turkey.

In Witness Whereof, the parties have caused this instrument to be executed on the 26th day of August, 2020.

Wildlife Systems, Inc.
By: X Greg Simons
Copy 1 - Client
Copy 2 - Outfitter (Sign & Return)

Hunter / Client
By: X__________

ABOVE > Client satisfaction often hinges on them clearly understanding what to expect from their outfitter. Documents, such as booking agreements and prep packets, are essential to ensure everyone is on the same page and that clients are properly briefed about various details associated with their trip.

In addition to a pre-hunt packet, a booking agreement is essential. This document should outline pricing, dates, inclusions, exclusions, payment and cancellation policies, and other important details of the trip.

When I generate a booking agreement, I email it to the client and copy it to my office manager, who then generates an invoice. She emails the invoice to the clients along with the appropriate pre-hunt packet. These procedures not only create the necessary paperwork to get the process going down the right path, but providing detailed information such as this is also a part of the customer service matrix; it is part of our operating culture.

When our clients leave their houses and are embarking on their hunting trip with us, we want them to be properly prepared with accurate and reasonable expectations when they arrive in camp and as they work through the days of their hunt. When our clients are properly prepared, our camp staff's jobs are easier, allowing them to successfully deliver their portion of the customer service portfolio.

DURING THE HUNT

I tell our camp staff, "Your part of our customer service strategy generally begins when you first make eye contact with the client—whether that's at the airport, in the driveway at the camp, or inside of the lodge." Again, first impressions count. A smile, firm handshake, or hug are powerful tools of engagement that tend to create a positive connection immediately.

At this point, whether it is a guide or the chef welcoming the clients, they are serving as the greeters, and they should deliberately focus on establishing plenty of positive energy and good vibes. If the greeter is in a bad mood and telegraphs their negativity, then the initial impression and atmosphere for the clients will likely be compromised.

The importance of this stage of the hunt cannot be overstated. Enthusiastic greetings and genuine smiles should be automatic with comments like "It's so good to see you;" "We've been looking forward to your hunt for a while;" "We hope you had a good trip to the ranch;" "Let me help you with that." And if your staff can make it personal by adding details such as the client's name, hometown, and acknowledging their status as a repeat hunter (if that is the case), all the better. This transition point is incredibly important.

Some hunting operations have their entire staff line up on the outside of the lodge to formally greet incoming hunters, providing hot or cold wet hand towels while the chef immediately offers a snack or refreshments. However, most hunting camps are not set up to provide this amount of coordinated, detailed service.

Everyone's most prized possession is their name. When it comes to relationship building and nuanced communication, try to remember the name of everyone in the camp—and refer to them by THAT name. Before the hunt begins, we provide a client roster to the camp staff, which can help staffers learn the clients' names before they arrive in camp. These subtle details are the difference-makers, so own them and refine them.

PROVIDING QUALITY CUSTOMER SERVICE WHILE CLIENTS ARE IN CAMP

GETTING SETTLED IN

When hunters arrive in camp, there should always be someone there to greet them. At that point, it is best to have a good idea of which clients are staying in each bedroom, if such planning is realistic. Shortly after the welcoming pleasantries, staff should help clients with their bags and gear and allow them to get settled into the room. Having drinks, snacks, or perhaps appetizers available, depending upon the time of day, is a nice way to allow the clients to relax and become comfortable.

ORIENTATION

An orientation is essential in a hunting camp. This activity covers important details of the upcoming hunt, informing your clients of the hunt's structure and your staff's commanding role in the process. Though it can certainly vary from hunt to hunt, there are a list of items that should always be covered during the orientation.

- Introduction and welcome
- Importance of communication
- Daily routine
- Safety procedures and gun policies
- Harvest allowances
- Wounded animal policies
- Meat and taxidermy options
- Meals, kitchen details, and food allergies
- Signed release forms
- Hunting licenses
- Open discussion and questions

CHECKING FIREARMS

I highly recommend that all clients check their weapons at the range to ensure that their guns and bows are shooting properly, especially on big game hunts. Considering the cost of a quality hunt and the effort that is required to travel across the country to attend these coveted trips, it always amazes me when hunters are reluctant to check their guns at the range. Even with hunters who drive, it is common for guns to need some fine-tuning on the range.

There are few things more disheartening for a guide than having a hunter fail to convert an opportunity into a harvest. If a gun is not sighted in, a proper shot is impossible from the get-go. While at the range, guides can also size up their hunters' capabilities and how safely they handle their firearms. From this point forward, the guides will then have a clearer understanding of how to best accommodate their client, which is all part of the customer service experience.

SAFETY

The most important customer service component in this business is human health and safety, plain and simple. Although I elaborate on this subject in greater detail in the "Risk Management" chapter, I cannot overstate the importance of safety in the customer service lineup of this business.

As I tell our support team every year, there are certain mistakes we cannot afford to make in this business, as they could cost someone their life. Safety and well-being should always be front and center in your operating culture.

TOP TIPS FOR CUSTOMER SERVICE

This "laundry list" of tips should prove to be helpful as you develop your customer service strategies.

- Always have a positive attitude.
- Remember your client's preferred name from the start and address them by that name; a person's name is their most prized possession.
- Communicate adequately.
- A smile is the most important thing you wear to work.
- Dress for the occasion.
- Be at your client's beck and call.
- Keep your feelings to yourself unless they are joy, happiness, or enthusiasm.
- Do not be late for breakfast because punctuality and a good, leisurely breakfast start the day on the right foot.
- Never argue or become combative with clients, unless it is a safety matter.
- Involve your client in discussions regarding hunt strategy when it makes sense, but never allow the client to dictate the routine.
- Even if there is "ground shrinkage" on harvested animals, always congratulate your client on their harvest and treat the occasion as a celebration. Do the same for other hunters in the camp, even if you are not serving as their guide.
- Show genuine concern for your client.
- Be a team player and speak respectfully about other staffers and your boss. Nobody likes or appreciates negativity, which darkens the hunt mood and camp atmosphere.
- Make the hunting experience educational when possible, providing interpretive discussions regarding game sign, plant and animal identification, animal behavior, area history, techniques for processing animals, etc.
- Maintain a clean vehicle. (Clean windshields, no trash, minimal dust on surfaces, etc.)
- Be properly equipped.
- Do not push your client beyond their physical capability.
- Have snacks and drinks available.
- A sack lunch in the field can be converted into a nice dining occasion with a little extra effort. All humans connect with food, so make it special when you can.
- Do not be a slacker, as it will be noticeable.
- Make eye contact during conversations. This is a 101-level communication technique.
- Avoid using profanity.
- Be cautious about discussing religion and politics, as there are plenty of landmines with those topics.
- Be confident, but check your ego at the front gate.
- Remember, the hunt is about the clients, not about you.
- Spend plenty time afield. Long days during spring, summer, and early fall hunts can create a temptation to keep clients in camp too long.
- Be extremely careful about behaving in any manner that may be perceived by some as showing preferential treatment. (This can be a challenging matter at times and is a delicate, but crucial, detail.)
- Guides and chefs should always strive to improve their craft. Their mastery ultimately is reflected in their customer service.

DEALING WITH DIFFICULT CLIENTS

You will have tough customers in any business or industry. Some people are hardwired to be difficult. It will always be this way, which raises the question, "Are there strategic ways to deal with these difficult people while maintaining them as part of your clientele?" The answer is "Yes, sometimes."

Here are some approaches for your support team to consider when these challenging clients are in camp.

- **SOLUTION MANAGEMENT→** If possible, identify the source of a testy client's dissatisfaction or annoyance and seek out solutions that remedy the situation. Finding solutions may require thinking outside of the box.

- **KILL THEM WITH KINDNESS→** Many of even the most disagreeable people will eventually "give in" when those around them smile steadily and greet their complaints with a willingness to please. Smile, be pleasant, be accommodating, and try not to show your own rising annoyance.

- **THE SKY IS NOT FALLING→** Maintaining perspective is important for the support team. When faced with a difficult client, keep your eyes on the big picture and the overall goal of customer service. It is important to realize that things are generally not as bad as they seem.

- **IT IS TEMPORARY→** Though you may have to live with a jerk for several days, remember it is just a few days—and then the jerk will be out of your life, and you can move on.

- **SHOW EMPATHY→** By placing yourself in your adversary's shoes, you can generally see things from the client's point of view, even if you do not agree with it. Nelson Mandela was a master at building bridges in the midst of conflict by using empathy. Showing empathy often requires checking your ego at the door and putting aside your personal biases in order to change the relationship and ultimately achieve a positive outcome.

- **CONFIDE WITH OTHER PERSONNEL→** As humans, we tend to find relief when we confide or consult with others. Private discussions not only provide a vent to release a little steam, but fellow workers may be able to lend some advice on how to work with a challenging client. You know what they say—misery likes company.

- **ANGER MANAGEMENT→** Do your very best to not wear your heart (well, your feelings actually) on your sleeve. People tend to communicate their emotions through comments, facial expressions, and body language, which we sometimes refer to as telegraphing. Antagonists often feed off such telegraphing, so practice disguising these emotions. Avoid confrontational discussions with testy clients unless safety is the issue.

- **TREAT IT LIKE A GAME→** Though this is stretching the mind a bit, one way to deal with difficult clients is to view the conflict as a game of personalities where your can-do, customer-centric spirit is pitted against their combativeness. If the client's unreasonable behavior gets the best of you, then your ornery client wins. However, if you can maintain quality customer service and a positive disposition, then you win. So be creative with your mindset, once again thinking outside of the box.

- **SAFETY FIRST→** Any behavior that compromises the safety of those around them cannot be tolerated, especially in the hunting business. Whether it is unsafe gun handling practices, bullish behavior around other clients that may lead to verbal or physical confrontation, or any other circumstances that put people at risk, company personnel should intervene. Intervention may ultimately lead to dismissing or evicting the client from the premises. There should be zero-tolerance for behavior that endangers people.

Unhappy clients and tough customers present an interesting and sometimes challenging dilemma. As humans, we want to wash our hands clean of unpleasant people. However, as a service provider, if you go the extra mile, it may turn the situation around. This "twist of fate" can create a magical outcome, especially with unhappy clients.

Many people occasionally want to be coddled or "put up with" and sometimes these same people deeply appreciate someone who goes the extra mile or perhaps simply hears them out and ultimately "makes things right" for them.

Making lemons into lemonade is often a matter of using the "F" word—"F" for flexibility. Obviously, your ability to bend depends on the situation, but a willingness to address unpleasant challenges often results in great outcomes. Simple things such as saying, "I am sorry," often cost you nothing, other than a bit of pride.

Providing concessions to earn an unhappy client's confidence may be an alternative that has short-term financial costs but yields long-term gains and loyal clients. Be creative, treat these difficult situations as an opportunity to build a long-term relationship, and over time you will likely find that lemonade stands have a place in your business strategies and service culture, but there will hopefully be no need for a lemonade stand on every corner!

AFTER THE HUNT

As they say, "It ain't over till it's over."

Small finishing touches often translate into repeat customers. It is a shame when all the pieces fall into place perfectly during a successful hunt, but unnecessary sloppiness at the completion of the hunt sends the entire process awry. Then instead of double thumbs-up, disgruntled clients give your operation a double thumbs-down—and tell all their family and friends.

Here is a list of some helpful suggestions to ensure the overall customer service experience is topped with a nice bow at the end of the hunt.

FINISHING TOUCHES

- Make sure that the clients are dropped off at the airport early to avoid mad dashes or missed flights.

- Ensure that capes and horns/antlers are either shipped to the client or expedited to the selected taxidermist with appropriate tagging and instruction.

- For rebookings, make sure that you have a rebooking policy that has been clearly outlined so that clients understand what those advantages look like and so they do not inadvertently miss out; this also helps ensure high client retention.

- "Thank you" notes and photos can be an excellent way of putting the proverbial icing on the cake.

- Tidy up around camp, even if a house cleaner is scheduled to clean the facilities. Leaving a bunch of loose trash around leaves a negative final impression. The same applies to the skinning and processing areas. Make sure that animal parts are properly disposed of and that all surfaces and floors are cleaned.

- Ask guides and chefs to provide feedback to the office or the proprietor on any noteworthy matters such as problems encountered, issues that may require additional attention, or clients' interests in rebooking their hunts.

- Provide hunt photos to the company office in a timely manner.

ABOVE > I believe African PH Ronnie Sparrow (center) was one of the most "strategic" guides I've ever hunted with during my international travels. Sparrow said he enjoyed guiding difficult clients, and approached the inherent challenges as a game. If Sparrow maintained his professional focus and continued to deliver unwavering, high-quality service despite the client's demands, Sparrow declared himself the winner. The best hunting guides possess both mental toughness and emotional control.

THE FREE THROW

And, last but not least, be nice. Yep, it is that easy—be nice!

There is a reason that "Do to others what you would have them do to you" (Matthew 7:12) is considered the Golden Rule. It works. People tend to treat others the way they are treated. That is Customer Service 101.

So again, be nice! It is a surefire way to advance the ball down the client retention field.

13 RISK MANAGEMENT

IN THE HUNTING BUSINESS, SOME MISTAKES CAN COST PEOPLE THEIR LIVES, SO NOTHING CAN BE TAKEN FOR GRANTED WHEN IT COMES TO SAFETY.

"There are certain mistakes we cannot afford to make. Otherwise, it could cost someone their life." Those are words that I share each year at our WSI company in-service meeting. I hope this observation creates context for the importance of the information in this chapter of The Hunting Business.

A year or so, after I formed WSI, I decided it was time for me to consider purchasing a liability insurance policy. I contacted a local insurance agent who was listed in the Yellow Pages and set up a time for a meeting. He asked me to come by the day before the meeting to fill out some paperwork. The next day, I sat down in his office and his first comments were something like, "Son, you could not have picked a profession that provides you with more risk and liability than this one. We can't write insurance for your company, as there are simply too many possible exposures that make your business too high a risk for us."

At that point, it became apparent to me that I was working in an industry that involved an almost endless list of scenarios that could potentially put people's lives in harm's way. Some 32 years later, the reality of the precarious nature of my business has only become more obvious and heightened my ongoing concern about properly dealing with this downside of my business.

Risk management is an attempt to control, as much as possible, future outcomes by acting proactively rather than reactively. Within this space, the proprietor is putting into motions steps to reduce both the possibility of a risk occurring and its potential impact. As a business owner or manager, it's extremely important to understand how to strategize how you minimize risk for your organization and ensure that you are being careful and conscious as you make business decisions.

The possible perils that define the risk profile of the hunting business are vast, including guns, knives, broken terrain, horses, UTVs, snakes, spiders, walking across the field at night, possible food allergies, alcohol consumption, dealing with strangers in mixed groups, encountered rabid animals, weather extremes, rivers and lakes, elevated blinds, etc. That is the bad news. The good news, however, is that there are some reasonable options that allow the proprietor to mitigate their risks and liabilities. I count my lucky stars that we have never had any serious injuries that have occurred on our hunts, though we have lost a few people to heart attacks, including my dear Mom who died while cooking on a hunt in 1990 at the tender age of 48. We have had many close calls, but I'd like to think that our attentiveness to this aspect of our business has served as a preventative for accidents and incidents that are ever looming in this industry.

Anyone and everyone who engages as a proprietor in the hunting business must construct some rendition of a risk management plan. Period. Such plans should be inclusive of written standards that help define the company's Best Management Practices (BMPs) that are intended to be deployed along the way. Such a plan is only as sound as the proprietor's or manager's ability to incorporate those practices through the breadth of the operation, which requires personnel training. I've referenced the importance of operating culture in multiple areas of this book, and nowhere in the vast assembly activities that span the business profile is operating culture more important than that of risk management and risk mitigation.

This chapter hits some high-points on risk management as it relates to the hunting business, but anyone who is involved in this industry should study and reflect deeply about there role in keeping everyone safe and out of harms' way, and what steps they must take to try and avoid associated problems.

INSURANCE COVERAGE

Considering our highly litigious society, appropriate liability insurance coverage should be a no-brainer for American hunting proprietors. Insurance coverage for commercial hunting programs can be expensive, and the premium rates tend to escalate with the addition of certain activities, such as using horses, UTVs, swimming pools, and boating. Regardless of the type, insurance is not an exciting overhead expense item, but as they say, when you need it, good insurance coverage can be a lifesaver. So make sure your coverage is appropriate for the scope of your operation and your limits are set high enough to adequately "cover your butt."

WAIVER DOCUMENTS

Outfitters and landowners may secure written and signed waivers from the hunters releasing the outfitter or landowner from negligent conduct. A waiver is defined as the intentional relinquishment of a known right. To be valid, the release provisions must meet certain standards and these standards vary between states and countries.

Statutes regarding business owner and landowner liability evolve over time. Texas for instance, passed the Texas Agritourism Act in 2015 that clarifies what landowners can do to provide added liability protection for various agritourism activities, including hunting.

As part of its provisions, the statute includes some standard language that can be built into a "waiver of liability" form. Although some people may say, "It is not worth the paper it is written on," it is always recommended that clients and/or guests sign a "waiver" that is also often referred to as a release form. I suggest that you consult an attorney to help you construct appropriate waiver language specific to your operation. Or you can consider other waiver clauses that have been reviewed and approved by legal professionals and use them as the basis of your release of liability form.

THE TALK

Another hedge against liability is an orientation presented to the hunters and guides before they ever leave camp to hunt the first time. This orientation, or what some of my camp staff refer to as "The Talk," creates a perfect opportunity to cover safety rules and to disclose any potential hazards. The Talk also sets the tone so the hunters know that the impending hunt will be run with structure and control. I cannot overemphasize the importance of this step of the process. More details regarding hunt orientation are covered in the "Customer Service Strategies" Chapter.

MARCHING IN STEP

When it comes to human health and safety, the enterprise's support team should have rigid protocols in the form of BMPs that define their procedures. BMPs do not have to be elaborate to be effective. In our business, we stick to the fundamentals as we have defined them.

WSI compiled and maintains a company handbook, a formal document that covers various company matters, including safety protocols. Furthermore, we host an annual in-service training session. The in-service training has proven to be an excellent platform for instilling and refining BMPs to help ensure that the support team becomes knowledgeable of these vital procedures and to encourage them to consistently implement them.

Among many other things, standard first aid and CPR should be part of this training regimen. As a side note, our annual training is also a great opportunity for our entire staff to socialize and get to know one another, which can be helpful when they find themselves together in camps across the state.

GUN SAFETY

When it comes to the risk and liability inherent in the hunting business, guns and gun safety are the big and obvious elephants in every room, every vehicle, every blind, and every pasture. It is imperative that your entire support team be "all-hands-on-deck" when it comes to enforcing appropriate safety measures.

TOP > Time on the gun range not only ensures that clients' guns are properly sighted in before the hunt, but gives staff the opportunity to evaluate how clients handle their guns. This insight into the client's skills signals how attentive and hands-on the guide needs to be to ensure safety.

Though the list below should not be considered complete, there are some basic gun safety rules that should ALWAYS apply.

BASIC GUN SAFETY RULES

- Treat every gun as though it is loaded.
- Every gun has two safeties—one that is mechanically operated and physically located on the gun, and the other that is positioned between the ears of the person holding the gun.
- No loaded guns in camp, in vehicles, or while climbing into or out of elevated blinds.
- Be particularly mindful and cautious when following up on wounded animals or placing additional shots after a miss because things can happen fast, and the adrenaline is generally flowing by this point.
- Recognize and respect transition points where firearm accidents often happen, such as getting in/out of vehicles, in/out of blinds, etc.
- Always carefully and clearly identify your target before pulling the trigger.
- Use extreme caution with low-flying birds when bird hunting.
- Wear eye protection when bird hunting or when practicing on the range.
- Recommend ear protection be worn.
- Instruct guides to remind clients about gun safety proactively and regularly.

Again, these safety rules represent a partial suite of items that the proprietor may include under a safety rules policy document. Do your own homework and design a safety list that you feel uniquely covers your situation well and build that document into your BMP plan.

GROSS NEGLIGENCE

As previously mentioned, liability statutes vary from state to state, but as a rule, the proprietor has a greater legal uphill battle when it comes to gross negligence as opposed to regular negligence. Of the two, gross negligence is more damaging because it implies a high level of apathy or indifference. Even in cases where victims cannot sue someone for regular negligence, they can still bring a case for gross negligence.

According to *www.law.cornell.edu*, gross negligence is, "A lack of care that demonstrates reckless disregard for the safety or lives of others, which is so great it appears to be conscious violation of other people's rights to safety. It is more than simple inadvertence, and can affect the amount of damages."

Those wishing to rely on liability insurance should contact their current insurance carrier to see if claims for gross negligence are covered by the policy. Likewise, if the claims are covered, see if the policy also covers punitive damages associated with a gross negligence claim.

When it comes to addressing concerns relating to gross negligence, if a proprietor knows of any preexisting hazards, then those hazards should be remedied before clients or guests can participate in activities where they may be exposed to those hazards. An example of an incident that might be considered gross negligence is when someone is harmed by a hazard that the proprietor knew existed, but did not remedy, which may include: gas leaks in hunting cabins, uncovered water wells, bulls or dogs that have previously shown aggression toward people, faulty steps on an elevated deer stand, and loaner guns that have previously malfunctioned. Bottom line, if you know that such hazards exist, take the time to remedy those matters.

HAVE A CONTINGENCY PLAN

Although no one ever wants to contend with an injury incurred by a client, guest, or staffer who suffered an accident while participating in an activity offered by your business, part of the BMP assemblage should include the "what to do" list should something go awry.

The following is a sample list of questions to ask before something goes wrong.

QUESTIONS TO ASK

- Where is the first aid kit?
- Where is the nearest Emergency Medical Services (EMS) center and how do I get there?
- Does my client have a medical history that I should know about, so that I can recognize or help understand certain signs of distress?
- How do I address hemorrhaging should someone suffer a major cut?

The above are simply a few examples. There are many other possible scenarios, so ensure that your support team ponders the breadth of things that could go awry. The bottom line for contingency planning is getting the entire staff to consider various scenarios and think, "What am I going to do if x, y, or z happens?" These possible incidents can be listed on paper and/or can be played out in person during an in-service training session. And always remember, it is one thing to have a scripted contingency plan, but it can be another matter to implement these practices when things go wrong in the field. The human brain tends to work differently when distress overload sets in, so part of the plan should also include the importance of trying to remain calm and steady.

In a commercial hunting operation, the "first responder" will likely be the guide or the chef. Your support team should deliberately try to envision possible circumstances so that they are as mentally prepared as possible should something occur. They need to recognize that it is not terribly uncommon for nonprofessional first responders to be so affected by accidents that they panic and/or go into shock themselves. Shock can lead to its own physiological problems for the first responder, but for the sake of brevity, the take-home lesson for the support team is that they should do their best to remain calm, focused, and respond appropriately and quickly to any emergency. Having a clear head can be the difference between life and death.

Having a solid risk management plan serves several purposes. First, having BMPs in place and recognized as part of the business' operating culture can be a difference-maker when it comes to ensuring the safety and well-being of everyone involved in any given hunt. Second, should a legal claim ever be brought against you because of an unfortunate circumstance or an accident, your ability to prove that you, as the proprietor, and your team have gone the extra mile by developing and implementing a sound risk management plan may be your best defense against such a legal claim. Furthermore, being properly prepared in this aspect of your business is the right thing to do, plain and simple. That being said, I suggest putting a risk management plan at the top of your priority list when developing your operating culture.

1 > All hunts should begin with an orientation, which WSI personnel occasionally refer to as "the talk," shortly after clients arrive. This allows staff to go over safety policies, daily routines, harvest allowances, and wounded animal policies among other things. The orientation also establishes that the hunt will be organized, structured, and professional.

2> Regardless of the risk management plan, hunting proprietors in the U.S. cannot be absolved from gross negligence. Any known, pre-existing hazards, such as an uncovered abandoned well, must be remedied before any hunts.

3> Perils in the hunting business evolve over time. With the range of Africanized honey bees increasing, this is simply one example of a naturally occurring hazard that rarely had to be dealt with 20 years ago. Like man-made hazards, this possible human health and safety matter should be promptly dealt with if you know that a hive is in-place where clients or others are likely to frequent.

4> Annual training for guides and chefs ensures that camp staff members are prepared to deal with an assortment of circumstances and that standard operating procedures are part of the business culture.

14 TAXIDERMY AND MEAT

EVERY BUSINESS HAS A "NOT SO GLAMOROUS" SIDE REQUIRED TO COMPLETE ALL THE TASKS AND STEPS THAT ARE PART OF THE BUSINESS PROCESS.

In the hunting business, an important and sometimes arduous step is that of taking care of game meats and capes/antlers/horns at the end of the day and upon completion of the hunt. This can be a huge exercise.

Shortly after I got into the hunting business, I visited with Dick Laros at his taxidermy studio in Allentown, Pennsylvania, in 1988. Dick, who was in his mid-fifties then, was a bit of a pioneer in the hunting industry. As I pointed out in Chapter One of this book, Dick was a booking agent for international hunting trips and an acclaimed taxidermist. He also owned the Lehigh Valley Outdoor Expo Sports Show.

As part of our conversation, we discussed North American outfitters' "workmanship" as it applied to skinning, caping, and meat preparation. Dick bemoaned the waning quality of work and attention to detail shown in skinning and butchering that he had witnessed in recent years. He observed, "The workmanship quality of skins and capes reflected, in part, the overall business integrity for many outfitting operations." In other words, those outfitters who produced sloppy work in the skinning shed were prone to do sloppy work throughout their operations. His comments left a lasting impression on me. As a result, I have tried to develop practices and instill high-quality standards as part of WSI's operating culture when it comes to this area of our work.

CUTLERY

Knives for working up game animals are central to this aspect of the process. I have always found it interesting that many hunters have a broad assembly of knives, some that carry hefty price tags when purchased. Many hunters are what would be characterized as collectors. But when it comes down to the knives that many guides use most commonly, those instruments are often inexpensive tools that are not flashy or high-end type knives by many people's standards.

KNIVES AND ASSOCIATED TOOLS

SKINNING

Knives commonly used for skinning most of the carcass on big game animals will often carry 3–4-inch blades that are mid-weight. These can either be fixed or folding blade knives—either serves the role well.

CAPING

Once the cape is down to the head and is ready to be "faced," most accomplished guides will strictly use a smaller, delicate type blade for this work. A 2.5—3-inch lightweight blade is often preferred for this more delicate work that requires finer precision.

MEAT

For quartering and deboning meat, most guides prefer a longer blade that is generally 4—6 inches. Also, a heavier blade or flexible blade that will not break when torqued is important with this work. Some people prefer using a relatively flexible fish filet knife when deboning big game animals, and I have become partial to this myself over the last few years.

Replaceable blade knives, such as Havalon brand, have become popular in recent years, and many of my guides use these knives. It is worth noting that these replaceable blade knives are generally surgically sharp with fine points. For someone who is not proficient with skinning and caping animals using these types of blades, it is easy to slice or punch a hole through the cape. Plus, with a slight slip, you can seriously cut yourself with these blades, so using utmost caution is important to avoid either of these types of mishaps.

Personally, my go-to knife that I have principally been using for 20-plus years is a 3-inch blade paring knife made by Dexter-Russell with a carbon steel blade. This is a relatively soft metal blade that holds an edge okay but sharpens easily. I recently ordered some of these Dexter-Russell knives as gifts and they were $3.05 each, so very inexpensive. I use these knives for skinning and caping and will occasionally use them for meat work. The knives that I use for caping, I only use for caping, and I am constantly touching them up with a steel and never allow them to get dull. My main caping knife is one I have been using for over 10 years without having to replace it, though I have put it on an electric sharpener a few times.

SHARPENER

There are many options on the market regarding knife sharpeners. With replaceable blades being so popular these days, I have found that most guides are not good at sharpening blades. I use a steel most of the time, and I try to avoid losing the edge on any of my favorite knives. I have an electric sharpener that has three grades of coarseness on the sharpening wheels. I have found these electric sharpeners to be easy to use and very efficient at quickly putting a razor-sharp edge on a blade, even with the hardest of materials.

SAW

For those guides who know what they are doing when it comes to breaking animals down, rarely is a saw needed. Quarters can be jointed with a knife. The main occasion that a saw is needed is when animals are being skull capped. I prefer a cordless electric Sawzall with a fine to medium tooth blade for cutting through bone. A regular meat or butcher's saw works well, but if you are working up animals on a regular basis, a cordless electric saw is the way to go.

TAXIDERMY

On big game hunts, this service cannot be overemphasized. Remember, for many of your clients, the mount from their hunts with your business is a daily reminder of your services.

While skinning the carcass is simple, proper caping is more technically exacting. Having a high-quality, usable cape directly affects the taxidermist's ability to produce a high-quality, realistic mount. The following are some key considerations during the caping process.

SKINNING AND CAPING

- Identifying the client's desired taxidermy outcome (shoulder mount, half life-size, life-size, or rug) and placing cutlines appropriately; the cutlines' placement will vary with the desired end product.

- Except for short-haired animals, dorsal cuts, those located along the back, are currently the preferred cutline on life-size mounts. Dorsal cuts on life-size mounts mean fewer seams and less sewing for the taxidermist. This takes a little more practice to master working the legs out of the skin.

- If you are making a belly cut on a life-size mount, as opposed to the dorsal cut, make sure that you cut alongside of the scrotum sack and penis on male animals, and make sure that the genital skin is left on the cape; do not remove and do not cut through the middle of this area.

- On shoulder mounts, always leave plenty of skin for the taxidermist, but it is not necessary to have the cape extend to the flank. Having an excessively large cape that extends to the flank can create a problem with freezer space and can also add considerably to the shipping fees, especially if you have to overnight a large frozen cape for an elk or other big animal. A circular cut about three inches behind the shoulder crease will provide ample skin and avoid problems for the taxidermist and for you.

- On rugs, do not forget to leave the feet on the skin. You can simply joint them off at the ankles, or you can use loppers or a saw to cut the bones to disconnect the feet or hooves. The taxidermist can turn the feet later.

- On horned animals, as opposed to antlered animals, the skin is tightly attached to the horns. Therefore, it is best to use the tip of your knife to make a circular cut around the horn's base that follows the contour of the hardened horn before you work the skin past the horns. In fact, it's not a bad idea to make this circular horn cut before making the V-cut on the back of the neck.

- On antlered animals, there is a distinct separation between the antler's burr and the skin. To free the cape from this portion of the antler, use the tip of a caping knife and a flathead screwdriver to pry the skin loose. This combination removes all of the hair and skin from the pedicel, the small bony structure that connects the antler to the skull. Be cautious not to cut through the skin where it attaches to the antler base.

- The eyelid and the eye glands require the most deliberate and cautious approach, especially when you are learning how to cape properly. If you are not careful, you will cut off the eyelid or the skin that is tucked into the eye gland. Using your thumb and index finger, protect the eyelid by pinching it and pulling it outward, as you carve the skin away from the skull.

- I like to free the lips before working the cape that far down by carving alongside or even against the bone as you pull the lips free from the skull.

- Avoid leaving excess meat on capes. Proficient, experienced professionals who have mastered the process of caping will not leave any chunks of meat on the cape; time and practice equals proficiency. With this said, proceed cautiously to avoid punching holes in the cape. Some of today's caping knives are razor sharp, and the areas where skin is thin, such as around the throat, can be especially challenging to get clean and leave intact.

- Do your best to keep cutlines clean and straight, as opposed to an irregular or zippered cut.

- For beginners, I suggest practicing caping animals that are not destined to be mounted. Until you become comfortable with the process, your efforts will likely be slow and awkward. So, practice this craft when the opportunity permits, and eventually caping will not be any more difficult than simply skinning a carcass.

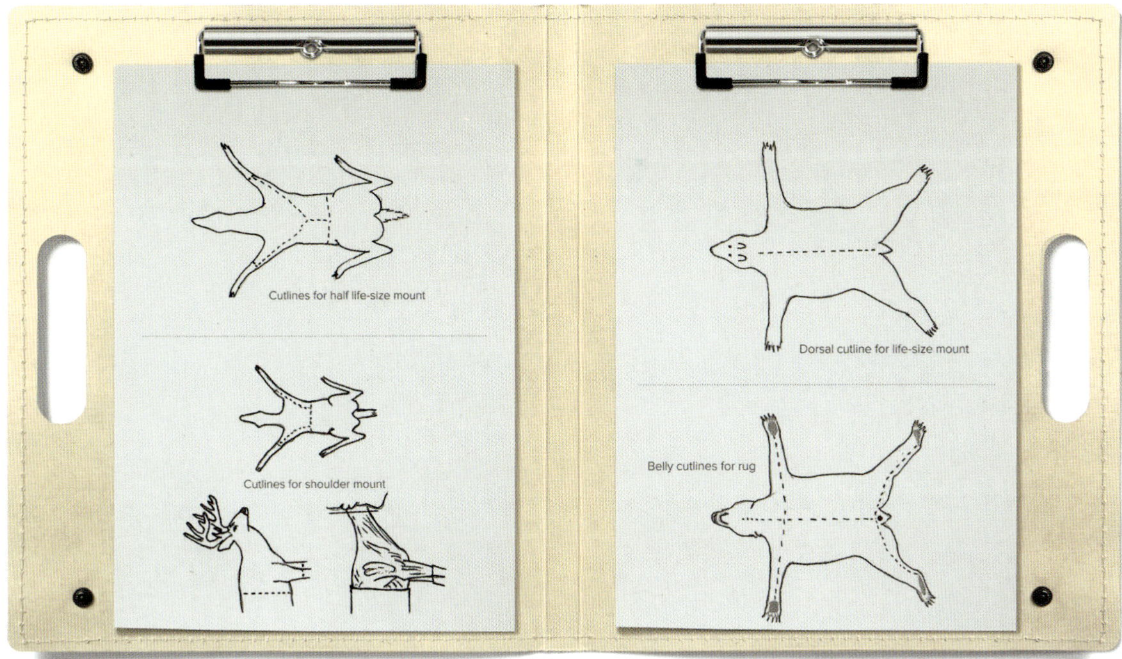

At WSI, we use heavy polybags for storing and freezing capes, but heavy-duty trash bags will suffice and are commonly used. Regardless, you should never place a warm cape in a plastic bag, seal it, and immediately place it in a freezer. Without proper cooling, the hair could slip or turn loose, ruining the hide. To properly cool the cape, just lay it in the cooler or freezer for ten to 20 minutes. Once it is thoroughly chilled, roll the cape up and secure it in the storage bag.

Labeling the packages containing the hides is extremely important. At a minimum, the label should have the hunter's last name. Ideally though, the label should include the hunter's first and last names, as well as the container's contents. It is not uncommon to have a cape for a shoulder mount and also have the back skin for a rug. They should be packaged separately and labeled accordingly, denoting which is which. Also, a hunter may shoot more than one deer on the same hunt that are all suitable for mounting. In this instance, the labeling should also include something like "Deer #1" and "Deer #2" that corresponds to similar tags on the antlers so the taxidermist can correctly pair the cape and antlers.

At WSI, we utilize a laminated tag with a pre-punched hole. Using a zip tie, we can attach the tag and securely seal the bag simultaneously. Some people use a permanent marker, such as a Sharpie, to write the information directly on the storage bag, but I have found that information written on the bag tends to rub off more easily than information written on a laminated tag with the same type of marker. To be completely safe, there is nothing wrong with doing both.

In locations without freezers or international destinations that require extended shipping periods, freezing the capes and hides may not be a viable option. Capes, in these circumstances, have to be treated much differently. Camp staff will have to turn the capes' nose, lips, ears, and feet and remove all flesh from the hides. Then the skins are laid out, liberally salted, and allowed to cure. This process removes all moisture and temporarily preserves the skin until it gets to the taxidermist and is tanned. This process is vastly different than simply freezing and shipping and requires added expertise to ensure that things are done properly so the hides do not spoil before the tanning process.

TOP > Guides MUST understand how to make proper cutlines when skinning or caping trophies destined for a taxidermist. Shoulder mounts, pedestal mounts, half-body mounts, life-size mounts, and rugs all require unique cutlines.

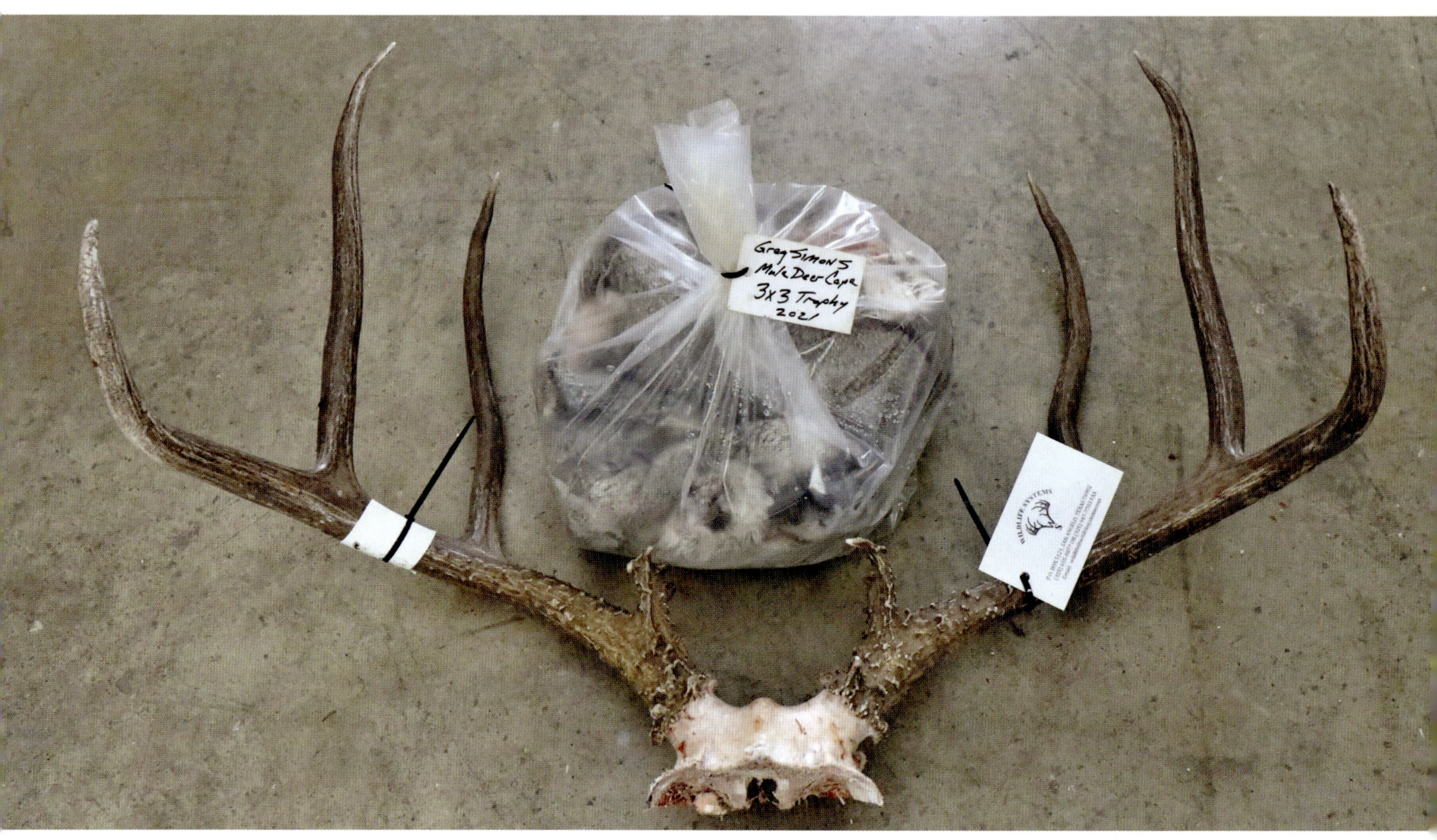

Getting the hides and antlers or horns to the taxidermist is not always simple. The simplicity of the process depends on the distance between the taxidermist and the outfitter's storage facility. The following is a list of tips to consider.

SHIPPING AND DELIVERY

- Stay caught up on shipping as much as possible. Allowing capes and horns to accumulate can potentially create many problems—including delaying the taxidermy work, occupying too much freezer space, and increasing the chance of capes being lost to fire, theft, or damage by a freezer malfunction.

- With that said, some international operations wait until the end of their safari season to take care of all their shipping due to their local logistics, but that is generally very different than an American outfitter who deals solely with domestic shipping.

- Shipping frozen capes overnight is expensive. At WSI, we charge a nominal service fee to cover the cost of our time, but the major expense is the shipping charges themselves. We invoice the hunters after the items are shipped.

- On a large frozen cape like a life-size aoudad or a shoulder mount elk, the shipping charges alone may be $500 or more. Before our clients leave, we ensure that they understand the potential expense so they do not get sticker shock when we send them the bill. For those clients who drive to our hunts and are using their local taxidermist, we do everything in our power to convince them to take the cape and other items back with them, excluding WSI from the delivery loop.

- Antlers and horns must be either crated or boxed. Furthermore, they need to be protected and secured. In fact, the tips need to be protected individually as well. Pieces of rubber hose or foam pipe insulation work well for placing over antler or horn tips, which protects them from breakage. It also helps prevent the tips from poking through the box and being damaged en route.

- We often stuff paper feed sacks into empty spaces, which helps secure capes and antlers in shipping containers. These multilayer paper feed sacks provide good insulation for frozen capes, so we will often take the cape that is still frozen inside of the polybag and slip it inside a feed sack to keep it insulated and soak up any moisture.

- For game such as elk, moose, kudu, and other animals that have large horns or antlers, it may be easier to split the skull cap and nest the antlers or horns together. However, if an animal is going to be officially scored for Boone & Crockett or Safari Club International, the skull cap cannot be cut before it is officially measured. For those skull caps that are cut, make sure to take an inside-the-beam and a tip-to-tip measurement of the spread so that taxidermists can use that measurement as a frame of reference when they fasten the antlers or horns to the form.

- Also, when nesting antlers or horns together inside the shipping container, it is best to bind them together with zip ties, cord, or tape, so they do not shift during shipping.

TAXIDERMY REFERRAL AND ARRANGEMENTS

Most outfitters have a taxidermist that they send work to on behalf of clients who do not have their own preferred taxidermist. I am a bit of a taxidermy snob in that I appreciate high-quality work. In my experience, some taxidermists do excellent work on certain species but fall short on other species. For instance, some taxidermists contract out their birds or fish but do mammals in-house. Then, there are certain species that are just more difficult to get right, whether it is ensuring the anatomical correctness of a pronghorn or the facial characteristics and expressions of cats.

Some larger shops have several taxidermists on staff who have their own specialties, which collectively allow that taxidermy studio to have breadth with its work. It is extremely rare to find a "mom-and-pop shop" where one or two taxidermists are excellent in all areas of taxidermy. Consequently, I work with multiple taxidermists. Taxidermists notoriously take a "long time" to complete their work. In my experience, most quality taxidermists normally take eight to 12 months from the time that materials are delivered until the mount is complete. I have heard of some taxidermists taking one to two years to complete their work. In my opinion, anything over 12 months is unreasonably long. If the work takes longer than 12 months, perhaps the taxidermist should limit the number of projects they take on or should find additional qualified help.

As a final point, I try to make it clear to our clients that once WSI turns the cape and antlers/horns over to a taxidermist that we are no longer involved. From that point on, the business arrangement is between the client and the taxidermist. Nonetheless, there may be extenuating circumstances where we are forced to get involved with the process to help facilitate things.

OPPOSITE-TOP > Developing an organized method for adequately labeling and packaging hides, antlers, etc. helps ensure these items are properly taken care of before they leave camp, which may prevent confusion or mistakes when they reach their destination. Always write the hunters' first and last names on labels.

TOP > To prevent damage to antlers and horns, it is important to develop and implement shipping protocols. Sections of rubber hose, zip ties, and packing materials are useful in the shipping process.

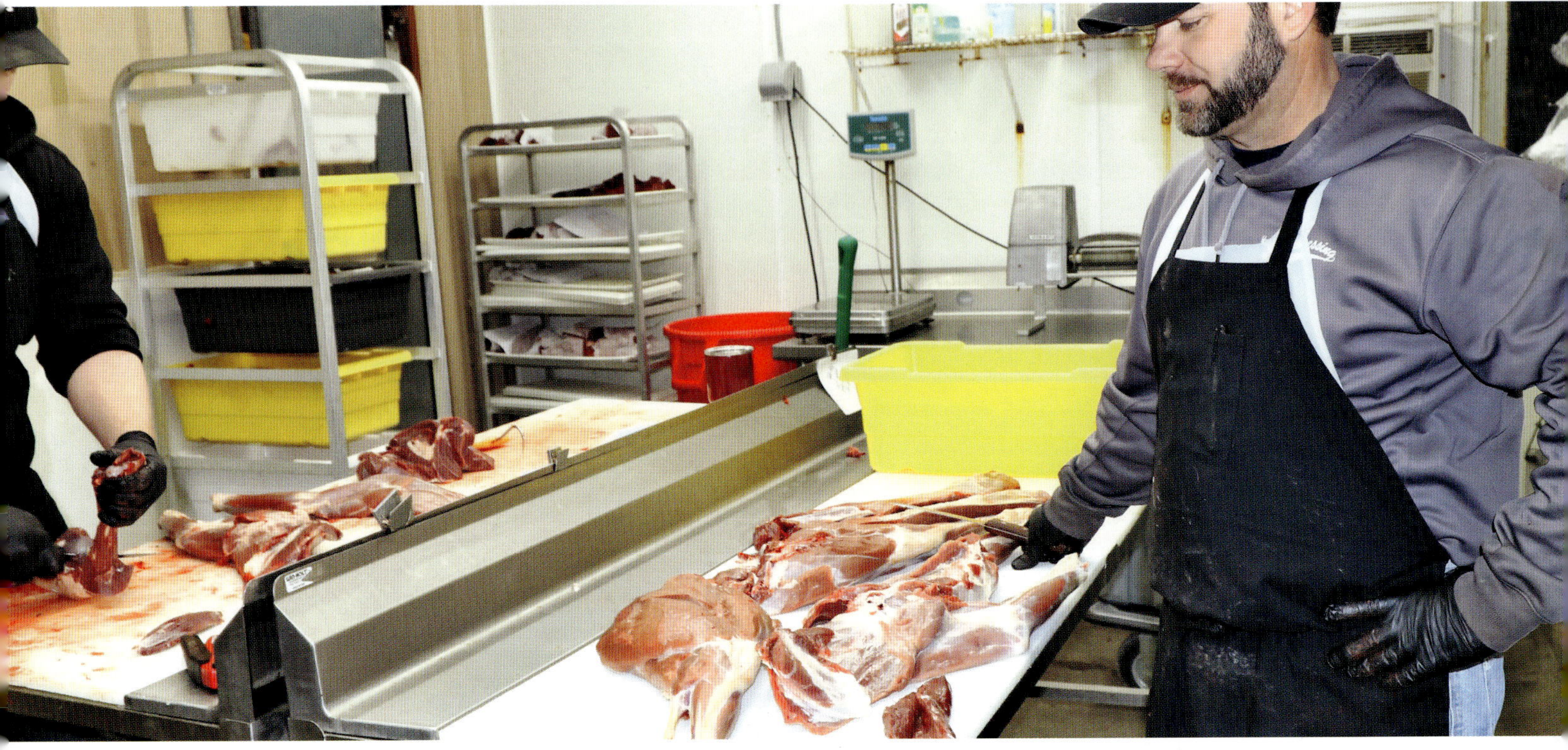

MEAT

Meat is an important part of any successful hunt. Properly processing and storing it to ensure quality and minimize waste is incumbent on the outfitting team.

FROM FIELD TO FREEZER

FIELD CARE

Ensuring the quality of the game meat begins shortly after the animal is taken. With big game animals, it is important that they be field dressed relatively quickly, especially when temperatures are warm. Many operations have their guides field dress the animals while they are still afield, but others require that the animals are dressed at a central location.

At WSI, we generally field dress big game animals in the field, away from infrastructure such as stands, feeders, and water troughs. Bringing whole animals back to the skinning shed delays carcass cooling and creates an unnecessary mess at the skinning facility, which in turn requires additional time and manpower to clean up.

Some clients insist on field dressing their own animals. I am fine with this because this is an important part of the experience for some hunters. However, generally it is the guide's responsibility to provide this service to the client.

Cleaning game birds, especially small birds such as doves and quail, is not quite as time sensitive as field dressing big game animals. As a rule, smaller birds can be left unattended for up to six hours, especially if temperatures are cool, but larger birds, such as turkeys, should be cleaned within three to four hours or placed in a cooler to be processed sometime later.

PROCESSING

Butchering can be labor intensive. In our camps, we have historically quartered the animals. If clients want their animals deboned, then we generally ask the clients to assist with that process if they can. However, with growing concerns of Chronic Wasting Disease (CWD) and ensuing regulations regarding transporting the meat of CWD-susceptible cervids into certain states, our WSI team is being forced to debone all deer meat that we are sending back with clients who hail from those affected states. Deboning requires an additional step and a bit more expertise, but there is no way around providing this service if it is required for clients to legally transport the meat across state lines.

If clients want the animals fully processed, then the carcass needs to be handled by a commercial processor. Either the clients or a WSI staffer can drop off the carcass. Similar to taxidermy work, once the animal is delivered to the meat processor, WSI is no longer part of the loop, and the business arrangement is between the client and the processor.

Wasting as little meat as possible should be a priority, as should keeping the meat clean and in good condition. As far as I know, all states have some type of "wanton waste of meat" laws, so people can get themselves into a legal tangle if they do not take care of the meat according to those local directives. As the proprietor, make sure you understand these laws; many people do not.

Moisture fosters the growth and spread of bacteria. When possible, we prefer to bag meat that is dry. To avoid a wet mess that can spread bloody water and bacteria over all the work surfaces, we prefer to trim off any soiled or dried crusts instead of washing the meat. If the carcass requires washing, I prefer to spray it while it is whole and hanging, and then allow it to dry before proceeding with processing.

PACKAGING AND STORAGE

Meat, like capes, has to be properly cooled and packaged. Trash sacks and Ziploc® bags are handy for packaging. We generally use white kitchen-sized trash bags for larger quarters and Ziploc® bags for backstraps and tenderloins. To prevent meat from souring, allow it to cool thoroughly before placing it in plastic bags, just as you do with hides and capes. Larger cuts of meat take longer to cool, and hindquarters tend to cause the most problems.

Meat should be properly labeled. With the emergence of CWD, there are likely some regulations that vary from state to state that may dictate the information that is required for each label. Typically at WSI, we use a permanent marker and write the hunter's full name on the plastic bag containing the meat. On animals that must be accompanied by a license tag, we insert the tag on the inside of the clear Ziploc® bag containing the backstraps. The tag is easy to find and read, making it easy for a game warden to check the meat and tagging without having to tear into any packages.

SHIPPING MEAT

At WSI, we have a long-standing policy regarding shipping meat—we do not do it. If our clients want their game meats, then they have two choices: they can either take the meat with them or it can be dropped off at a commercial processor, and the client can make arrangements for the processor to ship the meat once it is fully processed. Early on, we learned that shipping meat is a no-win proposition for us. We make sure it is clear from the beginning that we do not offer this service.

Providing a full-service outfitted hunt means the proprietor must be proficient at seeing that the meat is properly taken care of and that all trophy parts are properly extracted, stored, and sent to the taxidermist of the client's choice. Successful businesses, in any industry, focus on details, and this area of the hunting business requires a great attention to detail to ensure a quality hunting package from start to finish.

OPPOSITE-TOP > Understanding how game should be broken down and creating consistency in how your support team accomplishes this task helps create many efficiencies, ranging from saving time and economizing freezer space to avoiding meat wastage. Develop a functional system and replicate it.

15 HARVEST PHOTOGRAPHY

A BIG PART OF THE ROMANCE OF HUNTING INVOLVES PLANNING THE HUNT AND VISUALIZING THE ADVENTURE AHEAD. THEN THERE IS THE PLEASURE OF SHARING THE ADVENTURE WITH OTHERS, AND NOTHING PROLONGS THE EXPERIENCE BETTER THAN HUNT PHOTOS.

OPPOSITE
Larry Weishuhn
2019 Pronghorn
Brewster County, Texas
Guide - Don Richardson

In earlier times, photography commemorated only special occasions that helped define who we are and what we have done. These days, most people have "smart phones" with high-quality, built-in cameras, morphing photography into part of our daily routines. It is common for people to snap photos throughout their day, capturing the endless spectrum of daily life ranging from the exciting and memorable to the mundane. As a result, much of our modern communication is shaped as much (or more) by the images we take or view as by the words we hear, speak, or read. If you doubt this, simply create a Facebook post that does not include a photo and see what kind of response you get. Then pair those same words with a photo and compare that response to your previous post. I will bet more people engage with the second post than the first one by a large margin.

Images of the hunt are an important part of our ancient human culture, dating back to prehistoric times when our ancestors painted and scratched images on cave walls capturing their hunting stories. These were the earliest forms of art, giving rise to our human desire to express ourselves through documenting and recreating experiences of interest. As the existence of cave art proves, the importance of images as part of the hunting experience is nothing new. People, now more than ever, are visual creatures who respond to photos. In the "Professionalism" chapter, I discussed the necessity of self-policing the content and use of hunting photos so that we are better stewards of the hunting tradition and its future. Since I have already covered the need for better self-policing, I will not elaborate much further, except to comment on the evolution of quality harvest photos and the integrity involved with determining how the images are being used.

In my career, I have witnessed three distinct periods related to hunting photos. When I first got into the hunting business in 1987, most harvest photos that were taken by hunters were low-quality. The photos had poor lighting, bad backdrops, and too much blood and gore. However, that era predated social media and its ensuing flood of photos. Although we, as a hunting community, performed poorly as photographers, these distasteful images did not reach large audiences outside our own circles.

By the year 2000, hunters seemed to take more pride in their harvest photos and wanted to improve their quality. Around that time, quality cameras became more affordable, which helped nonprofessionals improve their photography skills and gave them the ability to take a good photograph without investing a large amount of money on camera equipment. At the same time, hunters began to recognize the impact that hunting photos had on hunting and its longevity, so we became better stewards of this craft.

This era continued from about 2000 until around 2015, when smart phones became popular. With the advent of MySpace and Facebook in 2003, social media got a toehold and then exploded onto the scene, changing our daily norms. Unfortunately, it seems as though the convenience of having a camera built into an ever-present phone has prompted people to take photos without putting much effort into the process. Using an actual camera seems to inspire people to take their photography more seriously than when they simply whip out their phones and fire off a few quick shots. The "quick click" often results in poor photos, which has been reflected in recent years with harvest photos. And with smart phones, it is way too simple to mindlessly upload poor-quality images onto social media platforms. As a result, I think the overall quality of harvest photos has regressed. Regardless of the evolution of harvest photos, they remain vitally important. And from a business standpoint, quality harvest photos are absolutely integral to promoting and marketing hunts.

Due to my ever-pressing, demanding style when it comes to harvest photos, WSI's guides sometimes refer to me as the "Photo Nazi," as I constantly push them to capture quality images. Out of roughly 30 to 35 guides who work with us through the course of the year, less than 20 percent are what I consider to be Grade A photographers, about 50 percent earn a B, and the others are C or worse. And that is with a considerable amount of training and pushing. Despite our ongoing efforts, our team's performance still falls far short in this crucial category. While this can be incredibly frustrating, I have concluded that most people are simply not "artsy" enough to be great photographers. Plus, there are some people who are too lazy to take the extra steps necessary to capture top-notch field photos.

I use a lot of harvest and miscellaneous hunting photos as part of our marketing efforts. These images are used in the e-blasts directed to our group list as well as on our website and in brochures. I often use these photos for magazine articles and PowerPoint presentations. Also, we generally send harvest photos to our hunters. I have found that this added touch helps extend their hunting experience, provides another reason to maintain communication, and potentially helps with client retention. Thus, harvest and field photos are essential to our marketing and other outreach efforts. For anyone considering outfitting as a business, I cannot overstate the importance of guides and other team members capturing high-quality photos.

TOOLS

CAMERAS

The primary tool of the trade is a decent camera. Phone cameras have improved significantly in recent years, but phone cameras are inferior to stand-alone cameras, plain and simple. Granted, when it comes to convenience, phone cameras are hard to beat and are certainly better than having no camera at all, but all hunting guides should invest in a dedicated digital camera.

Prices for small point-and-shoot cameras have steadily decreased in recent years. It is now possible to purchase a 20+ megapixel camera with built-in flash for less than $200. Many of these point-and-shoot cameras will take exceptionally nice harvest photos and general occasion photos. For people who really want to step up their photography game, digital SLR cameras with interchangeable lenses offer more reach and versatility. Because this is not a photography book, I am not going discuss camera options in detail. Suffice it to say, there are many good economical options available. As a rule, make sure the camera is at least 20+ megapixel and set on the highest resolution, which will likely be "fine" or "super fine." Plus, make sure that the camera has a built-in flash and use it.

COMB

A plastic fine-tooth hair comb serves two purposes. First, it is handy for properly grooming the animal's hair. Second, a comb is handy for removing dry blood from the hair. When blood is dried and crusted on hair, it will fleck off fairly easily by using a comb and/or scraping with a fingernail.

FORMULA 409 SPRAY CLEANER

Formula 409 Multi-Surface Cleaner does not contain bleach and works wonders for cleaning wet blood from hair. Spray, comb, wipe down, and keep using a combination of these steps repeatedly. In most instances, this process will remove all the blood from the majority of soiled hides. When blood has already dried, do not spray the cleaner until you have used a comb to scrape and fleck as much dried blood off the hair as possible. Then, liberally spray the area with 409 or a similar bleach-free cleaner and wipe. Repeat until the hide is clean. Water works okay, but I have found that a bleach-free cleaner such as 409 works best. Guides should always carry a spray bottle and a roll of paper towels in their hunting vehicles for this purpose.

PAPER TOWELS

Depending on the condition of the hide and the animal's size, properly cleaning soiled hides prior to the photo shoot may require a lot of paper towels. Trying to clean blood from the hide using a blood-soaked paper towel does not work, so do not skimp on clean, dry paper towels during the process. It is not uncommon to use an entire roll on a single animal, especially if the hide is messy.

TAXIDERMY EYES

After an animal has been dead for several hours, the eyes begin to recede. Using taxidermy glass eyes is a great way to provide more "life" to the image and offset the recessed eyes. Using taxidermy eyes is also a good way to eliminate the "eye glow" on freshly harvested animals. I suggest carrying two or three different sizes with you for different-sized animals. For instance, an elk will require larger glass eyes than a whitetail. If artificial eyes are used, it is essential to properly form the eyelids around the replacement eyes once they are placed within the eye sockets, or the overall effect may actually be worse. Learn to properly use this tool in order to get optimum results.

CLAY

When properly sculpted, modeling clay can be an excellent tool for temporarily repairing broken antler tines before taking harvest photos. Different shades of brown and tan are often needed to mimic the color and staining patterns of antlers. Some people are better at sculpting tines than others. I have found it best to roll the tine out, like you are rolling a cigar, and continue to roll it until it tapers on one end. Then mesh it in and around the broken stub's end and blend it in. Some points, such as brow tines, will often have more bumps, grooves, and uneven surfaces than others. Those textures can be recreated by using a toothpick or small stick and modeling the repaired tine's surface until it matches the opposite side.

TOP-LEFT > Although phone cameras have improved over the last few years, a dedicated camera is superior and provides more versatility. Digital pocket cameras, also known as point-and shoot cameras, take excellent photos and can be purchased for less than $200.

TOP-MIDDLE > To take harvest photos without an assistant, a camera tripod is a must. Plus, using a tripod and self-timer ensures crisp, sharp images.

TOP-RIGHT > Handy tools for obtaining quality harvest photos include Formula 409 Spray (without bleach), taxidermy eyes, paper towels, clay, and a fine-toothed comb.

PREP WORK, POSING AND OTHER TIPS

The prep work and proper posing of the animal is a big part of capturing good harvest photos. Here is a laundry list of suggestions.

GENERAL ADVICE

- Properly clean any dirt or blood from the animal.
- When possible, take photos before the animal has been field dressed. If an ungutted animal was shot through the chest, it may have a large quantity of blood spilling from the mouth and nose, soiling the animal's face. Try to elevate the animal's head to prevent it from laying in a pool of blood. To reduce the amount of blood leaking from the mouth and nostrils, temporarily stuff the back of the mouth and the nostrils with paper towels until it is time to pose the animal.
- Hunters should wear outdoor or hunting attire and remove their sunglasses if they are wearing them.
- The best way to ensure quality photos is to take a lot of pictures from different angles using multiple setups. With digital photography, the cost of film or processing is no longer a concern, so increase the odds of creating an exceptional photo by snapping numerous pictures.

SETTING AND POSITIONING

- Make sure that the backdrop is a natural setting, as opposed to buildings, vehicles, etc.
- Remove any distracting foliage that may interfere with the photo, such as excessive or tall grass that is standing between the photographer and the subject. While this may take a few minutes, it is worth it.
- Avoid laying the animal on bare ground. Animals are best shown laying in short grass or forbs.
- Pose deer and other big game animals in a pleasing manner. A deer should be lying on its belly with its front legs folded underneath, its head erect, and ears balanced.

LIGHTING

- If possible, take photos during the first two hours and the last two hours of daylight, when light and shadows are "softer" than they are when the sun is high in the sky. As professional photographers can attest, shooting pictures during these "golden hours" makes a huge difference in the photos' tone and color quality.
- Flash should be used at least 75 percent of the time to help mitigate harsh shadows. Use the flash when the sun is high, when the weather is cloudy, and at night.
- Nighttime photos with a flash are an excellent way to highlight the animal's antlers; the flash will silhouette the antlers and make them pop.

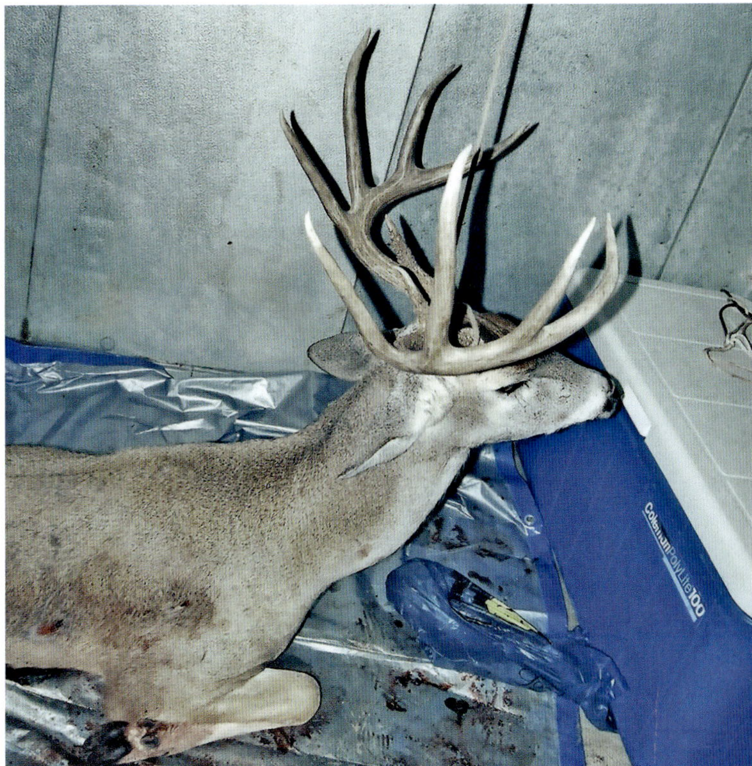

RIGHT > Properly posing big game animals before rigor mortis sets in and then allowing them to stiffen makes photographing the animal much easier. This deer, posed in a walk-in cooler with its head tied upward, is "resting" or stiffening to achieve the desired effect.

- Take photos of the hunter looking at the animal, as well as photos where the hunter is looking directly at the photographer.

- Position the hunter slightly to the side or behind the animal. Generally, it is best to angle the animal toward the photographer at approximately 45 degrees instead of positioning it in full profile or perpendicular to the photographer.

- Shoot different angles. The photographer should lie down or at least shoot some photos from an angle that "skylines" the animal's antlers. Again, it is best to shoot from various angles. I have gotten some good photos by standing up and shooting down at a slight angle that minimizes the amount of sky (and the amount of backlighting) in the background.

- Close-up photos are much more effective than landscape shots. Move in close and fill the frame with the animal and the hunter. However, when using a wide-angle lens, be aware that getting too close can make the nose of the animal look huge and distort the photo.

- Remember, using a wide-angle lens will make anything in the foreground look bigger than it is, which is a trick used to make horns and antlers look larger. Conversely, using a telephoto lens (50+ mm) will make anything in the foreground look smaller, so avoid using a telephoto lens when shooting harvest photos.

- When shooting straight-on photos of deer, tip the deer's head toward the ground so that the antler tines are oriented at an approximate 90 degree angle to the camera lens. On animals with curved horns, such as sable and scimitar-horned oryx, take profile shots of the head and horns. On animals with straight horns, such as blackbuck antelope and gemsbok, the nose should be pointing almost straight down or the animals should be photographed in profile; you do not need to have the animal looking toward the camera, with its horns pointing away, as this will make the horns look much smaller than they are.

MISCELLANEOUS FIELD SHOTS

While I catch myself harping on our guides to take plenty of good harvest photos, we often overlook capturing various other photos in the field and in camp. Interesting photos of people, equipment and other items not only help document various aspects of the hunt but also showcase the bigger story of the hunting experience.

When it comes to posting harvest photos on social media, it is a great idea to include miscellaneous photos to help shine the light on the hunting tradition and not focus solely on the harvested animals. Sunsets, game signs, equipment, close-ups of smiling faces, campfires, plated food, hunters sitting around the dining table talking and laughing, and guides with loaded pack frames in remote locations are all examples of images that help tell the story. It is really a matter of the guides, or someone else on the team, slowing down long enough to recognize and capture these shots.

PHOTO PERMISSION

Most hunters are perfectly fine with using their photos on websites, social media, brochures, etc., but some people, for various reasons, do not want their hunting-related photos being shared publicly. Most commonly, these are people who are invited to participate in a corporate hunting trip and are concerned with possible industry-related scrutiny. Other people simply do not want friends, acquaintances, or the general public seeing them posing with dead animals. Regardless of the circumstances, it is best that you develop a procedure where you check with your clients about their preferences regarding photos to avoid potential problems. The easiest way to accomplish this is through a simple questionnaire or form that all hunting clients are required to complete.

If one of these "attention shy" clients takes a high-quality animal, a guide can pose with the harvested animal or the client's face can be blurred in the editing process. Both solutions allow the proprietor to showcase the animal as part of the company's marketing efforts while protecting the client's privacy.

PHOTO ORIENTATION

Some species, depending on their antler/horn orientation, are showcased best in vertical photographs. The photographer should always be aware of how the subject is framed and the photo is composed, which helps avoid undesirable cropping.

TINE ALIGNMENT

On antlered game, always pay attention to alignment of the tines. Otherwise, you can make a 10-pointer look like a nine-pointer.

HEAD DIRECTION

Another comparison of how the angle of the deer's body and the direction of its head can make a difference in showcasing antler quality. Both nice photos, but one showcases the antlers better than the other.

HUNTER POSITION

When using a wide-angle lens in photos composed to showcase antlers or horns, the hunter should always be positioned behind the front portion of the animal. Typically, the animal should be angled toward the camera. These two photos show the same animal at a different angle. Note the orientation of head/body in relation to the camera.

GROUND COVER

It is best to pose the animals where there is ground cover, which can help avoid a "stiff-leg" appearance and can cover any soiled or bloody portions on the animal's underside. It helps create a softer, nicer look, as you can see here.

TONE QUALITY
VIA FLASH

On cloudy days and when the sun is at a high angle, always use a flash to help improve tone quality and reduce harsh shadows. Note the difference between these two photos.

NIGHT-TIME PHOTOS

Night-time photos taken with a flash can make antlers pop. The daytime photo of this mule deer is a better all-around image, but the night-time image literally and figuratively shines the light on the antlers.

MULTIPLE CONCEPTS

Avoid shooting all harvest photos with the same set-up. These images represent multiple photographic concepts, which make harvest photos more interesting and enjoyable.

BIRDS

Taking quality harvest photos of birds can require additional attention. As a rule, wet birds lose a lot of their iridescence and beauty. Feather color and iridescence is best captured with a flash on a cloudy day or when the sun is low and natural lighting is softened.

RESPONSIBLE PRACTICES

In the "Professionalism" chapter, I discussed social media's importance and how it helps shape society's view on hunters and hunting.

While I will not repeat myself here, I consider this topic to be very important, so I will add some tips on using images and text responsibly on social media.

SOCIAL MEDIA TIPS

- Do not post photos of animals that are excessively bloody or gory.
- Learn to use digital editing tools to crop photos or clean up unpleasant parts of any photo.
- While digital editing is not difficult and often requires little effort, it can help transform a distasteful image into a photo that is much more appealing.
- Harvest photos should only include people whose expressions suggest honor and respect for the dead animals that are in the photos. Images showcasing (or even suggesting) horseplay, off-color antics, "savagery," or any other images that dishonor wild game, hunters, and hunting by making light of taking an animal's life should never be posted on social media.
- As previously mentioned, include interesting photos of camp life, wild landscapes, plated food, camaraderie, and other aspects of hunting in the great outdoors to showcase the whole, multifaceted experience on social media.
- Carefully edit and proofread the text that accompanies the photos. Good grammar, punctuation, style, and content matter can help bolster the reputation of hunters and hunting.

In an era of information and sensory overload, "optics" are profoundly important in shaping the values and perceptions of society. Whether we realize it or not, cameras, editing tools, social media, discretion, and creativity are tools of the outfitting trade as surely as firearms and spotting scopes. They cannot be overlooked or underestimated when it comes to shaping the hunting community's future.

There are a few of my outfitting colleagues, as well as others that are in the conservation arena, who feel that hunters should not share any harvest photos on social media platforms. Their rationale is that the risk exceeds the reward regarding the net benefit of sharing these hunting images with the rest of the world. Though I understand their rationale, I do not agree with it. Part of the intrigue, beauty, and romance of hunting can only be captured and shared via imagery. Poor photos are a problem. Tasteful, quality photos are part of the solution. When you combine quality harvest photos with other interesting photos from the hunt and compliment them with well-written text, I think you have a great platform for effectively promoting hunting to hunters and non-hunters.

Hunting professionals have an even greater responsibility to lead by example and actively advocate for the appropriate use of our communication tools and techniques. Good photos, and the appropriate use of them, are not simply important marketing tools for selling hunts but also serve as informal advertisements promoting the importance of hunting as a conservation tool.

Wildlife
Systems

16 REGULATORY CONSIDERATIONS

THE NUMBER OF U.S. OUTFITTERS AND
GUIDES WHO ARE UNFAMILIAR WITH THE
LAWS AND REGULATIONS GOVERNING
GAME IN THE STATES WHERE THEY OPERATE
IS UNIMAGINABLE.

OPPOSITE
Finbar O'Neal
1999 White-tailed Deer
Irion County, Texas
Guide - Rob Ferguson

n the "Professionalism" chapter, I addressed the seeming lack of professionalism within the hunting industry in the U.S. From my perspective, a failure to understand all of the applicable game laws in a business's area of operation is a prime example of how our industry falls short here in the U.S. As professionals, it is incumbent on guides and outfitters to hold ourselves to a higher standard than the average hunter when it comes to knowing these important laws, conveying them to our clients, and ensuring compliance through best management practices (BMPs).

OUTFITTER AND GUIDE LICENSING

Legal requirements to become a licensed or registered outfitter or guide vary in every state and country. Understanding and complying with these requirements is fundamental to becoming a professional guide or outfitter who is operating within the law. Some states, such as Texas, have no requirements for entering the business nor an agency charged with regulatory oversight of the industry. However, New Mexico, Texas's next-door neighbor, maintains a strict set of requirements governing the licensing process for outfitters and guides.

The New Mexico Department of Game and Fish administers these regulations, which makes it extremely difficult for nonresidents to qualify for an outfitter's license. By making it almost impossible for nonresidents to qualify, the state has created a system that favors New Mexicans. One of the many requirements in New Mexico is, "paid property taxes or rent on real property in New Mexico; paid gross receipts taxes; and paid at least one other tax administered by the taxation and revenue department in each of the three years immediately preceding the submission of an affidavit to the department of game and fish." In my opinion, this is an example of onerous government reach. Generally, states that are made up of a large percentage of public land have some type of licensing requirement for outfitters and guides. Not surprisingly, licensing requirements are commonplace in the western states and much rarer in the eastern and southern states.

International outfitter and guide licensing requirements vary immensely. Many African countries set the highest standards in the world. In these countries, professionals are required to have the knowledge or education comparable to a wildlife or natural resources degree from a university as well as outdoor skills acquired by completing an extensive field practical. In my opinion, the capabilities and the professionalism demonstrated by African hunting professionals set the standard by which all others should be measured. Overall, it is far superior to what is normally found in the U.S.

At one point, I was licensed in both Colorado and New Mexico. Over time, due to various circumstances, I lost access to some of the private lands that were key to our operation, and I opted to allow my licenses to expire. In hindsight, I wish I had maintained those licenses because it would make it far easier for me to get back in the game in those states if the right opportunity came along.

TOP > Part of an outfitter's responsibility is helping to ensure hunting clients are following game laws. To that end, guides and outfitters should become intimately familiar with those laws.

BASIC GAME LAWS

As part of professional development 101, outfitters and guides should become familiar with these regulations and statutes that define legal hunting allowances in their area of operation. Most game laws are relatively easy to understand. Some of the areas that are often misunderstood cover tagging, resource documents, and record keeping. Generally, paperwork is not a "sexy" part of any business, but it should be a priority for proprietors to understand the legal requirements and have BMPs in place to ensure that their support team complies with these standards.

There is a spectrum of typical game laws, such as legal shooting hours, bag limits, evidence of an animal's sex, wanton waste of meat, season structures, equipment, firearms restrictions, and many other things that may vary from state to state. There is also plenty of minutia, but for those individuals who grew up hunting in a particular state, chances are good that they are already familiar with 90 percent of the existing game laws; but it is the other 10 percent that might be overlooked and cause someone grief. When outfitters and guides begin working in a new state, they should expect a considerable learning curve as they familiarize themselves with local regulations to ensure compliance. Again, it should be our duty as professionals to understand the basic laws that govern our practices.

TOP > In Texas, one of the most common violations occur when hunters mark out dates on tags instead of cutting them out as the law requires. Overlooking small details like this can create problems for the hunter and does not reflect well on the guide and outfitter.

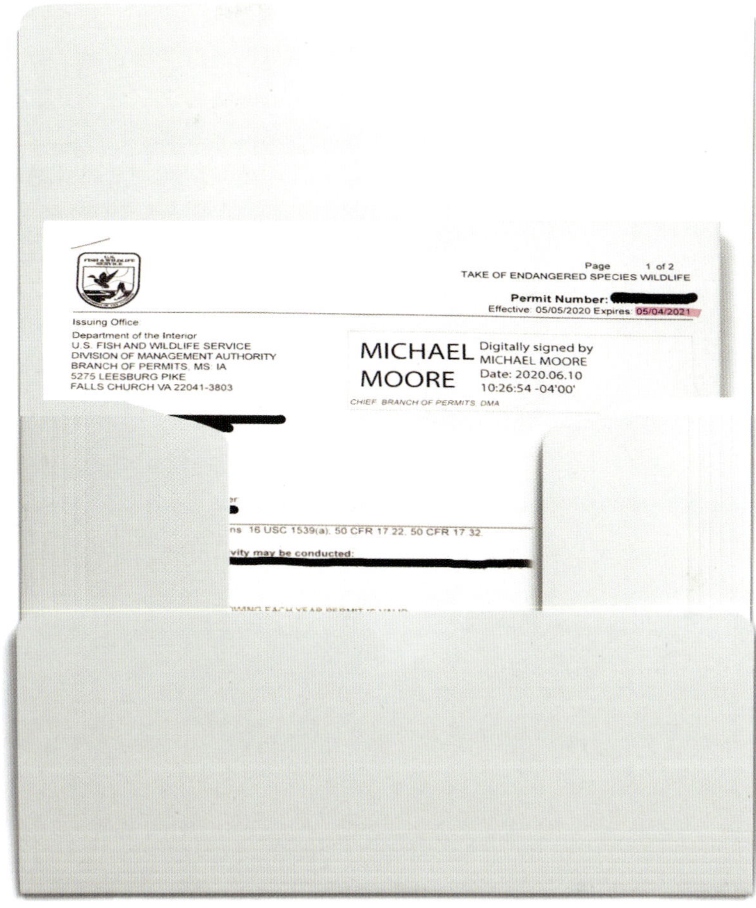

RIGHT > Federal wildlife regulations are sometimes more complicated. Working through the process generally requires more patience. Simple things such as receiving a response to an email or voicemail query can lead to frustrating times. In the U.S., as a rule, you can count on basic communication from federal agencies to be slower and less complete than that from state agencies.

FEDERAL LAWS

As outfitters and guides in the U.S., we normally deal with state laws as we conduct our business. However, there are also some federal laws that must be considered depending on the species. For instance, migratory birds, such as waterfowl and doves, fall under the auspices of federal law. This added regulatory layer does not necessarily create additional complexity, as these federal laws are effectively built into the game laws implemented by the states. One federal law of note is the Lacey Act. Enacted in 1900, it was the first federal wildlife law created in the U.S. The Lacey Act interacts with interstate commerce to combat the impact of poaching, interstate shipment of unlawfully killed game, and killing of birds for feather trade. The act was amended in 2008 to include products derived from illegally harvest plants. Designed to discourage illegal trafficking of these resources, the act has "big teeth" and should not be ignored.

With Chronic Wasting Disease (CWD) becoming more prevalent in some areas over the last few years, more states are creating new or additional legal restrictions on moving deer carcasses and raw venison. With any of the CWD-susceptible species in the U.S., which currently consist of white-tailed deer, mule deer, black-tailed deer, elk, moose, caribou, red deer, and sika deer, interstate movement in many states requires deboning as well as prohibiting the transfer of the brain or spine. I anticipate movement laws related to CWD will become even more prevalent as infection rates of this insidious disease continue to escalate.

INTERNATIONAL LAWS

A discussion about international laws and their intersection with the hunting industry is certainly more complex than considering basic game laws on a state-by-state basis. From a hunting standpoint, the Convention on International Trade in Endangered Species of Wild Fauna and Flora (CITES) is the big guy on the block of international wildlife laws. Effective in 1975, CITES is an international treaty created to help ensure that international trade in plants and animals does not threaten their sustainable survival in the wild. A state or country that has agreed to implement CITES is called a Party to CITES. Currently, there are 183 Parties.

Here in the U.S., under the Endangered Species Act, the U.S. Fish & Wildlife Service (USFWS) has been designated to carry out the provisions of CITES through the Division of Management Authority and the Division of Scientific Authority. Optimally, USFWS should be working with many diverse partners, including federal and state agencies, industry groups, and conservation organizations. Unfortunately, special interest groups, often led by animal rightists, have effectively "corrupted" the system. By operating outside the spirit of the process, the outcomes are often not friendly to hunting and place wildlife resources in harm's way. As a result, the department's culture and its policies have become less favorable to hunters and hunting. Unfortunately, this position undermines the vital role that hunting plays in global wildlife conservation while bastardizing the agency's function. In my opinion, the situation with USFWS is going to get worse before it gets better, that is if we ever see any righting of this ship that has veered widely off its course.

The most visible impact that CITES has on domestic U.S. affairs is the international importation of legally taken species. The USFWS often raises roadblocks for no good reason. As it currently plays out, American hunters can legally harvest animals in foreign countries only to encounter regulatory roadblocks created by the USFWS to impede the importation of that species. When this happens, the USFWS has effectively devalued the resource and ultimately diminishes conservation dollars generated by the legal and reasonable take of that animal. The species that are most vulnerable to these unreasonable policies include wild felines and other large charismatic species, such as elephant, rhino, and even hippo. Again, much of this is driven by special interest groups like the Humane Society of the United States, People for the Ethical Treatment of Animals, Center for Biological Diversity, and others. Collectively, they wield tremendous financial and political influence. Unfortunately, these groups are motivated more by emotion than the facts and proven history of successful conservation.

The most common impact CITES has on domestic hunting activities involves exotic species that require CITES permits. For instance, people must hold a Captive Bred Wildlife Permit to have and propagate red lechwe. In order to legally harvest a red lechwe, a separate Cull/Take Permit is required. Until recently, it was not difficult to work through the permit process, but over the last few years it seems as if the USFWS has been stricken with a paralysis that affects the issuance of new permits. Even getting answers to questions about expected permit timelines is difficult at best.

Fortunately, under President Obama's administration, a rider was attached to an omnibus spending bill that reinstated an "exception" to the permit requirements for scimitar-horned oryx, addax, and Dama gazelle. All three of these species have thrived because of conservation funding created through the sales of live animals, and hunting opportunities; both can incentivize private landowners to provide a home for these species and can offset costly conservation practices. In the case of these three exotic species, less permit red tape has resulted in a conservation success story for these species that do not fare well in their homelands. This is a conservation trifecta—and private landowners, hunters, and, most importantly, the wildlife resources are the big winners.

The regulatory side of any business can be a drag when it comes to understanding and adapting to the laws that interact with various businesses. But it should be a key focus of the outfitters and their support team to understand the regulatory framework that governs use and allocation of the game resources that support the hunting industry. These days, the ability to bone-up on these laws hinges on a simple internet search, as virtually all game laws are available on agency websites.

TOP > Regulated hunting by way of reasonable hunting laws helped restore many wildlife species, including wild turkeys, that were depleted in North America by the late 1800s. Such wildlife laws continue to help ensure sustainable health of wildlife populations for the benefit of future generations of hunters and other wildlife enthusiasts.

17 SUSTAINABILITY VERSUS DIMINISHING RETURNS

THE HUNTING BUSINESS RELIES ON WILDLIFE RESOURCES THAT ARE FINITE. SOME OF THESE RESOURCES CAN BE RELATIVELY BRITTLE WHILE OTHERS ARE MORE RESILIENT.

As outfitters and hunters, we deal with renewable resources that can be sustained and perpetuated through reasonable management, or they can be mined with little to no regard to the impact on the resource. As long as local wildlife populations are not depleted past the point of recovery, and as long as wildlife habitats are not completely destroyed on a large scale, outfitters have no regulatory mandates regarding the stewardship of wildlife. However, one can argue that outfitters, through professionalism and morality, have a responsibility to harvest animals and maintain habitats with a vision for long-term conservation.

I believe that when people use our wildlife commercially, there should be some checks in place to protect those resources and a professional culture within the industry to advocate for responsible use of those resources. My point is that outfitters should "do right" by the wildlife resources, and when that happens, it's also my belief good things come to those who make good decisions, or as my friend Shane Mahoney would say, "Doing well by doing good."

OFFTAKE

In regard to game animals, bag limits typically dictate what the legal harvest allowance is for each individual hunter. However, when it comes to private lands, the total allowable offtake from a specific property can vary immensely. In the U.S., the department of natural resources (DNR) in each state is typically the governing body that decides what the broad harvest allowances may look like between species, regions, and properties.

For instance, pronghorn harvest in West Texas is based on a landowner tag allocation, with landowners receiving a fixed number of pronghorn tags, which ultimately determines the maximum pronghorn harvest for that property. On the other hand, the legal mule deer harvest on that same property is restricted by the allowable bag limit for each individual hunter. Essentially, there are no laws preventing landowners from allowing every mule deer on the property to be harvested—and mule deer are what I would consider to be a brittle species. Fortunately, West Texas is made up of landowners who, by and large, are good caretakers of their wildlife resources. This in turn creates a management regime that helps ensure reasonable conservation practices of the area's mule deer.

In some African countries, the allowable commercial offtake of game animals on communal lands is generally restricted through a quota that applies to each huntable species; this establishes the maximum allowable harvest for the safari operation on that particular property.

These are just two examples of how different regulatory systems interact with the potential total offtake of animals from a particular property.

In hunting programs within the U.S., where outfitters are contracting for hunting allowances on private lands, landowners often set "sideboards" on allowable harvest as part of the outfitting contract. This arrangement is the landowner's method of protecting against excessive harvest. Plus, a quota system also helps ensure that the business arrangement between the landowner and the outfitter is fair and equitable. Landowners who allow outfitters to take an unlimited number of animals run the risk of being undercompensated for the value of the wildlife that is actually taken in relation to the lease price paid as well as the obvious risk to the sustainability of their game populations.

TOP > When times are good and the hunting markets are strong, hunting proprietors are prone to take a higher number of surplus game animals. Annual population surveys establish baselines that can help ensure populations are managed and not mined.

A quota system generally applies to big game animals and does not generally apply to game birds, with the notable exception of turkeys. Other than limiting the number of turkeys taken, it is unusual for landowners to restrict the number of upland birds and migratory birds that an outfitter may ultimately take off a particular property. Because some farmers view game birds as pests that depredate their crops, it is not unusual for farmers to want the outfitter and their hunters to harvest a liberal number of birds from their farmlands. Like so many things in this business, the number of animals an outfitter operating on private land is allowed to harvest varies depending on the culture and situation of the negotiating parties. Farmers and ranchers may view the situations differently and have different expectations. Harvest limits vary between big game species and game bird species. And the list goes on.

It would stand to reason that outfitters would harvest game conservatively on the lands where they operate because they and their clients should benefit from abundant and quality game populations in future years. However, people being people, there are some outfitters who become money hungry. Greed often precludes sound wildlife management, which generally results in heavy game offtake. Some outfitters do not manage money well. When finances are tight, those people may be more prone to take more animals than they would have otherwise. Whether it is fear or a lack of self-discipline, the "cash first" approach can lead to mining the resource instead of managing the resource. In these cases, landowners generally make a change by dismissing the outfitter or refusing to renew the business deal.

Over the last 30 plus years, the outfitters that I know who have developed sound reputations and have demonstrated their staying power in this business are generally those who, among other things, have a reputation of exercising sound conservation practices on the lands where they hunt. Some of the best hunting on private lands is on properties where the landowner is highly interested in protecting the wildlife resources on their property. As a result, the outfitters who earn reputations as good wildlife stewards benefit from positive word of mouth in the landowner community. When outfitters are sought out by landowners because of positive recommendations, they are positioned to grow their businesses and enjoy sustainability in a challenge-filled industry.

LEFT > These days, with the prevalence of game farms and pen-raised big game animals, some hunting proprietors run excessive numbers of animals on high-fenced areas. Exceeding the carrying capacity can lead to long-term damage to important habitats and can even result in soil damage. This shortsighted management can compromise the ecological fitness of landscapes and may require decades to recover after proper management applications are implemented.

HABITAT

When wildlife professionals reflect on the three most important factors in wildlife management, it is common to hear, "habitat, habitat, and habitat." Indeed, habitat is the cornerstone of healthy, sustainable wildlife populations. Fundamentally, it is always important to remember that the animal cannot be changed to fit the habitat, but sometimes the habitat can be changed to fit the animal. While there are many principles in the wildlife management matrix, none are remotely as important as the understanding that suitable habitat is the foundation for healthy wildlife populations. Any attempts to replace fully habitat with artificial substitutes will fail us and the resource time after time. However, habitat alterations and augmentations are often key in maintaining or enhancing functional wildlife habitats, so it is imperative that wildlife managers understand fundamental principles of habitat management.

As previously mentioned, plenty of publications provide road maps for successful wildlife management, so I will not delve into habitat management strategies here. However, it is important to remember that the four components of habitat are food, water, cover, and space. Each of these components is important, and they are interconnected in some fashion. When one component is lacking, the missing piece may serve as the limiting factor that prevents wildlife populations from reaching their full potential. As a result, managing these four components of habitat as one functional system is key.

From a management standpoint, we tend to focus on food and water more than cover and space. Through supplemental feeding and installing watering devices, we can help shape the supply of food and water for wildlife. Through brush and timber management, we can certainly affect the character and availability of woody cover. Through grazing management, prescribed fire, and discing, we can often affect grassy and weedy cover. These cover management strategies are often implemented without much strategic thinking. Sometimes they result from trying to increase forage production by opening brushy or wooded areas without giving much thought into how these habitat alterations may impact different types of cover. Some types of cover include security cover, thermal cover, fawning or nesting cover, and loafing cover.

Winter Storm Uri, which wreaked havoc on Texas in 2021, proved the importance of adequate brushy thermal cover for wildlife. Those ranches that had been sculpted and manicured to resemble city parks experienced a higher death loss for certain wildlife species because there was not enough cover for species to properly thermoregulate. This is just one example of why it is important to consider all four habitat components when trying to make wildlife habitat more productive for the species of interest.

Of these four habitat components, the one that is most often overlooked is space. Space requirements for habitability for various species of wildlife is also the least understood component. In time, I think we will see increased emphasis on this aspect of wildlife management. From an outfitting standpoint, high-fenced areas provide an example of how associated management programs can breach certain space requirements for big game animals. These fences essentially create a closed system. When we overcrowd the habitat on these fenced properties, especially by integrating various species of exotic ungulates with native ungulates, we run the risk of denuding the landscape. In addition, when we breach a population's space requirement, some degree of social or behavioral stress is created—and this is very poorly understood. Problems such as cannibalism may occur with captive birds, including pheasants and quail. Is this behavior a reaction to overcrowded conditions? I suspect that it is. As a veterinarian friend of mine says, "When it comes to animals, including people, 'dis-ease' equals disease." Does a lack of suitable space create dis-ease for wild animals? I am certain that it does, but this is hard to measure and quantify.

My main point? Professionals who are using wildlife commercially should have some understanding of the basic elements required to ensure the health and sustainability of wildlife. Many great hunting outfitters do not have college degrees in the natural resource field—and that is perfectly okay—but the industry should adopt an operating culture that advocates for the reasonable use of our wildlife resources, both through the offtake of animals and through an understanding of the importance of healthy wildlife habitats.

WILDLIFE AS A PUBLIC TRUST RESOURCE

The debate over who owns wildlife is not readily apparent to the masses. Make no mistake, though; the issue of wildlife ownership has shaped our wildlife culture in the U.S. beyond measure. It has also profoundly affected wildlife policy and game laws across the country. Ownership of wildlife resources varies immensely between countries, and the question of "who owns wildlife?" is one that will likely become more visible and more relevant as we move forward.

In recent years, attention has been focused on what is often referred to as the North American Model of Wildlife Conservation (The Model). The Model is actually not a model but a collection of tenets that are reflective of the philosophical foundation that has allowed North American wildlife populations to thrive since the early 20th century. During the 19th century, many wildlife species were exploited and almost depleted. Some species, such as the passenger pigeon, heath hen, and great auk, were lost altogether.

At one point, the passenger pigeon was perhaps the most abundant terrestrial vertebrate on the planet. In less than 100 years, the birds went from the peak of their population to extinction. Fortunately, by the late 1800s and early 1900s, the American wildlife revolution was set into motion by forward-thinking people like Theodore Roosevelt, Gifford Pinchot, George Perkins Marsh, John Muir, and others. This paradigm shift in how Americans approached the use of wildlife resulted in the most remarkable recovery and success story for wildlife that has ever been witnessed in mankind's history.

During the early 1990s, Valerius Geist began publishing and promoting the notion of The Model, and it slowly gained traction across the wildlife community. Later, Shane Mahoney and others helped refine the messaging strategy and educational language of The Model, and Mahoney has served as the most effective pitchman in leading the crusade to bring important visibility onto The Model through his prowess as an international conservation icon. In recent years, the tenets gained even greater visibility in other special interest circles, including the hunting world, and most mainstream conservation groups, many university wildlife programs, and most state DNRs now endorse and recognize these tenets as guiding principles for their value-systems.

THE MODEL'S SEVEN BASIC TENETS

1. Wildlife is a public resource

2. Elimination of market hunting

3. Allocation of wildlife by law

4. Wildlife can only be killed for a legitimate purpose

5. Wildlife species are considered an international resource

6. Science is the proper tool for discharge of wildlife policy

7. The democracy of hunting

RIGHT > *The North American Model of Wildlife Conservation* is like no other on this planet. Although The Model is not beyond reproach, the principles reflected therein are largely responsible for the most incredible wildlife conservation story ever witnessed on this planet.

An entire book and hundreds of articles have been published on The Model, so I will not dissect its various principles. However, for the sake of this book, I will take a brief look at the first tenet: Wildlife is a public resource. It is considered the foundation tenet and is often referred to as the Public Trust Doctrine (PTD).

PUBLIC TRUST DOCTRINE (PTD)

PTD HISTORY

North America's exploration by the French and English was largely motivated by the continent's abundant natural resources and an unfettered opportunity for individuals to exploit them. As the continent was being settled through the 1800s, a culture was evolving that placed tremendous value on the idea that wildlife was owned by no one and, in fact, was owned by everyone. These natural resources fueled emerging economies and livelihoods and added greatly to the quality of life in the U.S. Over time, the idea that citizens owned these wildlife resources became entrenched in the American value system, shaping our wildlife culture.

The Model's key component is the concept that wildlife is owned by no one and is held in trust for the benefit of present and future generations by the government. This common law basis stemmed through a U.S. Supreme Court decision in 1842 (Martin v. Waddell) that declared certain resources could not be taken into private ownership. This ruling continues to serve as the common law basis which some refer to as the PTD. Essentially, this doctrine is based on the idea that the states' wildlife resources are owned by citizens, and that these resources are held in trust by the state wildlife agencies not only to benefit the public, but for future generations as well. This is the legal foundation for authority in federal, provincial, and state wildlife agencies.

Public ownership through agency entrustment creates a strong platform for regulatory boundaries safeguarding against the abuse and possible depletion of our wildlife resources, as witnessed during the 19th century. This human connection to wildlife resources has shaped our American wildlife culture and created a conservation matrix that has served Americans and this country's amazing wildlife resources well.

PTD PRESSURES

As one might expect, there have been pressures over the last several decades that put PTD of wildlife in the U.S. at risk. These pressures are often associated with the commercial use of wildlife. The pressure most familiar to me involves ownership of white-tailed deer and mule deer in Texas that are held in private breeding facilities under a Deer Breeder Permit. What began as a bona fide cooperative effort between private landowners and research facilities, then referred to as a Scientific Breeder Permit, eventually resulted in many of these deer still being held in these privately owned facilities even after the research was finished.

To continue holding and propagating these held over white-tailed deer, landowners were granted a usufructuary privilege, which means that the landowners were given "ownership privileges" over those deer without having "ownership rights." As a result, these breeders could buy, sell, and trade these deer, but they did not have a legal deed or title. This is an extraordinary privilege. Frankly, a law that grants individuals the ability to possess and financially profit from a publicly owned natural resource seems to fly in the face of reason and logic, and it is counterintuitive. However, this was the deal that was created, so it stands.

In recent years, special interest groups have applied tremendous pressure to change the statutes and regulations in the deer breeding world in Texas and elsewhere. Much of this legislation that has been introduced, often in every succeeding legislative session, has to do with private ownership of the resource, transfer of regulatory authority from Texas's wildlife agency to an agriculture agency, commercial sale of venison from native deer species, eliminating external ID requirements on the captive-raised deer, and allowance of cloning, among other things.

In addition to being in direct conflict with The Model's tenets, these legislative efforts caused extreme chaos in the ranks of the pro-wildlife community. Largely, it is the deer breeders who support these liberalized allowances, and largely it is the pro-wildlife community who opposes such changes. To call the legislative debate on these issues that occurs every two years during Texas's legislative session a blood bath is an understatement.

On a few occasions when deer breeding-related legislation has been under debate, special interest groups have appealed to legislators to legally treat deer no differently than domestic livestock; some have used the term "personal chattel" to describe the historical ownership context of livestock. Earlier in history, livestock were occasionally referred to as personal chattel, tangible items of value that are not connected to "real property," such as land. At one time, livestock and items such as furniture, jewelry, and automobiles were considered to be chattel. As I understand, this did not include money or items used for business purposes. During that era, wildlife was not classified as personal property.

During the aforementioned legislative discussions, individuals who were opposed to privatizing deer by transferring ownership of breeder deer to individuals maintained that from a common law standpoint, wildlife in the U.S. were never considered to be personal chattel. According to them, this historic precedent was yet another reason why there was no legal basis to justify conveying these deer from public to private ownership, even though the permittee had already been granted the extraordinary usufructuary privilege of being able to buy, sell, or trade these publicly owned resources.

Obviously, wildlife as a public trust resource is a complex matter. Certainly, we can point to other examples where we, as a society, have "drifted" away from the PTD's principles of native wildlife being a public trust resource. Captive propagation and meat sales of bobwhite quail comes to mind. It is not difficult for a person to begin breeding bobwhite quail by purchasing "seed stock" from another breeder. That particular allowance is treated much differently than illegally trapping and possessing wild bobwhites. As a result, there is some "convolution" in the regulated use of this species, and it's this convolution that deer breeders will sometimes point toward when they try to confuse the discussions and advance their agendas on ownership of deer.

Not long ago, the American alligator was classified as endangered, but today this species is thriving in much of its traditional home range. Alligators, now classified as a game animal in some states, can also be legally raised in captivity for commercial purposes, including meat and hide production. Eggs from wild alligators can be collected for commercial purposes as well. While each of these practices is highly regulated on a state level, this is an example of a public trust resource that has been privatized in some ways and is being utilized commercially.

On the surface, one might surmise that this drift from the legal and historical precedent of wildlife being a public trust resource is simply a sign of the times, where our society's legal framework has been modified to allow citizens more latitude in monetizing the wildlife resources found on their land. One could also argue that this drift is eroding the foundation of The Model—the same model that led to wildlife's remarkable recovery in North America and continues to benefit these resources—and the American public.

PTD: WHY DOES IT MATTER?

So, what is the big deal about this shift in recent decades, where segments of our wildlife populations are either being legally conveyed to private ownership through statutes or are being treated as private property for commercial use, which is de facto privatization in some people's minds? I have already touched on this subject, and I am not going to delve too deeply into this complex and polarizing topic, but privatization of our public trust wildlife resources is such an important topic that it deserves some attention.

Discussing the stakes of wildlife privatization takes the conversation into deep philosophical areas that stretch people's understanding. Invariably the conversations turn to ripple effects, diminishing returns, unintended consequences, and innumerable other topics that litter the slippery slopes of "what if." Privatization of our wildlife resources and the consequences thereof is a topic open for interpretation, uncertainty, and confusion, and it will almost always lead to a heated debate in mixed settings. Despite the pitfalls, I believe the privatization of wildlife resources is one of the most important issues facing the wildlife community now and in the future. With that in mind, here are a few reasons why I generally oppose privatization of our wildlife resources.

1) AMERICAN WILDLIFE CULTURE

Historically, perhaps no other idea has shaped Americans' view of wildlife more than the notion that wildlife is not owned by the crown, but by the people, and that all Americans stand to benefit from healthy, abundant wildlife. The migration to North America by Europeans, most notably the French and English, to access and use these natural resources is embedded in the history of this country's settlement and inextricably shaped how Americans view and value wildlife.

Even though there are other countries that enjoy more wealth per capita than the U.S., there is no other country where its citizens value wildlife in the same way as Americans. When you look at what we spend annually on pursuing wildlife, through hunting, fishing, photography, nature tourism, and other activities, it is staggering. Because of their value systems, Americans integrate wildlife resources into their lives and create economies that are good for our country and are generally good for the resource.

While Americans often point toward "exotic" parts of the world, like Africa or Ecuador, and focus on how exciting those destinations can be from a wildlife resource standpoint, we, through hunting or tourism, largely fund the systems that help keep those international resources in place. Through our appetite to participate in wildlife-related activities, American wildlife culture has created a national and international conservation platform and is one of the cornerstones of global wildlife conservation. And, importantly, much of this hunger can be traced back to the unfettered access that early Americans had to the wildlife resources of this country.

2) RELEVANCY FOR WILDLIFE

As American society moves away from rural environments and our population has been enveloped by concrete and asphalt, our society has become increasingly distant from wild things, wild places, and open spaces. Coinciding with this demographic shift that began at the end of World War II, the general appreciation for our wildlife resources has been slowly eroding, presumably because a larger percentage of our citizens grow up with no meaningful relationship with the outdoors. Award-winning writer Richard Louv has explored this societal change in his work. Louv has focused on sharing research findings and personal interpretations on what he refers to as "nature deficit disorder." According to Louv, there are measurable and immeasurable consequences associated with lifestyles that are largely separated from green space and outdoors, and this disorder manifests itself through physiological and psychological health. Some of these human health issues include obesity, high blood pressure, anxiety, and depression, to name a few.

So what does privatization of wildlife have to do with these concerns over nature deficit disorder? One way to reinforce society's bond to our natural world is by making those resources relevant. In the case of wildlife, we create connections between people and game (or non-game) species. In my opinion, one of the most natural and effective ways to reconnect Americans and wildlife is by making it clear that we all have skin in the game. If wildlife suffers, all Americans suffer because those resources have shared ownership, even if it is just emotional ownership, with all Americans.

Adding to the idea of our Americana connection to wildlife, the late E. O. Wilson spent much of his career evaluating and discussing what he coined as biophilia. According to Wilson, humans are hardwired to want to connect to other living systems, such as that found through nature, perhaps reinforcing why early American wildlife cultures became inextricably intertwined with wild things, nurturing the biophilic values that led to where we are today with our value-systems involving hunting and wildlife. A natural tendency to want to connect to wildlife, combined with legal systems to utilize these resources in a meaningful way, undoubtedly help shape our modern-day American wildlife cultures.

Because we all have skin in the game, we should all take responsibility to ensure that federal and state policies consider the long-term sustainable health of these resources. Policy is shaped by the court of public opinion and through ballot box outcomes. When we make wildlife relevant to the general public, we also create a favorable opportunity for wildlife to have a fighting chance to be sustainable for future generations. Furthermore, it is my opinion that one of the quickest and most surefire ways to create an even greater disconnect between our society and our wildlife resources is for us to create policies that suggest that the public has no skin in the wildlife game and that there is no reason for these wild things to be relevant within the value systems of average Americans. With this in mind, I believe that anything that we do intentionally that compromises the long-standing American principle of wildlife being a public trust resource will result in further diminishing wildlife's relevance within our society. Some may dismiss this sentiment as philosophical conjecture, but I believe it is one of the biggest threats facing the sustainable health of wildlife in the U.S.

3) USURPED VALUES OF WILDLIFE

As part of the privatization of wildlife narrative, special interest groups, especially deer breeders, suggest these captive deer should be treated the same as privately owned livestock and that deer producers should be granted the same legal allowances as livestock producers. This presents multiple concerns.

Perhaps the biggest potential downside of allowing wildlife to be effectively converted into livestock is that the unique and important values tied to wildlife are replaced by the different, but equally important, values tied to livestock. When wildlife quits being wild and becomes a domesticated species, the special reverence for wildlife dies, plain and simple. By reclassifying deer as livestock, the deer breeders' narrow interest has been allowed to destroy the broad and long-term cultural values of our wild deer in the name of short-term financial gains within their industry. It's important that we do not allow the value systems of livestock to usurp the value systems of wildlife. Period.

4) LOSS OF APPROPRIATE REGULATORY CONTROL

When wildlife is legally privatized and classified as livestock, the next step in that unfortunate progression is for the state regulatory authority to be transferred from the wildlife agency to a livestock or agricultural agency. In addition to the aforementioned downside, another ancillary problem is the increased workload that is inevitably heaped onto an already understaffed agriculture agency.

Because of this, we potentially compromise food safety and other crucial protections for Americans by placing yet another unreasonable burden on the agency tasked with overseeing agricultural and food production. In addition, professionals who have been trained within the disciplines of agriculture production are now being tasked to monitor wildlife management and husbandry practices. Because their expertise lies in other areas, they may not be equipped to effectively regulate wildlife.

When we ask ourselves what the consequences of wildlife privatization may be and why it matters, we must explore the potential cascading effects that privatization may have on the long-term sustainable health of wildlife and the long-term sustainable health of people. As we are hopefully entering the post-COVID period, human health, both physical and psychological, are more apropos today than ever, and it is imperative that the public understand this logic regarding how wildlife privatization has implications tied to our lives, our lifestyles, and our health. Wildlife managers and enthusiasts are not the only stakeholders in this discussion; every single American has a stake in the well-being of our publicly held wildlife resources.

Yes, the stakes are that high and grave. Unfortunately, the complexity and philosophical nature of what is at hand makes it difficult to grapple with and convenient to push aside. Wildlife in the U.S. cannot afford to be ignored in these important conversations.

CONSERVATION VERSUS EXPLOITATION

The remainder of this chapter will focus on areas of concern that I have regarding practices and ideologies existing within the hunting and wildlife arenas. These observations are not intended to be personal attacks on individuals but are merely candid opinions or concerns that I and others have with the exploitation of wildlife, especially as it relates to hunting, hunting values, and our treasured hunting heritage. Today, we live in a world where terminology is used loosely, often by design, to fit the narrative of someone's agenda.

Although entire books have been written on wildlife conservation, for the sake of context, I would like to quickly reflect on Merriam-Webster's definitions of the terms "conservation" and "exploitation."

Conservation: *Planned management of a natural resource to prevent exploitation, destruction, or neglect.*

Exploitation: *An act or instance of exploiting. From a transitive verb standpoint, that meaning is described as: To make use of meanly or unfairly for one's own advantage.*

Now, let's look at Cambridge's definitions of these same terms:

Conservation: *The protection of plants and animals, natural areas, and interesting and important structures and buildings, especially from the damaging effects of human activity.*

Exploitation: *The use of something in order to get an advantage from it. For instance: The ruthless exploitation of the world's resources is rapidly destroying our planet.*

As part of my education in the wildlife field, I was taught that wildlife conservation is the "wise use of our wildlife resources through applied management." And from my biased perspective, wildlife exploitation infers the "unwise use of our wildlife resources that may ultimately damage the long-term health of those resources." By exploring the nuanced meanings and differences between conservation and exploitation, I hope to use the remainder of this chapter to create additional context regarding the matter of conservation versus exploitation.

During the 84th Texas Legislative Session held in 2015, there was a heated debate regarding a bill that would force the Texas Parks and Wildlife Department to implement rules for a Deer Management Permit involving mule deer. This permit would allow the capture of wild, native mule deer and placement of them in privately owned breeding facilities for propagation. The Texas Deer Association (TDA), a special interest group for deer breeders, spearheaded this legislation. Many other conservation groups opposed this legislation for various reasons, including the fact that mule deer were already residing in pens under a different permit, and those deer had not performed well over the years.

Many experts, including myself, felt (and continue to feel) that mule deer are more fragile than white-tailed deer. From our perspective, it makes no sense to capture healthy, wild mule deer and place them in small pens where their health will likely be compromised. Plus, many people, myself included, felt that we should not allow mule deer to go as far down the same path of domestication and intensive husbandry practices as whitetails. This bill, as with many of the other deer breeding bills, generated a heated debate that was played out on a House committee floor through testimony delivered by special interest groups. At one point, well into the testimonies, a high-profile wildlife consultant who is deeply involved in the deer breeding industry characterized those who opposed this bill as "preservationists" and those who supported the bill as "conservationists." In my way of thinking, his spin was the exact opposite of reality. The true conservationists, in my opinion, were fighting to keep fragile mule deer free-ranging and truly wild.

This play on words stuck with me. Since then, I have spent considerable time contemplating how game management tools can cross certain thresholds that may ultimately lead to an end product that redefines a practice in a much different light. It not only creates a different, generally negative connotation in people's minds, but perhaps is the factor that differentiates conservation practices from exploitation. A matter of semantics? Perhaps. At the end of the day, though, semantics matter. When we allow special interest groups with ulterior motives to intentionally confuse the narrative by misappropriating terms, then we are effectively entering a game of charades, using the proverbial smoke and mirrors to drive an audience toward the special interest group's point of view. I've dealt with similar situations when an organization is drafting a position statement and that draft language is being shaped by people of diverging stakeholder interests; there's a tendency for a play on words to be inserted into the language that allows one stakeholder group to achieve their desired outcome. When interpreting an assembly of words, context can be important in terms of what the intentions may have been at the time when such language, or play on words, were crafted. Words matter. Semantics matter. Context matters.

Gamesmanship like this is part of our human nature, and we might as well accept it for what it is, especially in the world of politics and public policy. Because gamesmanship is part of public policy when it comes to laws, rules, and regulations governing the sustainable health of wildlife resources, it is even more important that we recognize the differences between wildlife conservation and exploitation. The fine, subtle lines between the two can lead to vastly different outcomes, both short-term and long-term, for the resource. So frankly, I no longer have any patience for tactics that bastardize our game management world.

Over the last several years, I have been very outspoken about my concerns regarding the captive breeding of whitetails. Boldly expressing these concerns over certain practices that define much of what goes on in the deer breeding world has cost me friends and a tremendous amount of business. I have received death threats, I have been blacklisted by various industry companies, and I have opened myself to a tremendous amount of grief and criticism by openly sharing my opinions on this matter.

From a selfish business standpoint, it would have been less painful and more profitable for me to have simply gone with the flow and capitalized on the generous opportunities that were coming my way from about 2005 to 2010. During those years, I had the chance to develop commercial hunting programs centered on pen-raised deer. WSI dabbled in that market a bit, and our team could have easily shifted its focus to that emerging market, as we were likely the largest whitetail outfitter in the country during that era. But I chose to go a different route.

Knowing what I know now, if I had to do it over again, I would likely do the same. There is no doubt that my business would have been much more profitable if I would have done what many of my competitors did and exploit the opportunity that has since led to the exploitation of white-tailed deer at a level beyond comprehension. In fact, it is my opinion that the captive deer breeding industry is the greatest source of pressure on the long-term health of wildlife conservation.

THE (WHITETAIL) TIPPING POINT

For approximately 120 years, hunters and hunting have driven successful wildlife conservation practices in North America. During the last 100 years, funds derived from hunting have underwritten terrestrial conservation in this country.

Furthermore, for decades, white-tailed deer have been this country's most economically important wildlife species by a long shot; there is no close second place. It stands to reason, then, that anything we do that could diminish the health of, or compromise the broad and long-term values of whitetails would be considered taboo. After all, whitetails have been the pillar of our conservation funding mechanism for decades. Unfortunately, we have allowed egregious captive deer breeding practices to put our conservation crown jewel at risk, all in the name of growing bigger antlers and all driven by human greed.

50 Years of Texas Deer Management
Management Intensity Continuum

Least Artificial/Intensive → Most Artificial/Intensive

- Passive
- Basic habitat management
- Spotlight or Hahn surveys
- Aerial surveys
- Traditional harvest management
- Supplemental feeding
- Camera scouting
- High fencing
- Aggressive genetic culling
- TTT Permit (wild deer)
- DMP Permit (wild deer)

- Breeder Permit with live cover (registered deer)
- Feedlot feeding
- Pharmaceutical enhancers
- TTP Permit (euthanization)
- Artificial insemination
- Sexing of semen
- Soft antler scarification
- Embryo transfer
- Cloning

THE TIPPING POINT

THE TEXAS EXPERIENCE AND THE PARADIGM SHIFT

White-tailed deer hunting has been an important recreational and economic activity in Texas for many decades. This large, ecologically diverse state, which is approximately 96 percent privately owned and supports more than four million whitetails, has a long history of commercial hunting practices supported by what some would describe as progressive deer management.

The book *Producing Quality Whitetails* by Al Brothers and Murphy E. Ray, Jr., was originally published in 1975, during a time when the interest level in white-tailed deer from hunters, wildlife managers, and landowners was beginning to accelerate. From that point on, deer management practices evolved, expressing the ever-growing desire to produce bigger antlers. Initially, managers focused on basic herd management principles, such as striving for more maturity within buck herds and balancing sex ratios. Habitat management, such as brush work, water development, and rotational livestock grazing to improve range condition, followed.

Managers seeking more control over deer herds turned to high fencing. These closed systems provided a greater influence over the micro-ecology of those enclosed areas. Then people began implementing intensive feeding programs which elevated year-round nutritional planes for deer. Some deer herds responded to the superlative nutrition by producing larger antlers and increasing fawning and recruitment rates. Aggressively culling bucks became part of a "fine-tuning" process. Bucks with undesirable antler traits were eliminated in an attempt to sculpt age cohorts and manipulate the genetic profile of high-fenced deer herds.

The progression of management practices described above developed and matured over 20 to 25 years. During this time, antler quality within local deer herds often showed significant improvement, but generally speaking, the top end average Boone and Crockett scores increased no more than 10"–20" on mature bucks. Whitetails with 130"–140" in most areas of Texas were still considered relatively large in many hunting circles; bucks in the 170"–180" range remained rare, and very few bucks measuring more than 200" were taken around the state annually until 2000–2005.

Prior to the year 2000, the captive deer breeding industry was a cottage industry. In 1996, there were an estimated 227 registered deer breeders in Texas with approximately 12,000 deer in captivity at that time. Shortly thereafter, the captive deer industry in Texas grew rapidly. By 2011, there were 1,371 registered deer breeders with an estimate of almost 110,000 whitetails held in pens. In recent years, the industry's growth has not only flattened, but is now beginning to tick down.

Up until 2005, much of the industry trade was breeder-to-breeder sales. A large number of deer were sold as start-up inventory for newly registered breeders, and then existing breeders purchased additional deer from one another to either increase herd numbers within breeding facilities or to introduce new genetic lines into existing breeding operations. The value of deer from certain facilities with prominent pedigrees ballooned.

Bred does often fetched $15,000+ each. Select bucks brought considerably more, including a buck which purportedly went for $1 million. Semen straws, used for artificial insemination, sold for $5,000 or more. The huge prices attracted a lot of attention, spurring even more industry growth.

Also, until roughly 2007, most deer that were released from their pens to pastures were released to enhance the genetics of existing herds. However, it was also around this time that the shooter buck market began to creep into commercial deer hunting as a put-and-take practice. Bucks were grown out in the pen and released into high-fenced areas so they could be shot during the upcoming season, perhaps a few weeks after release. Many of these shooter bucks' racks were considerably larger than the antlers of those being produced "naturally" in the pasture, even these the upper-end of the size spectrum. Within a few years, harvesting a Texas buck that measured 200" or more went from being a rarity to being a relatively common occurrence.

Currently, there are hundreds of (but perhaps less than one thousand) bucks being harvested annually in Texas with scores of 200"—500" or more. The overwhelming majority of these are grown out in pens and released into high-fenced enclosures after their antler growth is complete. It is not terribly uncommon for two-and-a-half-year-old pen-raised bucks to score more than 200", with a surprisingly high number of two-and-a-half-year-olds scoring more than 300". In some areas of the country, there are a sizable number of pen-raised bucks with 600"+ antlers and at least a few that have topped out at more than 800". For comparison, the world record non-typical Boone and Crockett elk scores 478 5/8". Some of these monster whitetails cannot hold their heads in a normal, erect position due to their abnormally heavy antlers. In some eyes, these extreme genetic expressions in whitetails are no different from the genetic manipulations in farm animals which often attract the ire of animal welfare and animal rights groups.

Late in 2008, the Texas economy collapsed when the price of crude oil fell and the stock market crashed. In 2009, there was a major shift in the deer breeding and commercial deer hunting industries in Texas. The price of pen-raised deer fell to a point where a substantial percentage of pen-raised bucks were more valuable as shooter bucks than as breeder bucks confined within breeding facilities. For the first time, hunting operators could purchase large pen-raised bucks at a low enough price that they could still add a margin to the purchase price and then sell those shooter bucks in the commercial hunting market at a profit.

In my opinion, 2009 was the year that big pen-raised deer arguably became the face of the commercial deer hunting industry in Texas—and have largely remained that way today. Shooter bucks sustain the deer breeding industry in Texas and elsewhere. The shooter buck market drives the train in the deer breeding business.

These days, the primary economic driver in the deer breeding industry is no longer the breeder-to-breeder market, and it is no longer a market built on attempts at "improving" pasture genetics. The industry's viability depends on the shooter buck market, plain and simple. Interestingly, when deer were being released into pastures, primarily to enhance existing genetics, they were normally double ear tagged because the deer manager did not want the deer shot. At the time, the managers wanted to maximize the breeding life from those released deer. Since 2008, most bucks released into pastures are not ear tagged because the proprietor does not want hunters to be turned off by seeing tagged deer. In many cases, this attempt to mask the reality that these deer reside in pens until just before they are shot is nothing short of snake oil salesmanship.

A COLOSSAL DEBATE AND CIVIC ENGAGEMENT

Up until around 2010, deer breeding in Texas was a relatively quiet industry, hardly gaining any attention from outside industry circles. The TDA was formed to serve as a trade group for this growing industry, providing professional and political guidance for its members. As the industry continued to grow, concerns grew over trends in commercial deer hunting, but these debates and discussions generally took place behind closed doors and were out of the public eye. In 2011, this changed.

During the 82nd Texas Legislative Session in 2011, there was a host of deer breeding-related bills which were supported by deer breeding industry leaders. Many of the bills contained language addressing activities which historically were hot button issues within pro-wildlife groups. Some of these bills related to such things as privatization, commercial sales of whitetail and mule deer meat, due process for breeders violating regulatory and statutory standards, transferring regulatory authority from Texas Parks and Wildlife Department to Texas Animal Health Commission, allowing wild mule deer to be captured and placed in pens for propagation purposes, and elimination of external identification requirements of breeder deer among several other subjects.

The only contentious deer breeding-related bill that passed in 2011 was the mule deer bill. But, fortunately, the bill's author filed a letter of intent requesting that research precede the permit's implementation. To date, that research has not been conducted and the permit has not been implemented. This long list of deer breeding-related bills not only generated considerable attention from various individuals and conservation

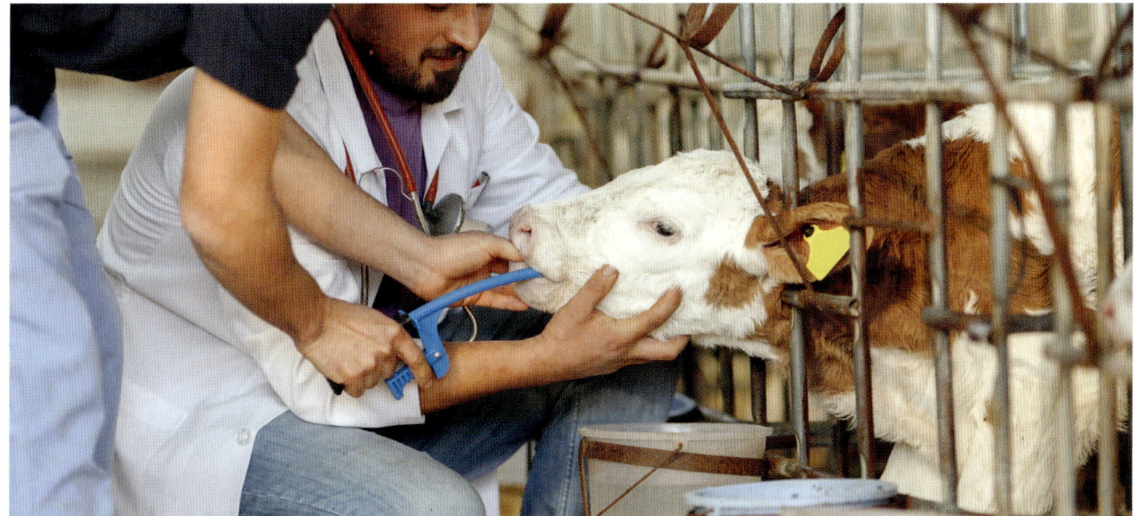

ABOVE > What are the consequences of allowing the unique values tied to livestock to usurp the unique values of wildlife? Further, what message do we send to a discerning non-hunting public when our game management practices look more like livestock husbandry practices?

organizations, but spurred a heated debate that, by the latter part of the session, prompted more people to attend committee hearings than had previously been the norm. The sleeping bear had been poked.

After 2011, during the interim between legislative sessions, the concern over what was taking place in the deer breeding industry continued to grow. Groups such as the TWA and the Texas Chapter of TWS focused more attention on advocacy efforts dealing with certain practices within the breeding industry. Additionally, concerned citizens acting on behalf of themselves took a more active role in helping to address these mounting concerns. The 2013 Texas Legislative Session was a repeated and amplified version of 2011. An emerging, active pro-wildlife community became even more organized to speak out against certain deer breeding practices and agendas. As many expected, an assortment of similar bills supported by leaders in the deer breeding community were introduced.

In an attempt to curb put-and-take deer hunting, or what many perceive as canned hunts, the TWA supported legislation that would have changed what has been historically referred to as the "Ten Day Rule." Essentially this rule requires that bucks be released at least ten days before the start of the earliest deer season in order to be legally hunted that season. This bill called for a three-year phase-in period that would have changed the pre-hunt time period from ten days to 60 days. The bill failed to pass, but only after it created tremendous resistance from the leaders of the deer breeding community. All other controversial deer breeding-related bills failed as well.

Over the last few years, the conflicts and debates between the deer breeding industry and pro-wildlife community have continued to escalate. Deer breeding industry leaders and activists have responded by spending a tremendous amount of money on public relations campaigns, which often include the economic impact of deer breeding using questionable figures.

As part of the communications strategy, old practices and tools have been renamed in an attempt to create a more favorable perception. Examples of this rebranding include: conservation fence instead of game-proof fence, stocker buck instead of shooter buck, farmer instead of deer breeder, high fencing instead of breeding pens, and intensive deer management instead of captive deer breeding. As I previously mentioned, semantics, wording, and context matter when trying to understand the picture. The deer breeding industry has also spent a tremendous amount of money on professional lobbyists, and some of their advocacy efforts could accurately be described as bullying.

SPECIFIC AREAS OF CONCERN

Depending on who you ask, the list of concerns over what has been taking place in the deer breeding industry is long:

- Human health and safety concerns, especially as it relates to possible consumption of venison potentially adulterated by drug residues. An assortment of medications are commonly used in the industry, most of which do not have the necessary research to identify adequate withdrawal periods in white-tailed deer and their venison

- Extreme practices such as unnecessary medicating, artificial insemination, bottle-feeding and hand-feeding, hunting in small enclosures, sexing of semen, and scarification of antlers and antler pedicles. These activities are not practiced by all breeders but are used by some to achieve certain objectives

- Animal health and welfare associated with certain practices

- Perception of canned hunting associated with put-and-take practices

- Fostering disease by concentrating animals and by transporting them. The increasing spread and prevalence of chronic wasting disease is now highlighting this concern

- Genetic degradation of wild deer herds as large numbers of deer are released from pen to pasture, co-mingling with native deer, perhaps compromising hardiness and immunity that natural selection has created over millennia

- Distorted expectations of deer hunters caused by bucks with unnaturally large antlers that have been pen-raised and harvested as part of put-and-take hunting programs

- Lack of reasonable disclosure to hunters who kill these animals about how these deer are grown

- Erosion of deer hunting markets due to the proliferation of artificial practices that kill the mystery and magic of hunting and turn off many hunters who are aware of the intensive manipulation required to produce these anomalies

- Diminished value of wild deer herds

- Damage to our hunting heritage

As a wildlife biologist and a proprietor of a commercial hunting operation for more than 36 years, I am convinced that the widespread release of artificially raised monster deer that are being integrated into commercial deer hunting is reducing the number of deer hunters who are willing to spend their money on annual deer hunts. In my conversations with deer hunters, they have observed that deer hunting does not have the same look and feel. It's my sentiment that this erosion of deer hunters has the ability to greatly impair our important conservation funding platform.

Any photo of a big deer now typically prompts suspicions about its origins and its rearing, regardless of the animal's background. By creating artificial experiences, we have reduced the mystery and magic associated with white-tailed deer and whitetail hunting. As a result, we are compromising the inherent value and sustainability of the crown jewel of our wildlife conservation funding mechanism.

CONSERVATION CROSSROADS

Current laws in many states favor a captive deer industry where we will continue to see nontraditional "wildlife management practices" push the upper limits for abnormally large antlers. Deer hunting markets will continue to respond to such changes. As we head further down this path of mass-producing giant deer through artificial supports, our deer hunting markets will continue to quietly erode.

Regulatory reform within the captive deer breeding business is long overdue. I am sad to say that I think many of our mainstream sporting/conservation groups sat back on their laurels too long without addressing this serious problem. Socio-political and financial pressures have deterred many in the conservation NGO community from confidently and courageously stepping up and proactively advocating for the best interests of our wildlife resources and hunting heritage when it comes to the problems associated with captive deer breeding. I get it; I understand the reticence for many of these conservation groups to step out there and risk creating chaos among their membership and potentially losing financial support from members and the industry, but at the same time, it is these same conservation groups that we must rely on to be a voice for conservation and a voice for ensuring our broad wildlife-related markets, such as hunting and angling.

I predict the non-hunting community will become less tolerant of private individuals who subject our country's publicly held wildlife resources to abhorrent practices that do not consider animal welfare nor conservation, all in the name of financial gain. Furthermore, as awareness increases about what is taking place in these breeding facilities and how these animals are being integrated into commercial deer hunting, I suspect that our hunting community will also become less accepting of such practices as well.

The ensuing cultural and political debate over the fundamental principles of keeping wildlife wild will pull into the mix a broad cross section of Americans who represent diverse stakeholder interests. I believe the intense debate and conflict will push this issue to a tipping point. The question of the day is which direction will things tip? Will the non-hunting community's support of hunting dip below a threshold that allows hunting to remain as a socially acceptable activity and a sustainable wildlife conservation force? Or will hunters once again rise to the occasion and speak up for reason and wildlife, just as our conservation forefathers did some 100-plus years ago? We are truly at a conservation crossroads.

So, much of this discussion circles back to the example of the 2015 House Committee hearing I mentioned earlier in this chapter, where the individual knowingly distorted the narrative by characterizing practices which largely exploit our wildlife resources as conservation practices. It is time that our hunting and wildlife communities quit tolerating intentional distortions and prevent authentic wildlife conservation from being hijacked by wildlife exploitation.

Again, we are truly at a conservation crossroads. What path will we take?

18 THE 8 M'S OF HUNTING

ONE COULD ARGUE THAT OUR HUNTING COMMUNITY, OVER TIME, HAS LOST SIGHT OF HUNTING'S FUNDAMENTAL ESSENCE. THE CHANGES IN THE WAY WE VALUE IT AND THINK OF IT ARE NOT SURPRISING GIVEN THE NUMEROUS CHANGES IN SOCIETY, LARGELY BECAUSE OF TECHNOLOGICAL PROGRESS.

OPPOSITE
Blake Barnett
2022 Free-Range Nilgai
Willacy County, Texas
Guide - Mike Lassig

The ever-changing tools, techniques, and technologies that define our lives ultimately shape our cultures and customs as well as the way we think and act. Our hunting world is not immune to the changes; it looks very different than it did 50 years ago. Our tools, techniques, and technologies for rearing and hunting game animals have morphed in unanticipated ways and to such an extent that many hunters question the legitimacy and integrity of certain practices and tools that seem to broadly define hunting these days.

One of the smartest people I have ever known is Dr. Bill Eikenhorst, from Brenham, Texas. Bill, a successful small animal veterinarian, is an avid hunter and a fierce pro-wildlife ambassador and advocate. He is also a good friend. Several years ago, Bill began to talk about "The Four M's of Hunting," which was later amended to include a fifth M and then a sixth. The most recent amendment added a seventh M, so then he and I referred to it as "The Seven M's of Hunting." Then, Larry Weishuhn pointed out that this list of tenets would not be complete without an eighth M, Memories, to which Bill and I fully agreed.

Over the last few years, I have added some well-considered words to this framework to help breathe even more life into what Bill and I feel serves as a litmus for hunting. As I was reaching the end of this manuscript for this book, I realized that my work would not be complete without sharing a concise version of The Eight M's of Hunting, so I added another chapter to include this framework.

MYSTERY

When the outcome of a hunt is almost certain, an integral property of hunting is lost because it is no longer hunting but something else more akin to shopping or collecting and the mystery is gone.

Among other things, this raises the question, "Can we know too much about the individual animal we are hunting?" Considering that remote cameras are now integrated into hunting, this allows us to become extremely familiar with our quarry's traits and habits. This may be the ultimate example of TMI, "too much information." Other examples of practices that may kill the inherent mystery of the hunt include small enclosures that allow little or no chance for escape and "domesticated" game that is no longer afraid of people.

These are simply a few examples of tools and practices that may lead to erosion of the mystery virtue of the hunt. And please do not misunderstand me, I'm not questioning the validity of the legal allowance of these things, but I do believe that there are collective and compounding effects of such elements that eventually provide too much certainty of the outcome of the hunt, ultimately eroding the important mystery property of the hunt.

MAGIC

Humans are able to connect with wildlife in indescribable ways. Kids and adults alike have always been fascinated with wild animals. This biophilic relationship that we have with these wild creatures—and that hunters have with their quarry—is magical. When hunters become too focused on a single aspect of the hunt, such as "collecting a wall-hanger," the "magic" is lost.

To fully experience hunting, hunters must not lose sight of the entire experience. Some parts of the hunt are physical, some are spiritual, and still others are emotional. There are components that can be measured, while others are intangible and must just be savored. The sum of all of these individual experiences creates the magic of hunting that keeps beckoning humans to the chase, and it's this magic that adds to retention of hunters.

ABOVE > Dr. Bill Eikenhorst, an intellectual giant and wildlife conservation champion, came up with the original components of The 8 M's of Hunting, initially consisting of five tenets. He and I engaged in on-going discussions, adding two more to the initial list, with Larry Weishuhn suggesting the eighth. I then committed these eight tenets to paper.

MAJESTY

Dignity, beauty, grandness, and splendor are inherent in God's natural creations. Man's ability to artificially push the limits of nature only tarnishes the majesty of these already amazing natural creatures. When game management practices look more like livestock husbandry practices, the unique values tied to wildlife are replaced by the agrarian values of livestock. This effectively destroys the untamed nature of wildlife and the majesty of wildlife is lost.

MEAT

Humans began hunting to harvest meat to survive. When food is no longer a motive, we have strayed far from hunting's defining purpose and have severely weakened our ability to defend the need for hunting.

Human decency has its boundaries, and taking an animal's life for no justifiable reason arguably breaches certain lines of decency in the eyes of a civilized society. Hunters must reasonably use their harvests and avoid wanton waste. And from a figurative standpoint, when the hunt lacks substance, it lacks the "meat" that provides the legitimate platform to support hunting.

From an advocacy standpoint, there is not a more defensible aspect of hunting than the food or meat part of the hunt. Every single living being can relate to food, and we must do a better job of capitalizing on this communication cornerstone.

MATURITY

"Maturity" does not simply relate to growing big deer. In the grand scheme of things, maturity is a virtue that our hunting community must embrace if it is going to survive.

When I reflect on the advanced tools, techniques, and technologies that we use to produce and harvest game animals, I am reminded of my friend Bill Eikenhorst's statement, "The edge of intensity cuts both ways, often resulting in unintended consequences." In a mature hunting community, the tools and techniques du jour—and their consequences—should be considered as we move forward.

MONEY

For hunting to continue to be relevant, it must remain economically significant to help justify its existence. The economic impact is demonstrated at various levels, including community-based conservation where local citizens, especially in rural communities, reap the benefits of hunting-related expenditures, which helps create relevancy in the eyes of the public. Money derived through excise taxes, license and tag sales, and other hunting-related expenditures supports the conservation efforts of state and federal wildlife agencies. Also, free enterprise markets allow private landowners to benefit from fee-based hunting programs which incentivize private lands stewardship.

Furthermore, the success of businesses across industries today, often hinges on the public's perception that those industries meet certain Environmental, Social, and Governance (ESG) standards. If we are going to ensure sustainability of the conservation funding that is tied to hunting, we must consider the importance of public perceptions and public acceptance and how such societal pressures ultimately shape the financial outputs that are tied to hunting; several of these Eight M's of Hunting interact with public perceptions.

MATERNAL

There is no stronger drive to protect than the maternal instinct of a mother protecting her progeny. Whether such behavior is prompted by an emotional bond for the offspring, or whether it is biologically hardwired to ensure procreation of the species, the presence of the maternal instinct to protect is undeniable. Similarly, it is my opinion that our innate sense to procure food, to "hunt," is also fundamental to our human DNA; it is part of who we are, though it may not be part of what we do. And because our drive to hunt is fundamental to our existence, the hunting community has an obligation to protect our hunting heritage and pass it on to the next generation, as surely as a mother is responsible for protecting her young. Protecting our legacy as responsible hunters should serve as a shared sense of duty.

MEMORIES

The importance of acquiring pleasant memories afield cannot be overstated as a fundamental benefit of hunting. Your memory interacts closely with your emotions, and vice versa. Positive memories can bring you peace and perhaps provide healing from those memories which are not so pleasant. Positive experiences gained in our natural world, including those associated with hunting, do not just allow us to enjoy recalling and sharing our stories, but the time spent outdoors has proven to be beneficial to human health, both physically and mentally. And as suggested in the Maternal section of this chapter, our hunting community should refuse to allow these special memories associated with hunting to become a thing of the past.

An entire book could be dedicated to The Eight M's of Hunting, and perhaps someday that will happen. However, this discussion is an overview of the principles that should serve as a litmus test for hunting. These tenets should shape a currently undefined list of best practice standards—the same practices that allow hunting to pass the test of public scrutiny, the same practices that keep wildlife wild, and the same practices that protect the hunting experience's integrity. When the hunting community cannot check off each of these eight boxes affirmatively, we, in my opinion, are failing our tradition, ourselves—and future generations. Regardless of the conceptual framework we might use, our hunting community needs to examine ourselves and our practices proactively if we are going to keep up with and remain relevant in a rapidly changing world, a world that has grown more distant from hunting. Or, as I have been saying more frequently in recent times, until we learn to play the game smarter, it will do us no good to play the game harder.

I believe we are at crossroad today, similar to that faced by sportsmen in the late 1800s when they took on market hunting. At that point, saying "enough is enough" showed a hunting community embracing mature decision-making for the greater good of wildlife and humanity. Is our hunting community mature enough today to allow self introspection to be a guiding light in making adaptive decisions that ensure sustainable health of hunting? Only time will tell.

ABOVE > Memories. Gib Surles and Bobby Jarvis, best friends since their college days at Texas A&M, pictured here with Gib's 174" Boone and Crockett whitetail that he killed in December 2021 at his South Texas lease. They have been making memories like this every year for over 40 years.

19 ROLE OF NGOs IN HUNTING

RARELY ARE HIGHLY SUCCESSFUL BUSINESS OWNERS SIMPLY DRIVEN BY THEIR BUSINESS MISSION. OFTEN OTHER MOTIVATORS KEEP THINGS EXCITING AND DRIVE THOSE PEOPLE TO BE HIGH PERFORMERS IN VARIOUS FACETS OF THEIR LIVES.

t is my observation that many of these high-energy, ambitious individuals find an energy pill through volunteer work, and this volunteer work often creates a counter-current reciprocating synergy between their business efforts and their volunteer work—one helps fuel the other.

Not long after I graduated from college, I found myself at an odd stage in my life. In college, I was hyper-focused on professional development. My college years were very satisfying on many levels, including a little bit of partying. Most importantly, college helped me determine the path I wanted to take as I fledged my own business.

After a few years of getting my feet under me, I found my work as a private wildlife biologist and hunting outfitter left me unfulfilled. Please do not get me wrong, it was exciting to see things begin to come together and witness the successes created by our small support team. Business was growing, new opportunities were emerging, and my dreams of being an entrepreneur in the wildlife world were taking shape. I was happily married, and we were putting down roots in our new hometown of San Angelo. I was living the American dream. Nevertheless, something was missing. Since entering college, I was driven to "make a difference" in the wildlife world, but through my new business, I felt like my work was inconsequential beyond my family, clients, and employees.

I initially joined the Texas Wildlife Association (TWA) when I was a senior in college in 1986. While attending a Texas Trophy Hunters Association show in the Dallas Metroplex, I came across the TWA booth, an organization formed the previous year. The organization was advocating for private landowners' rights, was pro-hunting, and was focused on game species. These priorities checked off some boxes for me, so I joined.

After graduating from college and starting WSI, we were living on a shoestring budget, and my time was limited, so I let my TWA membership lapse for a year or so. Rejoining TWA in perhaps late 1988, I attended my first TWA convention in 1989 at the then Y.O. Ranch Hilton in Kerrville, Texas. Attending that event was a personal paradigm shift that changed my life. At that TWA event, I realized that through this organization I could "make a difference" in wildlife conservation. For years, I simply attended TWA conventions and various other TWA events. I was still leveraging my modest amounts of cash to grow my business and had little spare cash or spare time to devote to TWA. But as time went by, I became more involved, serving on various committees, donating my time, and donating hunts for fundraising.

I became involved as a regional chair for TWA, and then a director, and eventually ended up serving on the executive committee. In 2001, I applied for TWA's CEO position and was passed over for someone who was a better fit. In 2011, I had an opportunity to serve as a TWA officer, which is a six-year commitment, culminating in serving a two-year term as TWA President. During the last few years, I have had the honor of serving as president of the Board of Trustees for the TWA Foundation, which is responsible for raising money for the natural resource education and hunting heritage programs. I have also become involved as an executive committee member with the National Deer Association, and most recently as a board member of the Dallas Safari Club. Frankly, it was a non-governmental organization (NGO) that provided me with something that was missing in my life—the opportunity to contribute toward something that was, and still is, exceptionally fulfilling. It is safe to say that had I not found TWA and become involved with this impactful organization, I probably would no longer be in the hunting and wildlife profession.

An NGO is any non-profit, citizen-based group organized on a local, national, or international level, operating independently of the government. These days, and for the sake of this discussion, an NGO is often a special interest group, sometimes but not always serving as a pressure group advocating for a particular mission. In the hunting world, we often refer to these as sportsman's groups or conservation groups. Some of these sportsman's groups include Rocky Mountain Elk Foundation, Ducks Unlimited, National Wild Turkey Federation, Safari Club International, Dallas Safari Club, Pheasants Forever, Quail Coalition, Texas Bighorn Society, National Deer Association, and many others. In the wildlife world, we have groups like The Wildlife Society, Sierra Club, Wildlife Management Institute, and National Wildlife Federation among many others. There are also similar trade groups, such as Archery Trade Association, National Shooting Sports Foundation, Texas Deer Association (TDA), Association of Fish and Wildlife Agencies, and others. You also have animal welfare and animal rights groups, such as the Humane Society of the United States, Center for Biological Diversity, People for the Ethical Treatment of Animals (PETA), and others.

Though each of these four categories of NGOs advocate for wildlife, their values and positions do not fully align, even though the first three categories tend to be more similar. Individually, all four categories of these stakeholder groups represent large numbers, both in people and funding. Taken collectively, the number of people and the amount of money represented by these groups is staggering. It raises the question, "Why can't we, especially with sportsman's groups, trade groups, and wildlife groups, do a better job of identifying common ground and working together to achieve similar goals?" Though I do not have a good answer to this question, one of the reasons I have chosen to accept the opportunity to wade into the leadership circle of three of these organizations is so that I can better understand why NGOs tend to stay in their own lane, investing little time and effort on trying to synergize their efforts between various similar groups.

Depending upon who you ask, you'll likely get a different answer regarding the role that NGOs play in this important game of conservation, and more specifically, the role that they play in advancing the need for education, advocacy, and outreach for hunters and hunting.

UNIFIED VOICE

Over the years, people have asked me, "What can I do to make a difference for wildlife and hunting?" As time has passed, my reply to this question has become an easy, stock answer: "Become involved with one of the conservation groups that aligns with your interests and values."

Millions of hunters, fishermen, and outdoor enthusiasts across the country are passionate about their pastimes. By serving as advocates for conservation and hunting, individuals can indeed "move the needle" in a positive direction. Moreover, by serving through an organization, individual efforts are amplified and their impacts multiplied. The coordinated programs of these NGOs create synergies from the collective contributions of their members and constituents.

As the late anthropologist Margaret Mead summed up well, "Never doubt that a small group of thoughtful, committed citizens can change the world; indeed, it's the only thing that ever has." The spirit of Mead's observation is the very essence, beauty, and meaning of today's conservation groups.

OUTREACH AND EDUCATION

I shared some thoughts earlier in this book regarding Richard Louv's work on nature deficit disorder. Perhaps the single greatest global challenge facing humanity today is the conservation of our natural resources. As hunters, many of us understand the importance of hunting in this conservation matrix, especially as a funding tool. However, as Americans have become removed from rural lifestyles and less aware of the importance of our natural resources, our collective knowledge about natural resources and natural resource management has diminished. Wild things, wild places, open spaces, and hunting have been marginalized at best and rendered completely irrelevant at worst.

In order to reshape the value system of society, we should begin with a more effective education that raises awareness of the natural world. To get natural resource education materials built into required curriculum in public schools at the junior high and high school levels is nothing short of an act of Congress. Using education to create a paradigm shift in regard to how we value our natural resources would best be accomplished if we could reach the masses through mandatory formal education. Perhaps we will see some changes along those lines in time, but for now, educating the public about our natural resources and management of said natural resources will require a variety of creative options.

1 > Special interest groups, also known as pressure groups, are instrumental in shaping public policy. Here, I, along with other leaders of the Texas Wildlife Association, met with then-Texas Governor Rick Perry, during the 84th Texas Legislative Session to discuss various wildlife-related issues.

2> I believe one of the hunting/conservation community's greatest weaknesses is the lack of coordinated efforts between those conservation groups that share similar missions. In my opinion, the future of hunting largely rests in the organizations' ability to "lower the walls of their silos" and work together more closely. This screenshot lists the organizations that are members of the American Wildlife Conservation Partners. This clearly illustrates the broad (albeit incomplete) assembly of NGOs that share similar missions—a massive amount of strength just waiting to be collectively applied.

3> Natural resource illiteracy and its attendant issues are the greatest challenges faced by humans as we determine the future health of our societies globally. It is important that the general public make intelligent decisions affecting natural resource and wildlife conservation. Education and leadership development programs, such as the Texas Brigades youth camps, are great ways to provide positive impacts on these fronts. Wildlife biologist Ty Bartoskewitz is shown here providing instruction to teenagers at North Texas Buckskin Brigade youth leadership camp.

4> Advocacy for our hunting heritage requires funding. NGOs raise millions of dollars each year dedicated to various conservation initiatives, including advocacy.

AWCP ORGANIZATIONS

American Woodcock Society | Archery Trade Association | Association of Fish & Wildlife Agencies | Backcountry Hunters & Anglers | Bear Trust International | Boone and Crockett Club | California Waterfowl Association | Camp Fire Club of America | Catch A Dream Foundation | Congressional Sportsmen's Foundation | Conservation Force | Council to Advance Hunting and the Shooting Sports | Dallas Safari Club | Delta Waterfowl Foundation | Ducks Unlimited | Houston Safari Club | International Hunter Education Association - USA | Izaak Walton League of America | Masters of Foxhounds Association | Mule Deer Foundation | National Association of Forest Service Retirees | National Bobwhite & Grassland Initiative | National Deer Association | National Rifle Association | National Shooting Sports Foundation | National Trappers Association | National Wild Turkey Federation | National Wildlife Federation | National Wildlife Refuge Association | North American Falconers Association | North American Grouse Partnership | Orion – The Hunter's Institute | Pheasants Forever/Quail Forever | Pope and Young Club | Professional Outfitters and Guides of America | Public Lands Foundation | Rocky Mountain Elk Foundation | Ruffed Grouse Society | Safari Club International | Shikar Safari Club | Sportsmen's Alliance | Texas Wildlife Association | The Conservation Fund | The Wildlife Society | Theodore Roosevelt Conservation Partnership | Tread Lightly! | Whitetails Unlimited | Wild Sheep Foundation | Wildlife Forever | Wildlife Management Institute | Wildlife Mississippi

Over the last ten to 15 years, more conservation groups are channeling a larger share of their energy into education programs for adults and youths. Ideally, it is best to target all sectors with these education programs, but resources can be scarce and program reach generally has its limitations. With the limited resources available, in my opinion, the two groups that should be targeted are policy makers and junior high students who are still in a formative period of their lives. When it comes to the younger generation, there are several opportunities to help shape personal values and interest, but by their junior year of high school, many have already established their own values and opinions. In my opinion, return on investments through these deployed resources diminishes beyond the sophomore or junior year in high school; values that have lasting impacts must be formed before people reach this period of their life, generally speaking.

Policymakers, such as state representatives and state senators, are generally naive or uninformed when it comes to natural resource issues. As a result, special interest groups often target these policymakers with slanted agendas that may be less about facts and truth and more about "selling a bill of goods" that may not be in the best interest of natural resources or hunting.

Ideally, outreach and education should reach, by design, all sectors of our society, but limited resources rarely allow for such broad strategies. So, being a bit more laser-focused with resource deployment is important in being effective on this front.

WILDLIFE POLICY

I am by no means a public policy expert. However, I have been actively involved in policy at the state level through the Texas Legislature since 1999. Primarily, I have provided testimony to House and Senate committees, but I have also helped raise political action committee (PAC) funds, worked with lobbyists, assisted with writing bill language, created talking points for grassroots and membership participation, and been involved in various other public policy related activities. Although this can be exciting and provocative, politics can be a slimy process, full of underhanded deals and tactics, blatant corruption of the process, dirty gamesmanship, lies, deceit, you name it. However, that is how the proverbial sausage gets made, and if you want to effect change at the legislative level, then you better learn to make sausage.

The ability for special interest groups, such as conservation groups, to influence public policy should never be underestimated. These groups are occasionally referred to as pressure groups for good reason. Most pressure groups have PAC funds that are used to show their support for state representatives and senators. Most conservation groups have meager PAC funds compared to certain trade groups, such as those in the energy, construction, medical, and transportation industries. However, a few trade groups in the wildlife world, such as the TDA, have relatively large PACs. PAC funding and the ability to influence legislators' positions on issues are only a small part of what goes into the sausage.

Paid lobbyists are integral to the process. A lobbyist is a person whose job is to try to influence public officials, usually for or against a specific policy. Lobbyists typically are employed by special interest groups that want public policies to favor them and their causes. In the pressure group world, strong lobbyists are worth their weight in gold, and most of the smaller groups cannot afford to hire some of the big name lobbyists. In fact, there are some groups that cannot afford a lobbyist at all. Those small groups will often lend ancillary support to larger and better-funded groups by joining forces with the larger group to help expand its reach.

Lobbyists often know how to gain access to elected officials, either directly or through the officials' staffers. During session years, legislators are pulled in many directions. Lobbyists are better equipped to navigate barriers and gain access to officials than the average concerned citizen. When bills are being reviewed, there is often considerable lobby action that takes place. Paid lobbyists often help negotiate and broker the necessary deals that allow certain bills to gain traction.

Although professional lobbyists play a vital and unique role, individual citizens can exert influence by contacting the elected officials who live in their districts, especially at the state level. Legislators have a duty to serve their constituents who live in their districts. Phone calls and emails to the elected officials' offices area where the grassroots connect and shape public policy. At this level, the NGOs can help organize such grassroots efforts by providing contact information and talking points on various relevant issues.

LUMPING VERSUS SPLITTING

There are many special interest groups that represent hunting and wildlife. When you throw in all the state or regional chapters that are subgroups of the parent organizations, it creates a huge suite of groups—and people—who are charged with deploying those organizations' missions.

When you create a large assembly of special interest groups that share similar values and missions, then it is common to see some friction. People have different leadership styles and levels of professionalism. Values may differ, even within the same organization. As a result, their efforts may prompt dissent and/or become counterproductive. Furthermore, these groups often compete for the same financial resources within the same geographical area from the same pool of donors whose personal interests align with that of the organizations. The constant barrage of solicitations these potential donors receive from similar interest groups can lead to "donor fatigue." At best, a larger number of similar special interest groups allows greater reach and increased human capital. At worse, it can lead to unfriendly competition and may ultimately result in in-fighting and dissension.

It is quite interesting to me how a new special interest group can form. As an NGO grows, and/or as new issues emerge, it is common for some members of an organization to feel as though their specific interests are not being represented well by the organization. In this case, sometimes a group of dissatisfied members may split off from the existing organization and form a new organization intended to best serve their unique needs.

The TDA, formed in 1999, is a case in point. Prior to then, TWA was the state's "umbrella" wildlife organization representing private landowners and a variety of wildlife enthusiasts on many fronts covering a vast number of issues. As the deer breeding industry began to rapidly grow during the mid to late 1990s, it became apparent that TWA was not representing the deer breeding industry's viewpoints and needs as closely and sufficiently as many deer breeders thought necessary. Several active TWA members, including some old guard TWA leaders, split off and formed TDA, which is a single-issue interest group focused solely on captive deer breeding. In my opinion, it was the appropriate thing to do.

ATTEMPTED COUP

For years after its formation, TDA enjoyed increased membership as the industry continued to grow. Over time, the organization's financial strength grew as well. The organization's PAC and lobbying efforts were particularly well funded.

After several years of gaining strength, TDA became more outspoken regarding its desire to seek regulatory and statutory reform to benefit the captive deer industry and the association members' interests. During that same time span, TWA began to speak out about certain deer breeding issues that were concerning to the organization's members. From roughly 2005 to 2010, tension between TDA and TWA began to escalate.

During the 2011 Texas legislative session, TDA pushed several hot button issues. During that session, there were several bills relating to the privatization of wildlife and transfer of regulatory authority from the Texas Parks and Wildlife Department (TPWD) to Texas Animal Health Commission. In addition, a bill allowing wild mule deer to be captured and placed in privately owned pens for propagation purposes was introduced. These hot button bills garnered a lot of attention from various individuals in the pro-wildlife community and prompted significant debate in committee rooms at the state capital.

TWA was caught off guard by this flurry of deer breeding-related bills and did not engage deeply during that session. The only concerning bill that passed was the mule deer DMP bill, but it was "hamstrung" when the bill's author attached a letter of intent as the bill made its way to the governor's desk. The letter of intent provided guidance by suggesting that before any permits were issued, research be conducted to provide the scientific basis for writing the rules governing the permit. In addition, the language in that bill was permissive, saying that TPWD "may" issue such a permit not that it "shall." TPWD intended to allow research to shape the permit's rules. To date, the research has not taken place, and the wild mule deer capture permit has never been implemented.

After the 2011 Texas legislative session, it became apparent that TDA was planning to implement a full-court press in 2013 to pass a huge suite of bills related to captive deer breeding. Some of the bills that were eventually introduced during that session related to the privatization of deer, the transfer of regulatory authority, the commercial sale of native deer meat, forced implementation of the mule deer DMP, deer breeder "Bill of Rights" bill, the elimination of a required external ID on released breeder-deer, and various omnibus bills for a total of 17 deer breeding-related bills. During that same time, TWA vetted and solidified its position on most of these issues, creating a clear understanding of where TWA stood. TWA eventually opposed all the deer breeding bills that were introduced.

The 2013 session was a chaotic fight between the deer breeding industry and pro-wildlife advocates. Turmoil reigned during the hearings of those bills in both the Senate and House committees, which often lasted until midnight. The atmosphere was extremely tense, divisive, and volatile. The public policy work consumed a lot of energy and money. At that time, I was the TWA Vice President and in line to assume the presidency at the TWA convention in July of that year. Previously, WSI had worked with some deer breeding operations. As I became more outspoken about my personal concerns regarding some facets of deer breeding, I was painted as a hypocrite and ultimately blacklisted by various folks in the outdoor industry. At that point, it made sense that I, at least temporarily, suspend WSI's affiliation with deer breeding programs to avoid the perception that I was saying one thing while doing another.

Just prior to the TWA convention, there was a well-organized effort by TDA operatives to "introduce" an individual to run against me during the officer election at the convention. For several weeks, this individual was promoted using egregious tactics that included someone essentially stealing the TWA membership list. The TDA operatives reached out directly to TWA's directors and members, creating an immense amount of confusion and chaos. TWA was forced to spend a considerable amount of money to hire legal counsel and a CPA firm to provide professional, objective oversight of the election process at the convention. At that time, TWA had roughly 185 voting directors. With a standing-room-only crowd, it was the best attended Directors' Meeting that the organization had ever witnessed.

TDA attempted a bona fide coup to assume some degree of control over TWA. Fortunately, the majority of TWA's directors recognized the source of the pressure and the underlying motives for the disrupted election. During the election, through proxies and ballots cast in person, approximately 135 votes were cast. I garnered more than 90 percent of those votes.

After the 2013 convention, TWA lost a small number of members who were primarily deer breeders. In my opinion, the association became a stronger advocate for our values and positions related to deer breeding than it was before. And we, at TWA, became stronger wildlife advocates in general. While TWA is not an anti-deer breeding organization, it has over time staked out clear positions on certain issues related to captive deer breeding. The organization has continued to successfully assist in killing the hot button bills that TDA has continued to push.

The conflict between TWA and TDA provides a lengthy example of what occurs when similar special interest groups are lumped and split. Their missions are not always congruent, and their paths are not always parallel. Ideally, all special interest groups advocating for hunting and wildlife would work together in a more cohesive and coordinated fashion, whatever that might look like—perhaps looking quite different between various effective scenarios. By doing so, we would have a stronger front against those people who seek to destroy our hunting heritage and valued traditions.

The NGO world is vital to our efforts to effectively advocate for hunters' rights and serve as a voice for our important wildlife resources. As I previously mentioned, to maximize the efforts of our diverse special interest groups, we must look for ways to create better synergy through a more organized strategy, as well as by bundling our resources collectively to create stronger, more efficient platforms.

The American Wildlife Conservation Partners (AWCP) is a consortium of approximately 50 organizations that represent the interests of millions of American hunters, conservationists, professional wildlife and natural resource managers, outdoor recreation users, conservation educators, and wildlife scientists. Ideally, a consortium like AWCP should serve as a common platform for this broad suite of NGOs, allowing them to easily work together and advocate for our common causes more formidably.

Though AWCP has helped create a place where these groups can communicate and share thoughts that provide a better understanding of our challenges, it is my opinion that our broad conservation world still falls miserably short when it comes to maximizing our collective efforts. We must do a better job at finding ways to play in the same sandbox peacefully and strategically with purpose and design. We must learn to play the game smarter if we are going to continue to win future battles while serving as hunting and wildlife advocates. I expound on this topic in greater detail in this book's final chapter, "The Future of Hunting," as I examine some thoughts on key strategies for carving a successful path for hunters as we move further into the future.

20 **LESSONS FROM COVID-19**

THE EMERGENCE OF COVID-19 CAUGHT THE WORLD UNAWARE AND UNPREPARED. THE PANDEMIC FOREVER CHANGED INDUSTRIES AROUND THE GLOBE, INCLUDING THE HUNTING BUSINESS.

COVID-19 had been in the news for some time but appeared to be nothing more than a slight distraction in our lives. In a matter of days, COVID-19 turned this country on its head like never before. Prior to the pandemic, it was unfathomable that federal and state executive orders could—and would—shut down a large portion of America's economy and bring people's lives to a standstill. In short order, broad travel restrictions, border closures, shelter-in-place orders, empty buildings, empty airports, and empty lives were the order of the day. The eerie scenes seemed almost as if they were carved out of an Alfred Hitchcock movie, but that is exactly what unfolded. The entire world watched in confusion and chaos during this unprecedented time.

As I make these final edits, I doubt that there is anyone who can fully understand the complexities of what we have seen through this global pandemic, but there are certainly lessons to be learned on many fronts from these challenging times. Among many other things, COVID-19 has taught us that fear can control our society. It has also taught us that the window for inciting fear, and the time it takes to create a shift in our comfort levels, is amazingly small. We have proven that when pressures, such as human health, fear, and the idea of social injustice, are applied with enough intensity, radical change within our society can occur within days. Considering that the political and cultural standards that have defined our country were shaped over a period of more than 200 years, it is mind-boggling to think that so much can unravel in mere days—not months, years, or decades, but days. It is important that we, as Americans, take time to consider, evaluate, and understand the changes as well as the process and speed of changes that occurred.

So, what does this mean for our hunting world? To be honest, I am still trying to digest it all. From my perspective, if a radical, politically motivated group can force the elimination of our historical identity by tearing down statues and defacing our collective identity, all while handcuffing law enforcement, then I think it is safe to say that similar pressures can also be applied to other areas of our society. The targets and motives will depend on the goals of certain special interest groups. Groups, such as those with anti-hunting agendas, are certain to be paying attention to the strategies that have been used to successfully force change during the COVID-19 pandemic. I predict anti-hunting groups will adopt similar strategies, including bullying, inciting anger, and provoking fear, to advance their agendas. If the radical left successfully forces Americans to wash away America's historical identity, then they can certainly force the elimination of our important hunting heritage.

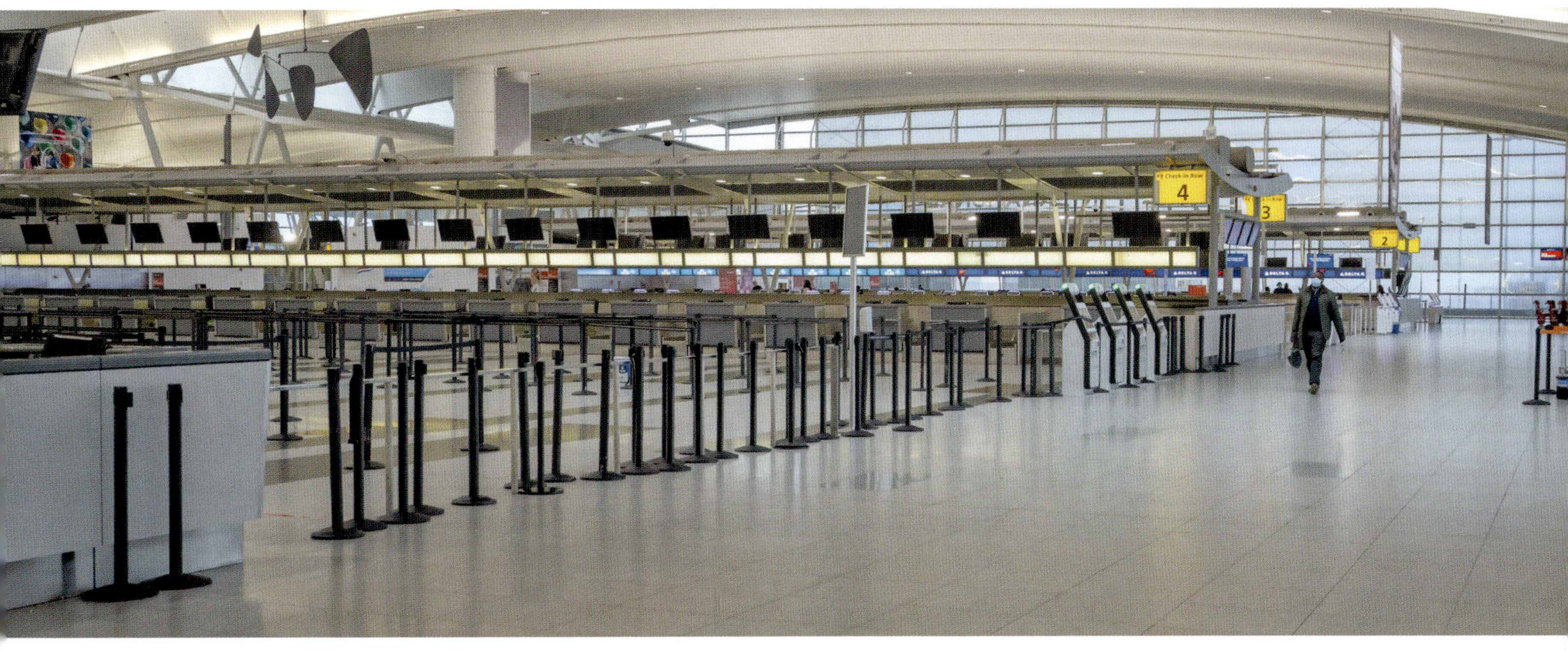

For decades, hunters, as one defense strategy, have showcased the historic role that hunter-conservationists played in the American wildlife conservation revolution. We often point to Theodore Roosevelt as the most influential political figure in shaping natural resource policy and protecting the natural resources we continue to enjoy. While Roosevelt is undeniably an American natural resource hero, during the throes of the 2021 social injustice protests, approval was granted to remove a statue of Roosevelt from the American Museum of Natural History in New York on the basis that this statue could be considered offensive and potentially interpreted as promoting white supremacy. If a special interest group can effectively force that kind of change, then there are no bounds to such politically motivated work. It raises the question whether future generations will have any clue of the role that hunter-conservationists have played in securing the health and welfare of wildlife in this country. This is very concerning.

In my opinion, COVID-19 has been a political boon for the radical left to advance an agenda of moving our government and society toward socialism. One can quickly look at the countries that have socialist and communist regimes and see that hunting is almost nonexistent. It appears socialism is gaining tremendous momentum in much of our society right now. As people continue to use this pandemic to advance political agendas by controlling

ABOVE > COVID-19 held the world hostage in 2020, shutting down international travel in many parts of the world for over a year and curtailing domestic travel for several months in the U.S. Although the jury is still out on the pandemic's long-term effects, it appears that the silver lining is that Americans responded to the lock-down by connecting or reconnecting with nature. This prompted an unprecedented increase in outdoor-related recreational spending. Is this phenomenon a paradigm change or pendulum swing?

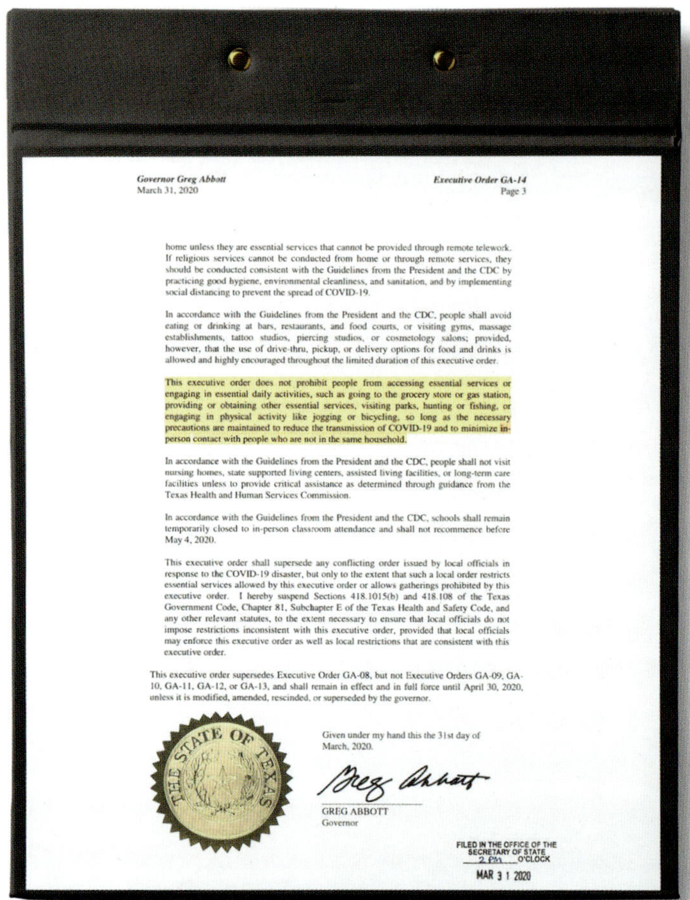

Governor Greg Abbott
March 31, 2020

Executive Order GA-14
Page 3

home unless they are essential services that cannot be provided through remote telework. If religious services cannot be conducted from home or through remote services, they should be conducted consistent with the Guidelines from the President and the CDC by practicing good hygiene, environmental cleanliness, and sanitation, and by implementing social distancing to prevent the spread of COVID-19.

In accordance with the Guidelines from the President and the CDC, people shall avoid eating or drinking at bars, restaurants, and food courts, or visiting gyms, massage establishments, tattoo studios, piercing studios, or cosmetology salons; provided, however, that the use of drive-thru, pickup, or delivery options for food and drinks is allowed and highly encouraged throughout the limited duration of this executive order.

This executive order does not prohibit people from accessing essential services or engaging in essential daily activities, such as going to the grocery store or gas station, providing or obtaining other essential services, visiting parks, hunting or fishing, or engaging in physical activity like jogging or bicycling, so long as the necessary precautions are maintained to reduce the transmission of COVID-19 and to minimize in-person contact with people who are not in the same household.

In accordance with the Guidelines from the President and the CDC, people shall not visit nursing homes, state supported living centers, assisted living facilities, or long-term care facilities unless to provide critical assistance as determined through guidance from the Texas Health and Human Services Commission.

In accordance with the Guidelines from the President and the CDC, schools shall remain temporarily closed to in-person classroom attendance and shall not recommence before May 4, 2020.

This executive order shall supersede any conflicting order issued by local officials in response to the COVID-19 disaster, but only to the extent that such a local order restricts essential services allowed by this executive order or allows gatherings prohibited by this executive order. I hereby suspend Sections 418.1015(b) and 418.108 of the Texas Government Code, Chapter 81, Subchapter E of the Texas Health and Safety Code, and any other relevant statutes, to the extent necessary to ensure that local officials do not impose restrictions inconsistent with this executive order, provided that local officials may enforce this executive order as well as local restrictions that are consistent with this executive order.

This executive order supersedes Executive Order GA-08, but not Executive Orders GA-09, GA-10, GA-11, GA-12, or GA-13, and shall remain in effect and in full force until April 30, 2020, unless it is modified, amended, rescinded, or superseded by the governor.

Given under my hand this the 31st day of March, 2020.

GREG ABBOTT
Governor

FILED IN THE OFFICE OF THE
SECRETARY OF STATE
2 PM O'CLOCK
MAR 3 1 2020

LEFT > I believe one of the ways WSI coped with the chaos in the early days of COVID-19 was researching, understanding and keeping up with the regulatory allowances governing travel. When Texas Governor Greg Abbott signed Executive Order GA-14 on March 31, 2020, it declared hunting and fishing as an essential daily activity, providing a clear path forward for WSI. In my opinion, the team's time-consuming diligence in this area allowed WSI to avoid catastrophic business impacts.

our society through fear, I can see the possibility of a bona fide socialist regime running our country in the next decade. If that happens, it is likely that hunting, as we historically know it, will be a thing of the past. The prospect is scary, but from reading the tea leaves, we are unfortunately pointing that way. Obviously, these are my personal opinions, and I am not trying to push them off on anyone else. We all know what they say about opinions.

The clear and obvious impacts that COVID-19 has had on the hunting world are immense and highly varied around the globe. Unfortunately, virtually all of my colleagues who operate a hunting business outside of the U.S. lost most, and in some cases all of their business in 2020 because of travel restrictions and concerns. In some countries, much of their business was largely lost in 2021 as well. As one would expect, some of those businesses went under, and many are trying to hold on as they replenish their financial stability. I cannot imagine how any business can remain viable after losing two consecutive years of income. The cascading effects of lost hunting revenue are huge. In most areas of Africa, safari revenues provide the money to support anti-poaching efforts. The money is also vital for drilling water wells for humans, livestock, and wildlife. Communal areas and local people rely on those safari revenues to help undergird their fragile economies. Lost safari trade not only translates into a conservation funding crisis, but a humanitarian crisis as well.

Here in the U.S., the impact of COVID-19 on our hunting world has been very different, at least for now. For WSI, from about March 15th through early May 2020 it was utter chaos. We had more than 100 hunters from 12 different states booked to hunt with us during that time. Several weeks were spent trying to understand legal allowances for travel and integrating enhanced risk management strategies into our routine. Our team spent hundreds of hours on the phone trying to sort out each situation and all of its related contingencies. That six-week period was the most unpleasant and stressful period of my career. However, our commitment to understanding the process as it was evolving, and staying hyper-focused on retaining as much business as possible, ended up paying off. We retained much of our booked business during the throes of the pandemic with very few hiccups. We weathered the initial storm and came out of May with both nostrils above water. Maintaining our focus and drive, we plowed through the remainder of 2020.

By mid-May of 2020, our business began to spike. For the most part, this increased business activity was being driven by international hunting cancellations. Money that was already dedicated to hunting began shifting from international destinations to domestic ones, and a piece of that pie landed squarely on our awaiting plate. Then we began to receive calls from people who were spooked by potential beef shortages. Those people were interested in hunting animals such as nilgai that are large and palatable. The demand for various hunts continued to escalate through the summer, and by September/October it reached a climax. Thankfully, the heightened demand for hunts carried forward into 2021 and then on into 2022, and as of this final edit in July of 2022, I can say that I've never seen another lengthy run of strong business activity like this one.

On April 1, 2020, I predicted WSI's worst year in the business. We were not only dealing with the fears and chaos of COVID-19, but we were also in the early throes of an oil/gas industry crash, which has historically resulted in a soft economy and reduced spending on leisure trips like hunting. Despite all the challenges, 2020 ended up being a record sales year for WSI and 2021 was even stronger, with 2022 being on an equally good trajectory.

In 2020, presumably in response to COVID-19, hunting license sales were up in every state in the U.S. This is the first time that has happened in many years. In addition, virtually all outdoor-related product lines have been tallying record sales since mid-summer of 2020. This certainly raises the question—What has been driving this activity? I think there are several contributing factors.

CONTRIBUTING FACTORS TO SALES INCREASES

1. The international cancellations and travel hurdles have certainly shifted the market to domestic hunting opportunities.

2. Because of the "lockdown," a high percentage of Americans stayed at home, which limited their spending and allowed them to accrue more discretionary cash than normal; many of those people deployed that money into the hunting market by the latter part of 2020.

3. Gun sales skyrocketed in 2020, with more new gun owners than ever before in this country. Some of those new gun owners wanted to put their firearms to use, so various shooting sports, including hunting, provided viable options for using their guns.

4. The lockdowns likely created, even if it was subconsciously, a desire within Americans to reclaim their lives. When the ability to enjoy things they had previously taken for granted was denied, I suspect that society's mindset was "retooled." In my opinion, the freedoms and luxuries that were taken away forced people to reassess what was important to them. Ultimately, it resulted in people wanting to connect or reconnect with the outdoor world, which increased our collective appetite for hunting, fishing, camping, boating, backpacking, and enjoying the pleasures that cannot be found in the confines of four walls.

I think we can look at the things I just mentioned as the silver linings of COVID-19, but the quick shifts raise some questions. Do these market changes reflect a paradigm shift that is long-term, or do they reflect a classic pendulum effect where the interest swings to an extreme high point and then almost as quickly swings back to its pre-pandemic level? Currently, there is an unprecedented opportunity for our professional hunting and wildlife communities to attempt to understand these market changes and learn how to leverage these emerging opportunities. Some state agencies and NGOs are evaluating this data as it emerges. It is no secret that our hunting community must learn to play the game smarter. In my opinion, this is an opportunity for us to do just that—seizing the moment and channeling our efforts to ensure a clearer understanding and a positive outcome.

Our outdoor world has always been a place where many people seek solace in times of stress and adversity. The pandemic, through shelter-in-place orders, effectively robbed many people of the freedom found in the outdoors. Even though people have moved into metro areas and away from the outdoors, a human's DNA is hardwired with a desire to connect to the natural world. I believe this proved that human health, physical and mental, requires the ability to connect with nature at some level, and I think there are some deep, emotional, and spiritual benefits derived from such relationships with our natural environments. The recent spike we have seen in the amount of time and money invested in outdoor recreation is undoubtedly a form of healing from the stresses and pressures that were created through the lifestyle suppression that began in 2020. It is also a classic example of how humans often take things for granted until those things are taken away from them. Basic shelter-in-place orders and being denied the enjoyment of customary activities is certainly an example of losing a basic freedom—freedom to escape the pressures of life. I think it is safe to say the pandemic has forced us to learn more about ourselves on many fronts, including our innate need to connect with nature.

Even at the time of this final edit and fine-tuning of this book in July of 2022, we have yet to enter into what I think can be described as the post-COVID, so nobody can fully understand how our American and global value-systems will be shaped through this entire pandemic period, but I think it is safe to surmise that we are in the early stages of the most profound environmental movement that our country, or any other, has ever witnessed. Alternative green energy, carbon emission offsets, regenerative grazing practices, sustainability, and the emphasis being placed on ESG investing are simply a few examples of groundswell changes and pressures that are bubbling up. Trying to reconcile what all these evolving changes mean and how they will translate into continued paradigms of the future is mind-twisting when one begins to read deeply into this mix.

LEFT > Unfortunately, travel or trip cancellation insurance is rarely booked by hunters who spend large sums of money on hunting trips. Even after COVID-19 wreaked havoc on all areas of the travel industry, clients still seldom purchase this type of protection.

One of the more surprising aspects of this pandemic as it relates to the hunting business is that traveling hunters have not changed their customary practices regarding their interest in purchasing trip cancellation insurance. We have been promoting the importance of this type of protection to our clients for over 20 years, dating back to the international travel interruptions that followed the terrorist attacks on September 11, 2001. Even though there are many insurance plans that do not cover pandemics, there are programs these days that do offer such coverage. But none the less, there are simply very few people that take advantage of these insurance products. Inevitably, when we have someone that inquires about their options and consequences when it looks like they may have to cancel, the first thing I ask them is, "Did you purchase trip cancellation insurance as we recommended?" Rarely have they done so.

Humanity is complex and unpredictable. I would have never imagined America (and the world) could—or would—shut down like it did in 2020. Furthermore, I would have never dreamed that we could shut down our economy for several months and then emerge, generally speaking, as vibrantly as we seem to be at this point. This is a testimony to how resilient Americans can be, but at the same time, we have proven there are change agents who can alter our world beyond imagination in a matter of days—and that scares me. We live in a "microwave time," where heat can be applied quickly and invisibly and transform life as we know it, and this should serve as a stark reminder that hunters must vigilantly and effectively advocate to maintain their role as conservators of wild things and wild places.

21 THE FUTURE OF HUNTING

THIS IS THE FIRST BOOK I HAVE WRITTEN, AND IT MAY BE MY LAST. I LAUNCHED THIS PROJECT OVER TWELVE YEARS AGO AND THEN SUSPENDED IT WHEN I GOT ABOUT 50,000 WORDS IN. THEN ABOUT FOUR YEARS AGO, I DECIDED TO SCRAP THE INITIAL MANUSCRIPT AND START OVER.

This closing chapter, "The Future of Hunting," is the most important chapter in this book. As you know, the four previous chapters covered some heavy material, including issues related to sustainability, conservation, the role of NGOs, lessons from COVID-19, and other topics that are inextricably woven into the future of hunting. I have already presented considerable information regarding where we have been and how we got here, so I will close by discussing how I believe our hunting community must approach future challenges if we are to remain relevant in a changing world.

CONTROLLING THE NARRATIVE

The late Nigerian novelist Chinua Achebe once famously quoted an African proverb that says, "Until the lions have their own historians, the history of the hunt will always glorify the hunter." I suspect that Achebe's point was reasonable when he brought the proverb to the attention of the masses, but I wonder if he anticipated that those "historians" would someday include the ranks of uninformed social media pundits, fake news promulgators, and a host of forces defying conventional wisdom and shaping the narrative in unprecedented ways. Furthermore, "the history of the hunt," in most cases, no longer glorifies the hunter. In fact, hunters rarely control the narrative defining how American society views hunters, hunting, or the merits of the two.

During its most recent cycle, "The National Survey of Fishing, Hunting, and Wildlife-Associated Recreation," conducted by the USFWS every five years since 1955, revealed an alarming statistic. From 2012—2016, hunting license sales across the nation dropped by almost 20 percent. This drastic reduction in hunting license sales paints a seemingly ominous picture for the future of this pastime that for more than 100 years has served as the chief funding mechanism for terrestrial wildlife conservation and as an important part of America's cultural fabric since the nation's founding. The percentage of Americans who hunt is now slightly below four percent. When just four percent of the population engages in a pursuit, when do they and their preferred pursuit become irrelevant to the rest of society? I suspect we are staring that threshold in the face, right now.

Contrary to the decline in hunting license sales from 2012—2016, the U.S. did see a relatively strong spike in hunting license sales during the pandemic years of 2020 and in 2021, which provides renewed hope. With that said, if we are going to honestly assess the strength and stability of our hunting community today, we cannot simply rely on "one or two good years" as our barometer. Rather, we must look at long-term trends. In that context, the general track record with hunting license sales in the U.S. since 2012 is indeed alarming. Now, our hunting community can simply fret over "better days gone by" or we can—and should—explore the reason for the decline in hunting participation over the last decade or so. And as a community, we should do a better job of controlling the narrative surrounding hunting, including policing the messages and images we broadcast to society at large.

CONTROL THE NARRATIVE

SOCIAL MEDIA

Like it or not, social media has quickly emerged as the medium of choice for most of society's daily "news and information." This largely uncensored and unedited communication tool holds a vast sea of material. At any point, a single incident or post can "go viral" and shape the public view of any issue du jour.

"Cecil the Lion" is a prime example of how social media participants can write hunting's narrative and shape its future using a single incident. In this case, social media erupted with the news of the death of Cecil, a 13-year-old male lion that lived on the Hwange National Park in Zimbabwe. Even though the lion was legally harvested with a compound bow outside the park by Dr. Walter Palmer, an American dentist, the fact that the lion was known to range at times within the park and the fact that the cat was radio collared for research was enough to create a public backlash. The global reaction was swift and harsh. Hunting and hunters were scourged on the whipping posts of public opinion. If public attention is ever focused on the egregious deer breeding practices that emphasize big antlers at all costs, the outcry prompted by Cecil the Lion could very easily become outrage on behalf of Bucky the Deer.

I am not a social media expert, but I think that hunters, individually and collectively through NGOs, need to use social media more wisely and more deliberately. It starts with being better stewards of our online content, whether it is hunting photos, hunting stories, comments on other hunts and harvests, on anything else that can shape someone else's opinion of our cherished tradition. I see plenty of garbage posted by hunters which paints a poor image of hunting, especially distasteful photos that create or reinforce stereotypes of hunters as bloodthirsty, immoral, and trashy. When it comes to sharing wholesome stories or messages that clearly articulate the beauty of the hunt and illustrate hunting as a conservation tool, we fall short. Although we understand the hunting narrative better than anyone else, we are often our own worst enemy and provide those who do not understand or value it with additional ammunition to attack it.

AMPLIFYING MESSAGES THROUGH NGOs

Historically, hunters have banded together by affiliating with various sportsman's groups. We can point to many NGOs as shining examples of hunters raising money and channeling sweat equity into causes that are good for hunting and good for our wildlife resources. Our hunting NGOs seem to fall short, however, when it comes to working together in a manner that aggregates resources, land creates synergy and efficiency. There is a separate section later in this chapter that expounds on the importance of collaboration between NGOs, but I would be remiss to not mention the role that NGOs must play in "controlling the narrative" if our hunting community is going to win the war on public messaging; in fact, messaging campaigns will only succeed if conservation groups are working in concert to amplify a voice that effectively resonates with the public.

SHAPING PUBLIC POLICY

In order to affect the most change or maintain the strongest defense, it is crucial for the hunting community to control the narrative by telling hunting's story from our perspective in the public policy arena where the laws, rules, and regulations governing wildlife and hunting are written. While democracy is designed so the will of the people is expressed through elected officials and appointed policy makers, special interest groups, who strategically control the narrative, position themselves to advance their agendas. Unfortunately, the hunting community is not generally well-organized when it comes to showcasing hunting's story through media outreach, public testimony, legislative relationship building, and general education. While we are making some progress in this area, we continue to fall short.

Societal opinions and pressures often shape public policy. These days the non-hunting community tends to apply more pressure than the hunting community. Hunters need to learn to play the game smarter. Collectively, there is not a good reason why our hunting community, through the leadership of NGOs, cannot better control hunting's narrative within the public policy arena.

Unfortunately, state wildlife agency employees have their hands tied when it comes to expressing their opinions to their state legislatures. As public employees, staffers must remain neutral. Historically, when these agency experts go out on a limb and assert their expertise on policy matters, some special interest group will cry foul. It often results in expensive, time-consuming legal wrangling that drains agency resources. As a result, citizens must shoulder the responsibility and engage in these policy proceedings. Unfortunately, our pro-wildlife groups have not carried the weight to the extent necessary. Again, we need to do a better job of controlling the narrative.

Controlling the narrative, regardless of the issue at hand, can certainly be oversimplified. I recognize that there are many more pressures than those I have discussed in this chapter that are affecting the future of hunting. However, the bottom line is that our hunting community must strive for excellence as we step up to microphones and media channels and tell the story of hunting while attempting to control the narrative. We must do a better job with public relations. We must generate stronger messages that are part of better strategies and repeat those messages on many fronts. And we must do a better job of managing our own troops. Otherwise, we will lose the battle!

R3 INITIATIVES
(RECRUITMENT, RETENTION AND REACTIVATION)

I would be leaving a glaring gap if I discussed the future of hunting without mentioning the concept of R3: Recruit, Retain, and Reactivate. Many R3 initiatives have been launched across the country over the last few years. I have reviewed several of the R3 plans, and there are some similarities in each of them. Within the last few years, Texas Parks and Wildlife Department crafted perhaps the most practical and easy to understand document that I have seen thus far.

An entire book could be written on R3 strategies regarding hunting, but I am simply going to share some personal thoughts and opinions regarding the importance of recruiting, retaining, and reactivating those hunters who have taken a sabbatical from the tradition.

HUNTER RECRUITMENT

ABOVE > Robust participation in U.S. hunting in the future will largely hinge on the success of the many R3 initiatives that are being implemented around the country. Recruitment, retention, and re-activation all serve important roles. Getting kids involved in hunting is critically important, but it is only one ingredient in the necessary recipe.

CHILDREN

Plenty of studies show that certain values become imprinted during the formative periods of our lives. By the time we finish high school, if not sooner, certain cultural values and customs that largely define the remainder of our lives are solidly established. As Americans continue to become more urbanized, a larger percentage of our population is disconnected from rural activities, including hunting.

To become hunters, most young people need a mentor such as a parent, grandparent, uncle/aunt, or family friend to introduce them to the sport. Unfortunately, most kids these days do not have a relationship with an adult who is an active hunter, which creates a barrier to entry. In my opinion, lack of experienced mentorship is the elephant in the room regarding hunter recruitment. Until we figure out how to provide kids with mentored hunting opportunities, we will struggle to refill our ranks.

Over the last ten to 20 years, some excellent youth hunting programs, such as the Texas Youth Hunting Program created by TWA and TPWD or the Jakes Program administered by the National Wild Turkey Federation, have emerged. These programs are designed to create affordable and convenient options for kids to participate in hunting and other shooting sports. We need to look for ways to increase the size and impact of these types of programs so that their efforts are not just blips on the radar.

To get kids interested in hunting, we may need to use a graduated approach and start them out in other shooting sports, such as archery, trap, skeet, sporting clays, or even plinking cans with BB guns. Once young people have been involved with recreational shooting, I think that a percentage of those kids will have a greater interest in experiencing hunting. Fishing is another indirect portal of entry into hunting, and fishing is often less expensive and offers easier access for new and young anglers. And lets face it, fishing is the aquatic form of hunting, but our hunting/angling cultures evolved through a bifurcated lineage along the way, and we now view these activities as distinctly separate practices.

Kids are the future of hunting. As a result, our hunting community, despite any existing challenges, must develop better strategies for introducing young people to hunting and getting them into the field.

WOMEN

It stands to reason that once women get involved in hunting, the rest of the family will likely follow. I suspect there is some, if not a lot, of truth in this idea.

In recent decades, the emergence of hunting programs geared toward women have engendered enthusiastic participation. These successful programs again raise the question: How do we increase the scale of these programs so they have greater reach and impact? Breaking down cultural barriers that may have discouraged or prevented women from hunting is where stronger engagement begins. In recent years, I think we have made great progress in this area.

To foster more participation by women in the outdoors and hunting in particular, product manufactures, product dealers, service providers, NGOs, and agency personnel are all actively contributing to a concerted effort to create interest and programs that bring women into our hunting community. Again, we have seen progress, but we fall short of where we need to be in terms of broad participation.

COST

How many times over the last few decades have we heard a comment like, "Hunting has become a rich man's sport?"

We can deflect or downplay this by saying things like: "It is also expensive to go to Disney World;" "Trophy hunting is expensive, but small game hunting is not;" "It is a matter of prioritizing your values on where you spend your discretionary dollars," or any number of other responses.

These responses, however well intentioned, are meaningless. If—and when—the majority of people perceive that hunting has grown too expensive, then, that is the reality. And indeed, the cost of hunting often prevents many Americans from becoming active hunters, plain and simple.

When it comes to open access and cost, we have state and federally owned lands where public access is provided. Some public areas are come and go. Others require a permit, and still others are limited entry areas where a lottery system determines who can hunt there. These public areas are generally more affordable, and cost is typically not considered to be a barrier to entry.

Some hunters complain that many of these public areas are overcrowded, and the hunting quality is often not very good. Other hunters, who diligently explore all options and seek out more remote and less crowded locales, maintain that quality opportunities exist on these public lands for those who are willing to make the extra effort.

We also have privately owned lands where the public is not allowed or is only allowed by invitation or through a fee-based system. Hunting on private lands offers a classic conundrum for many. Trespassing signs prevent access onto private property and are certainly fundamental to private property rights in this country. Obviously, these private property rights are an important part of the American fabric, and yet, many of these same privately owned properties offer fee-based hunting programs that allow the public restricted access to the land in exchange for a payment. The downside to fee-based hunting is that many potential hunters cannot afford the fees associated with some private hunting opportunities.

One of the upsides to a fee-based access system is that the profit created through these free enterprise markets incentivize private landowners to maintain wildlife habitat on their land. Many of these landowners become active land stewards, implementing management practices that improve the diversity, abundance, and health of both game and non-game species. Some of the highest quality hunting in the U.S. is found on well-managed private lands. In the hunting industry, we must wrestle with the conundrum that arises when the matter of limited public access is weighed against the elevated stewardship of the wildlife resources on these lands.

Most economists say the balance between supply and demand will ultimately dictate the cost of hunting on these privately owned lands. If our hunter numbers continue to decline faster than the supply of hunting on these private lands, then one could reason that the access fees for hunting these properties would eventually drop, making such fee-based hunting programs more affordable to the hunting public.

It remains to be seen whether an economic-based relationship realistically applies to this scenario. Thus far, even though hunter numbers are declining in some areas, I generally have not seen the prices drop, with the notable exception of guided whitetail hunts in some regions. As I previously mentioned, I believe price drops for whitetail hunting are more closely associated with the effects of the captive deer breeding industry's artificially and intensively mass-produced monster whitetails that have tarnished whitetails in the eyes of many hunters. Nonetheless, cost will always be a factor governing the participation in any activity. It is what it is—and it certainly applies to hunting.

In my opinion, the hunting community should do a better job promoting and "monetizing" small game and game birds as more affordable hunting options, thus fueling hunter recruitment.

SMALL GAME

Unfortunately, somewhere along the way, we appear to have lost interest in small game hunting. At one point, small game and game birds played a large role in training young hunters and recruiting them into the hunting culture. As best as I can tell, my generation was the last generation where rabbit and squirrel hunting were the most common portals into hunting. During the 1960s and '70s, a large portion of America was still rural. It was not uncommon for American kids, ages six to ten years, to grab their BB guns, .22 rimfires or .410 shotguns and head to the field, often with no adult supervision. My friends and I did it—and we lived in a sleepy suburban community just outside of Dallas. These days, it is almost unheard of for six to ten-year-old kids to have those opportunities and freedoms.

Previously, this "free-range" mentality shared by parents and children helped foster an interest in hunting, which led to hunter recruitment. Back then kids generally started out hunting squirrels and rabbits before moving to big game species such as deer when they were older. Over time, small game hunting declined and deer became the introductory species for many young hunters and other newcomers. Whitetails tend to be prolific game animals. With the rise of quality deer management practices over the last 30 to 40 years, shooting does has been emphasized as a herd management tool that also created an assortment of opportunities that are often more affordable and readily available. As mentioned previously, deer are often the point of entry for most new hunters these days. This is neither necessarily a good nor bad thing. However, from my vantage point, it appears that introducing new hunters to our tradition through big game instead of small game has some pitfalls.

Kids who grow up throwing rocks at various objects in the field tend to develop good hand-eye coordination, and the same thing applies to kids who grow up regularly shooting a BB gun. Because .22 rimfires and .410 shotguns are often lighter and shorter, they are easier for young hunters to handle, which makes it easier for youngsters to become comfortable handling and proficient at using a gun. Small caliber guns also have less recoil, so it is often easier to establish good shooting techniques for inexperienced shooters. Then, when these hunters begin shooting larger caliber guns, the transition is an easier and more fulfilling one. The idea of younger hunters working through a graduated process serves retention well, in my opinion.

Animals with big brown eyes can be problematic for some first-time hunters. Some people have anthropomorphic values and attach human attributes such as emotions to animals. A percentage of new hunters may find it disturbing to walk up to their first deer harvest, encounter a majestic animal with a large face, big eyes and long lashes. They may be stricken with such remorse that it turns them off hunting forever. On the other hand, small game animals, such as rabbits, squirrels, and game birds, do not typically elicit the same emotions or psychological responses as bigger animals with human-like features. Because of this, I think smaller animals provide an easier "acclimation" for new hunters. Plus, cleaning a deer involves much larger quantities of blood and innards, which people with sensitive stomachs may find off putting.

If a person's first car is a new luxury vehicle, it will be hard for that person to ever get excited about purchasing a used economy car. It is just human nature. Whereas, if a person's first vehicle is well-used and shows plenty of wear, then that person may be ecstatic about their next vehicle being a low mileage, clean vehicle. It is likely they will appreciate a new vehicle more when they can eventually afford one. I think there are some similarities between buying vehicles and experiencing hunting, at least when it comes to delayed gratification and satisfaction. I think that new hunters who start off with big game generally find the idea of hunting rabbits or squirrels less exciting, or maybe even beneath them. And I think it is a mistake to allow young hunters to shoot trophy-quality animals too early in their hunting careers, because it tends to limit their ability to appreciate hunting for what it should be. Kids who are fortunate to bag a trophy class animal (of any species) early on may place too much emphasis on size and score instead of enjoying the hunting experience. In my opinion, "too much, too soon" can also result in premature attrition because those young hunters lose interest and move on to something else that is more exciting to them.

From my perspective, small game hunting is a great way for new hunters to move confidently into the hunting experience. Then as their skills, appreciation, and appetite mature, big game hunting provides the proverbial icing on the cake and incrementally develops their appreciation and love for hunting, ultimately creating deeper appreciation for hunting and increasing longevity or retention as a hunter.

LOCAVORE MOVEMENT

Over the last decade, a new trend has emerged within a segment of the hunting community. These hunters place more value on the game meat as a "trophy" instead of antlers or horns. Furthermore, this evolving value within hunting reflects the progressive foodie movement that has emerged within our culture.

The foodie trend most relevant to hunting is sometimes referred to as the locavore movement. As part of the locavore movement, hunters want to actively collect or hunt the food and process it themselves. In this regard, the locavore movement is similar to homesteading, which is another recent trend that promotes a lifestyle of self-sufficiency.

Today, locavores are one of the fastest growing segments of our hunting community. When we discuss hunter recruitment, we must explore these fertile sources and strategically develop ways to cultivate their interest and participation. It is one thing to embrace an opportunity, but it is another to actively nurture such opportunities. Fortunately, we are beginning to see programs, such as the Wild Harvest Initiative, that showcase the benefits of food derived from hunting and fishing. The broad benefits of harvesting and consuming fish and game have never been calculated on a large scale in North America.

By clearly demonstrating that foods derived from wild fish and game have legitimate benefits, such as providing plentiful lean, unadulterated protein and adding a local food source that can be considered part of national food security, we can promote hunting and fishing in a new, effective way. And if our society widely accepts hunting as a responsible, respectful activity that yields meaningful benefits for human health and life, then it can change the discussion surrounding hunting and conceivably create new opportunities to attract and retain hunters. (I will expound more on this "food part of the hunt" later in this chapter.)

HUNTER RETENTION

When we contemplate the future of hunting through the number of hunters and their participation, we tend to focus much of our attention and funding on recruitment. In business development, many companies become so engaged in recruiting new clients that they overlook the benefits of maintaining their existing clients. The adage, "It is less expensive to keep an existing customer than to find a new one," is valid in our hunting world.

While I am sure there are current statistics that clearly illustrate hunting recruitment and attrition rates, this book is not designed to delve deeply into the science behind these big issues. Suffice it to say, we in the hunting community cannot afford to ignore the strategies for hunter retention. I will even venture to say that the average participation of newer hunters, such as the millennial generation and others who have become involved with hunting over the last 20 years, is likely much shorter than those who were born prior to 1970. Again, these are generalizations, but these opinions are based on a lifetime of experience garnered from being around hunters on a daily basis.

Some factors, such as financial barriers, impact recruitment as well as retention. While I have addressed a few of these items, I also want to address a few pressures in today's culture that impact our ability to retain hunters for longer periods of time.

FAMILY INVOLVEMENT

In recent years, the American "nuclear family" and its historic role in our culture has garnered a lot of attention. Through much of our modern history, the traditional nuclear family implied a male husband/father, a female wife/mother, and two or three children making up a family unit. In this now-stereotypical structure, the man served as the primary breadwinner while the woman was a stay-at-home mom who managed household affairs and reared the children.

This family structure assumed that the father and sons would spend time together doing "masculine" activities such as carpentry, yard work, and hunting, while the mother and daughters would engage in "feminine" pursuits such as cooking, cleaning, and sewing. Granted, I have painted the "accepted" family culture broadly to illustrate some points, but generally this culture did not encourage females to become hunters. Over time, the traditional American nuclear family has evolved into something quite different. Today, single parent families are common, traditional gender roles are neither accepted nor clearly defined, and our lifestyle is fast-paced and ruled by digital technology.

It is less common for young men to have a father figure who can help mentor their participation as hunters or anglers. Children often spend less time with their mothers because it is common for women to work outside of the home. On top of the evolving family structure, most families now live in urban or suburban areas. This new family structure does not have a convenient point of entry to usher young people into hunting or fishing, nor does it favor them finding their way into the outdoors.

Obviously, this evolving structure does not favor hunter recruitment, but just as importantly, it does not favor hunter retention either. There needs to be someone within the family to encourage and facilitate hunting opportunities for the kids. Without mentors, even young hunters who have been exposed to the tradition during their childhoods will likely cycle out of hunting during their teenage years and never return. I have no easy answer, but I think part of addressing the broad challenges of hunter retention is first identifying the pressure points.

CULTURAL ACCEPTANCE

In this country, we live in a value-driven society where sociopolitical pressures, which are essentially the same as peer pressures, often shape our lives and our activities. These collective values ultimately shape what mainstream America deems as being acceptable practices versus those that are not.

When society decided because of health concerns that it was no longer "cool" to allow tobacco in public

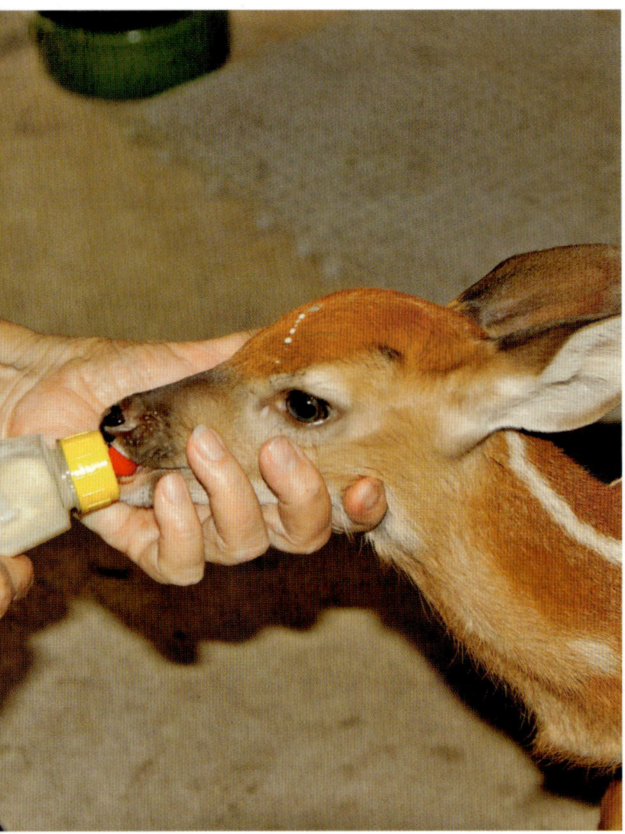

settings, those practices largely went away. What happens if hunting is ever considered uncool in the context of society's shared value system? It is alarming to consider how social pressure could be applied to squeeze the life out of hunting. In just one instance, existing hunters may choose to stop hunting because they are concerned by the potential scrutiny or perception of the people around them.

Social pressures undoubtedly are one of the strongest forces working against hunter retention, and this can also be just as easily applied to concerns over hunter recruitment. As previously mentioned, we must begin taking a harder look at hunting's "critical mass," the point where hunters become such a small minority of our population that our tradition becomes irrelevant to our fellow Americans, despite hunting's conservation benefits. My gut tells me that we are nearing the tipping point that is not favorable for hunting.

DIMINISHING RETURNS

Speaking of tipping points, I have explored some of the downsides to commercial captive breeding of white-tailed deer. I think there are certain features of the deer breeding industry that accelerate declining interest in whitetail hunting.

No doubt when certain elements of mystery and magic are removed from the hunt, hunting loses meaningful components that make it appealing to hunters. Do the highly intensive and highly artificial methods used to mass produce monster deer diminish the mystery and magic associated with hunting whitetails and devalue this resource? Yes, of course they do. It has been happening for several years. When the industry breached certain acceptable thresholds some years ago, the broad, once insatiable appetite for whitetail hunting noticeably diminished.

Of course, hunters who lose interest in whitetail hunting may not cycle out of hunting completely, but considering that whitetails have been the keystone American game species for 100-plus years, it is not far-fetched for us to see whitetails as potential change agents for both hunter recruitment and hunter retention. With whitetails being hunters' longtime favorite quarry, anything compromising the sustainable values of whitetails and whitetail hunting can further reduce hunter participation and retention over the long haul.

Along with the concerns that I have raised regarding the "whitetail tipping point," I will add that we in the broad hunting community owe it to ourselves to be our biggest critic. We must be hyper-aware of our own practices and attitudes that can destroy hunting as we know it. Self-searching discussions aimed at self-regulation are extremely difficult because it puts people within our own ranks in the crosshairs. At the end of the day, though, hunters can either be a part of the process and solution, or hunters can simply be by-products. It is this type of self-introspection and self-governance that led to the American conservation revolution dating back 100—130 years, resulting in the greatest wildlife recovery in the history of this planet. Thus, the idea of hunters self-governing with successful outcomes is not a new idea.

When we contemplate the broad continuum of wildlife management and hunting practices, there are points along that continuum that lead to diminishing returns and potentially negative outcomes. Our hunting community should explore those thresholds and identify shared boundaries so we can avoid the costly consequences of operating in the problem areas. Why shoot ourselves in the foot by promoting and accepting practices that diminish the properties which make hunting special and spiritual? When the mystery and magic of the hunt is gone, people will move on to other things, and hunting will be enshrined as a once golden pursuit of bygone days.

HUNTER REACTIVATION

When hunters cycle out of hunting "prematurely," it raises the question: What can be done to rekindle their interest and get them re-engaged in hunting? Reactivation is the third R3 component.

Personally, I feel that reactivation is easier than recruitment. Once people have enjoyed a taste of hunting, I suspect it will take less effort to get them back in the hunting community than recruiting people who have never hunted, and therefore do not know what they are missing.

When I consider people who were once involved with hunting and have cycled out prematurely, I think of kids who did not have an adult mentor to help foster ongoing opportunities. I also think of young adults who, because of the demands of developing their careers, establishing young families, and rearing children, simply cannot afford the time or money to get afield. I think of the millennial generation who were exposed to the tradition but grew up without a meaningful relationship with the outdoor world, making it easy to drift away from hunting because it was not ingrained in their culture and lives.

Time, finances, cultural disconnect, family priorities, and even peers are all external pressures that may drive hunters away from hunting. Perhaps this attrition is a sign of the times, but the good news is that these lapsed hunters have experienced hunting. Unlike complete novices, they have some basic skills, a respectable level of aptitude, an understanding of what hunting entails, and familiarity with the pleasurable experience that it can deliver through camaraderie, time in nature, and fresh, healthy protein.

So, what change agent might reconnect these inactive hunters? First, I anticipate a "demographic realignment" that may work in the hunting community's favor. While the baby boomers, born between 1946 and 1964, are now of a certain age, many of them still maintain a physically active lifestyle. Baby boomers have reared their children and typically enjoy a degree of financial security. As a result, these people in their late fifties, sixties, and even into their late seventies are positioned to be our most active hunters for a short term in the near future. Of course, because of the march of time, this generation will begin to lose their physical strength, and they are more likely to die than other age groups.

Then there is Gen X, who were born between 1965 and 1980. Many of them still have kids at home or in college. They are still in their professional prime and are still very focused on family and vocation. A large number of Gen X'ers once hunted but have since cycled out.

I believe the hunting community is currently contending with a timing gap. By 2025, a portion of Gen X will have reached a degree of financial independence and will have finished rearing their children, which will free up their time. I believe that over the next five to ten years we will have a very fertile pool of Americans who could likely be reactivated as hunters when they begin to look for ways to spend their newfound time and money. In my opinion, some of these people will organically reengage with hunting, but not all will. As a hunting community, we should identify opportunities and ways to usher the lapsed hunters back into our tradition.

We have developed some great youth hunting programs, such as the Texas Youth Hunting Program. Why not use those existing, successful models and create some hunting programs geared toward the "old timers?" Frankly, this age group is easier to engage for various reasons, and its members are also more likely to immediately take their place as hunters, which not only increases our ranks with potential advocates but provides financial resources for conservation. When we invest time and money in recruiting youngsters into hunting, we plant some important seeds in hopes of long-term growth and rewards. Potentially, we are looking at decades before they mature into active hunters. We need a pipeline for all generational cohorts to ensure sustainability and stability. It appears that we stand to gain more immediate dividends and returns on investment by focusing on reactivating the baby boomers, who could also be encouraged to serve as mentors to their own family members or other young acquaintances, and re-engaging Gen X'ers over the next five to fifteen years. Texas Wildlife Association recently launched its "Adult Learn to Hunt," which does not necessarily speak to retention, but this program certainly recognizes the idea of a stronger, immediate ROI with efforts being deployed to recruit new adult hunters, as opposed to younger hunters, though both are important.

Then there are the millennials who were born between 1981 and 1996. This cohort represents a new breed, one which our hunting community is not accustomed to accommodating. Many people in this generation did not grow up in a traditional nuclear family and have had very little meaningful interaction with our natural world. If they have had hunting experience, it is likely superficial. As a result, they are not versed in firearms or woodcraft, nor are they hunting savvy. Generally, millennials are still developing their careers and rearing young families. Currently, they do not have much free time or financial security. At first glance, the millennial cohort does not appear to be a fertile ground for recruitment or reactivation.

However, and it is a big however, millennials are defining and driving American food movements, including locavorism. Access to game meat will be the most likely portal for reactivating these inexperienced, lapsed hunters or engaging new hunters. Locavores also covet the opportunity to harvest and process their food, making them the most reachable millennial subset when it comes to hunting. Steven Rinella, through his MeatEater show and podcasts, has clearly demonstrated that there is a huge contingent of people who are interested in hunting for food, many of whom are millennials.

Reactivating lapsed hunters through their interest in procuring food provides an obvious and relatively convenient foundation on which to build programs. In Texas, we have an abundance of dove, waterfowl, and small game on public and private lands, an overpopulation of white-tailed deer and an explosively growing population of damage-inducing feral hogs, and we need hunters to help manage their numbers. With some concerted thought and effort, I think we can leverage these opportunities to grow our ranks and retain their interest in hunting for the long-term because humans must eat. Currently, people outside the traditional hunting community are expressing excitement and interest in game meats, so we need to take advantage of this opportunity. If we do not build on this opportunity, then our own apathy will have helped lead to our demise.

Gen Z are those Americans who were born between 1996 and 2015. They represent the largest cohort of our general population, but they are even more disconnected from our natural world than the millennials. While there is not much opportunity for reactivation within this age group, there is plenty of room for recruitment, although they are likely the most challenging generation of all time when it comes to hunting engagement.

The R3 lineup showcases the importance of creating sustainable populations of hunters to protect our conservation funding model, which ultimately ensures a positive future for hunting. Recruitment, retention, and reactivation is the basic model for success, but we must work smarter and harder to identify and implement practices that allow us to hit on all three aspects concurrently over long periods of time. Obviously, this is easier said than done, but this three-pronged approach is indeed the basic recipe for more success.

BRAIDING OF NGOs

Currently, I serve on boards for Dallas Safari Club, the National Deer Association, and the Texas Wildlife Association. Although my volunteer work requires an immense amount of time and energy, I hope to better understand how these similar special interest groups can "braid" their work together, creating synergies and increasing traction for the groups' similar missions. When I look at the website of American Wildlife Conservation Partners (AWCP), I see roughly 50 members of that consortium who have similar missions, some that are almost completely congruent, and others that overlap to some degree. Collectively, the aggregated strength of this assembly represents an immense amount of horsepower, financially, intellectually and otherwise. If these groups collectively strategized, worked closely together, and synergized their efforts, the harnessed capacity would exceed that of the extreme animal rightist groups that spend every day trying to kill hunting. Unfortunately, conservation groups, like most NGOs, operate in silos, doing their own thing and rarely working together in meaningful ways. In fact, sometimes there is so much jealously between members and leaders of some of the organizations that share almost identical missions that they waste energy throwing rocks at one another instead of working toward common goals. This is a shameful reality.

I want to better understand the dynamics of these organizations and how like-minded groups can collectively leverage our resources; hence, I often spend more time on volunteer work than my professional pursuits. It is my opinion the future health of hunting largely rests in the hands of NGOs and their engaged members. Anti-hunting groups have proven their ability to direct the outcome of public debates influencing social values. Pro-hunting groups have the same capacity, if we choose to use it. What these outcomes ultimately look like may directly reflect the gamesmanship of those on one side of the issue in comparison to those on the other. Make no mistake, engaged special interest groups will push the needle one direction or the other; the needle will not remain static and certainly will not find a comfortable, balanced place at the midpoint.

Anti-hunting and animal rights groups such as the Center for Biological Diversity, the Humane Society of United States, the Animal Liberation Front, and People for Ethical Treatment of Animals are thought leaders and influencers who would like hunting to cease today—not tomorrow—today! Then you have groups that are conservation activists who recognize and often promote hunting's role in global conservation. Whether hunting is accepted or shunned by society will likely depend on the point of view of the NGOs whose public outreach, education, and messaging campaigns prevail. Historically, groups who are antagonistic toward hunting have been more effective than our mainstream hunter/conservation groups.

As I was writing this section, I could not decide whether "braiding" or "weaving" best expressed the importance of our conservation-oriented NGOs working together more effectively. When I conducted a Google search on their respective meanings and I was delighted to find the symbolism and spiritual connotations associated with the act of braiding on the Angelica Balance website. According to the article I read, there are seven values which are tied to the act of braiding: societal status; learning to communicate; patience; wisdom; focus; accepting external opinions; and oneness of thoughts. If our conservation NGOs would embrace these intangible benefits and braid their individual work into a stronger whole, hunting and its future would benefit.

For the life of me, I cannot understand why our NGO community is not actively seeking ways to braid our efforts. Our track record for hunting advocacy demonstrates that our community has not crafted a cohesive plan to work together, and that is indefensible and not acceptable in my opinion. It should not be that difficult, except that humans are difficult. Our egos and personal agendas often overshadow our altruistic desire to

ABOVE > With the revitalized emphasis on the meat or food part of the hunt, I believe that promoting the importance of wild-harvested foods is the strongest future advocacy platform for hunters.

direct our intellect, resources, and energy to the common good. Until we work together more effectively, the hunting community will struggle to remain relevant in a society that is being influenced by those groups that are dedicated to crushing hunting.

WILD–HARVESTED FOOD AS AN ADVOCACY PLATFORM

About 15 years ago, when I saw the first television network fully dedicated to cooking, I thought, "Cooking 24/7? That will never last." Boy, was I wrong. In fact, today, there are several food networks—and they are exceptionally popular. In hindsight, I should not have been surprised because food is so central to our lives and lifestyles. Since the origin of mankind, procuring and consuming food has defined who we are and what we do. If early humans remained plant eaters, our path as a species would have been much different—and this discussion regarding the importance of hunting would not be necessary or relevant. The world as we know it would not remotely resemble what it does.

Hunting and meat consumption have undoubtedly shaped modern humanity. Our brain and its cognitive capacity that developed over millennia influenced by a meat-laden, protein-rich diet is one defining feature. Furthermore, the roots of philosophy, art, spirituality, social status, competition, and so many other aspects of modern humanity can all be traced back to the early days of hunting.

Over the last few decades, we have seen the emergence of foodie cultures across affluent societies. People have begun to connect, or actually reconnect, to their food more intimately. As I mentioned earlier, an increasing number of Americans, dubbed locavores, place great value on locally produced organic foods and have an interest in harvesting and processing these foods, and locavores represent one of the fastest growing segments of hunters.

History has a way of repeating itself, and that appears to be happening within hunting. Historically, the quest to procure food drove humans to pursue and kill game; the current trend is turning that direction. Frankly, this is refreshing. As someone who has spent his entire adult life working in the hunting business, it is revitalizing to hear clients discuss tasty, nutritious game meats with the enthusiasm once reserved for inches of antler or horn.

Steve Rinella, whose MeatEater brand has developed an almost cult-like following, vividly illustrates the public's interest in the food acquired through hunting. To Rinella's credit, he's a great communicator whose personality and style is a perfect fit for his subject matter, but the runaway success of his efforts—TV, books, podcasts, and speaking engagements—prove there is a huge, real market of people who are keenly interested in foods acquired by hunting.

This renewed interest in hunting for food provides new hope for securing hunting's position as a socially acceptable activity. I am especially enthusiastic about the work that Shane Mahoney, who popularized the North American Model of Wildlife Conservation, is doing through the Wild Harvest Initiative (WHI). WHI is an intensive state-by-state data collection effort designed to estimate the annual yield of recreationally harvested game and fish (fresh and saltwater) meat. No similar dataset has ever been collected. Although this initiative is in the mid-stages, the metrics generated suggest a huge amount of organic, wild meat is being produced. When combined with other wild-produced foods—nuts, berries, fungi, and edible plants—it appears the yield is large enough to contribute to national food security.

At the same time, WHI is also working to answer the questions: What changes would have to occur on the landscape to replace this wild-produced food through traditional agriculture? How many acres of wildlife habitat would need to be converted to farm fields? How much pesticide and herbicide would be required for such conversion? How would these conversions negatively impact other ecosystem services, such as carbon sequestration, naturally occurring water and nutrient cycles, essential pollinating plants, and the endless, almost indescribable impacts on vast ecological functions of the land and atmosphere?

If we can determine that naturally produced wild foods add to our nation's food security, we hunters and conservationists then have a new platform to promote and advocate the importance of wild places in human health and nutrition. If we can create such a platform to conserve wild places, we then have a stronger and more relevant (and defensible) platform to showcase the role that responsible hunting and angling play in conserving those wild places. It is a matter of connecting the dots, and the assembly of dots is not protracted—it is a relatively easy to follow equation.

While most Americans do not understand the true meaning of conservation, they—and every person on earth—can relate to food. Again, we have to connect the dots and bridge our messaging. Wild places equal food and human health. Hunting and angling, the means of harvesting wild food, equal conservation funding; conservation funding equals sustainability of wild places and wild food. The equation is not complex.

So, I hope you can see why I am excited about the work of WHI. In my opinion, the information being generated through WHI may very well hold the key to opening the door that we have been searching for over the last several decades. Left to me, every conservation group, state DNR, industry leaders and academic institutions would be supporting the work of WHI—it's that important.

Let me reiterate that harvesting food is the most defensible part of hunting. Plenty of surveys clearly show most Americans support hunting for food. Thus, it makes sense for us to shine the light on this aspect of hunting. Whether it is field to fork programs, sharing game meats through hunger initiatives, promoting the high nutritional value of wild game meats, or creating formal NGO campaigns that celebrate the food part of hunting, we must wave this flag proudly and often. Again, our hunting community must learn to play the game smarter.

SUPERFUND

For some time I have suggested that our hunting and angling community would be well-served by a national initiative designed to deploy a messaging campaign promoting the importance of hunting and fishing. Why not create a superfund that is large enough to engage a variety of media platforms to reach the public on a recurring basis and help shape public perceptions that are more favorable to hunting?

The superfund could be financed using a small percentage of Pittman-Robertson and Dingle-Johnson dollars that are allocated to all states, a small percentage of hunting and fishing license sales, contributions from NGOs, contributions from companies within the hunting and fishing industries, and private philanthropy. These sources already generate conservation dollars. If we only consider money generated through Pittman-Robertson, Dingle-Johnson, and hunting/fishing/trapping license sales, the total is more than $2 billion annually. Using just one percent of that total is $20 million per year. Using revenue from the other listed sources, that number could realistically double. In my opinion, an ambitious, aggressive concept could generate more than $100 million per year. A fund of that size is large enough to move the needle of public opinion.

To keep overhead low and the management simple, I would suggest establishing a trustee who oversees the fund's management and elect a board of financially astute individuals to ensure appropriate fiduciary oversight. An annual percentage of the superfund's cash generation could be dedicated to building a large endowment that adds resiliency to the ongoing initiative. Between earnings from the endowment and the cash generated annually, it would be possible to create a strong, impactful national messaging campaign that harnesses social media, radio, TV, and print media. If we could, then, engage a cadre of popular celebrities, including professional athletes, actors, and singers, to carry our message, I believe we could construct an effective education and advocacy campaign that could make a difference for the future of hunting and angling.

Okay, I will admit that I am oversimplifying this concept, but this is not nuclear physics we are discussing. As I think about it, I have to ask why have we not already gone down this path? Why are we not playing the public opinion game smarter? I fear we are making it much harder than it needs to be.

ANTI-HUNTING PRESSURES

For many years, our hunting community has discussed the anti-hunting movement. At times, I think the name "anti-hunter" has been bandied about so often and so loosely that our pro-hunting community simply defaults to talking about concerns over the anti-hunting movement without really trying to understand how these special interest groups evolved over time and what motivates their antagonism toward hunting.

Modern American society is sensitive to animal welfare, and social media has helped cultivate this American cultural value. Most people are offended by animal cruelty, especially if it involves pets. Over time, concern has expanded to include livestock and other animals. The images of animals in distress that appear on social media elicit strong emotions and sometimes prompt people to support pressure groups or NGOs that are created to address concerns over the treatment of animals. The overarching concern for animal welfare may occasionally be distilled into more radical special interest groups including animal rights and animal protection. To better understand the emotional dispositions and agendas of these groups, it requires defining some of the features that characterize these groups that fall along a continuum sometimes separated by shades of gray.

CATEGORIZING ANIMAL-USER VALUES

ANIMAL WELFARISTS

These people tend to advocate for humane practices that reduce the stress and suffering of animals caused by human interaction. They may advocate for pets, livestock, test animals, or any other animal for that matter.

From most people's perspective, animal welfare is a human responsibility to ensure the well-being of animals in their care, such as providing proper housing, humane handling, medical treatment, disease prevention, management, and feed. Proponents of animal welfare believe that humans can utilize animals in industry, entertainment, sports, and recreation as long as the animals receive reasonable care. They also seek to improve the welfare of animals through the regulation of animal-centric sports such as horse racing and endurance riding. The proponents acknowledge that animals also have interests, but their interests can be exchanged for human benefits as long as the benefits for humanity justify the sacrifice.

Animal welfarists are likely to approve hunting for meat but may tend to have reservations about "sport" hunting unless they are educated about the importance that hunting plays in conserving game. Pragmatism often defines this group's values and advocacy efforts. A large percentage of hunters can be categorized as animal welfarists, as most hunters are compassionate and support reasonable and ethical treatment of animals, both domestic and wild.

ANIMAL RIGHTISTS

Animal rightists believe there is no distinction between humans and animals, and that the two have equal and similar rights. Proponents of animal rights believe humans have no right whatsoever to use or utilize animals and that animals have rights that cannot be exchanged or sacrificed for the benefit of others. However, animal rights advocates do not hold the position that the rights are absolute; like humans, animal rights are limited.

Animal rightists also maintain that animals should not be used for food, entertainment, or experimentation. Animal rights groups promote laws and regulations that would prohibit activities that utilize animals, such as

horse racing, rodeos, hunting, medical research, raising animals for food, and using animals for recreation and entertainment. They also reject all forms of animal use no matter how humane.

Some animal rights proponents have also opposed the animal welfare reforms because they believe that by "improving the conditions under which animal exploitation occurs," the reforms impede progress toward full animal rights. Animal rights groups often adopt extreme tactics as they attempt to advance their agendas by disrupting lawful activities and sometimes inflicting property damage. This is a group that we normally characterize as extremists. A few NGOs that fall into this animal rights category include the Center for Biological Diversity, the Humane Society of United States, the Animal Liberation Front, and People for Ethical Treatment of Animals. Even within this mix of groups, there are differences of opinions that fall within their continuum of more extreme values, so it is not unusual for people within these groups to object to broad brush characterizations.

ANIMAL PROTECTIONISTS

Philosophically, this group falls somewhere between the animal welfarists and rightists. Animal protectionists, such as Jane Goodall, who is a well-known example, consider some uses of animals to be unacceptable while others are acceptable. The reasons vary greatly. For instance, an animal protectionist might express concern about trophy hunting as being "killing for entertainment or pleasure," but that same person might support subsistence hunting or killing to procure food. Some animal protectionists may advocate for additional welfare considerations for primates, elephants, cetaceans such as whales, dolphins, and porpoises, and some bird species such as parrots and corvids due to their advanced cognitive abilities.

TOP-LEFT > Hunters must govern ourselves better; otherwise, hunting will lose public policy battles. Support of hunting from the non-hunting public directly relates to how non-hunters perceive and interpret our actions as hunters. When the practices, even fringe ones, that characterize and define our hunting culture are described as bizarre, unethical, or indefensible by the non-hunting public, hunting loses the battle (and potentially the war), plain and simple.

TOP-RIGHT > The anti-hunting movement is well-funded, ambitious, and strategic. Until hunters learn to play the game smarter, the number of people who would like to see hunting wither away will continue to grow.

Going back to Cecil the Lion, animal protectionists would disapprove of trophy hunting as the hunter's motivation, which prompted Cecil's death. The same people might approve of breeding lions in captivity for conservation and ecotourism purposes, as long as the confinement program met certain thresholds for the lions' well-being.

The issues prompted by animal rights and animal welfare philosophies are very familiar to those who utilize animals in industry, entertainment, sport, or recreation. As society has changed from agrarian to urban, distinguishing between animal rights and animal welfare has become paramount. For the hunting community to work across the aisle with special interest groups, we must identify where common ground may exist as well as where the discord is most apparent.

Hunters represent about four percent of our American population, while anti-hunters have similar numbers. Animal rightists are not all anti-hunters and this subset of our population are more abundant than those who actively try to kill hunting. Animal protectionists likely represent a larger subset of our population than hunters or animal rightists. Animal welfarists represent the greatest number of people,

ABOVE > Aldo Leopold was one of the great visionaries in the conservation world, and many of his observations and interpretations remain relevant today. Leopold often relied on observation and introspection to better understand the dilemmas of his era. Today, more than ever, we hunters need to take a hard, honest look at how we must adapt to a rapidly changing environment and culture.

APPEALING TO THE MASSES

Again, hunters must learn to play the game smarter because people are watching. When the guns we use, such as AR platform rifles, look more like military guns than traditional hunting rifles, what signal does that send to non-hunters? Whether we recognize it or not, many people have opinions about who we are, what we do, how we do it, and whether our means and methods create an "unfair advantage" for hunters. If animal welfarists choose to use "unfair advantage" as their measuring stick to determine hunting's legitimacy, then our tradition is toast based on the means and methods of today. Yes, I know a large percentage of gun owners and hunters feel that it should be their legal right to use the gun of their choice to hunt, including AR platform rifles—I get it—but most Americans do not.

Furthermore, when our game management practices began to look more like animal husbandry because they include techniques such as artificial insemination, vaccinations, bottle-feeding fawns (that are later shot by hunters), sexing of semen, and even cloning, we must ask ourselves, what does this look like to mainstream America? Intensive practices that produce bucks with antlers so large that the bucks cannot hold their heads fully erect and sometimes suffer from frontal bone or pedicel fractures due to the enormous weight of their manufactured antlers are most assuredly perceived as an animal welfare matter to almost everyone except those who are involved in breeding monster deer.

When we in the hunting community, through captive deer breeding, possibly risk human health and safety by allowing people to use off-label drugs on animals without ensuring an adequate withdrawal period before those animals are legally hunted, our irresponsible behavior or complicit silence may as well be signing our own community's death warrant. We can do better. We must do better. We must play the game smarter. To coexist and remain acceptable to the public, including animal welfare groups, we must check our egos and our biases at the door and realize that a measure of self-reform is better than broad reform forced on us through the ballot box. Hunters are ill-prepared to win the modern public policy game. It will only get worse unless we look at ourselves and our practices closely and implement our own reforms.

Policy is not the only pressure that can end hunting as we know it. Public peer pressure often shapes our personal choices, including how we spend our recreational time. Public peer pressure dictates what is acceptable in mainstream America versus what is repulsive and unacceptable. Do the actions and images of hunters today create a general appearance of a wholesome, reasonable, and attractive activity?

Acclaimed wildlife conservationist and public figure Shane Mahoney has suggested that various special interest groups whose missions involve using animals, including our game resources, will be well-served if we can put aside our swords and work together for the benefit of the resources at hand. While I am not sure how realistic it might be for groups like the Dallas Safari Club to work with extreme groups like the Humane Society of the United States, I can see groups like the Dallas Safari Club creatively cooperating with groups like the Sierra Club and other moderate conservation groups. And why not? Why should special interest groups that truly appreciate and respect animals—game and non-game—not join hands to create policy and public outreach efforts that benefit the resources that we all value? As we braid the work of mainstream hunting/

conservation groups and strengthen our connections, can we also include some of these more extreme green groups? I think there is hope. The health of this world and the health of humans are one and the same, so there is too much at stake not to braid as inclusively as possible.

THE CRYSTAL BALL

So what does all of the material I presented in this chapter mean? What does the future hold for hunters and hunting? Although I think we have failed to control and leverage the narrative, historically the strongest argument for continuing hunting has been the fact that money generated through hunting license sales and excise taxes on sporting goods has been the principal funding source for terrestrial wildlife conservation. Conservation funding is incredibly important. It takes money to manage, protect, and conserve our wildlife resources. Conservation does not happen on its own accord without cause or cost.

On August 4, 2020, President Donald Trump signed into law The Great American Outdoors Act (GAOA), ending a decade-long battle to reauthorize and fully and permanently fund the Land and Water Conservation Fund. This fund, originally established by Congress in 1964 to reinvest royalties from offshore oil and natural gas development into public access and recreation on publicly owned lands, was essentially hijacked over time. Through GAOA, it is anticipated that this fund will permanently authorize some $900 million annually to ensure the health of public lands and recreational access to them. Many are hailing this as one of the greatest achievements in modern-day conservation funding. In some ways, I would have to agree.

At the end of the day, though, what does this new funding mechanism mean for hunting? Are there unintended consequences for hunters and hunting? Does this new conservation funding source diminish our ability to suggest that money generated by hunting is the primary funding source in the U.S. for wildlife conservation? If so, is our strongest advocacy platform for hunting now substantially weaker? I do not know the answers to these questions. I readily admit that voicing such questions will raise criticism from others who say that this logic is nearsighted and greedy. And perhaps it is, but this is one more factor potentially working against hunting, just one more straw on the camel's back. And this is all the more reason to explore the idea of using food security as the new platform for advocating the benefits associated with hunting that include helping conserve wild places that produce important organic foods.

The international hunting industry is fragile right now. For years, the animal rightists and anti-hunters have been chipping away at our ability to hunt and import certain game species from international locations. Some species, such as large cats, elephants, rhinos, giraffes, and polar bears, appeal in strong and unique ways to the public, and they are more likely to prompt policies that shut down hunting and other revenue generating activities. Countries that adopt policies eliminating the legal hunting and importation of these animals also kill the economies associated with the species-specific hunting trade. In recent years, safari operators have been hammered by restrictive policies.

On top of the local, regional, national, and international policies that have negatively impacted hunting operators in foreign countries, COVID-19 is also negatively impacting the hunting industry in these same areas. More than 90 percent of international hunts were canceled for 2020, with a hangover-effect that lingered through 2021. For some operators, COVID-19 has been the final "nail in the coffin," and they have gone out of business. COVID-19 alone is not a deal breaker for international hunting, but it is a significant added pressure.

Although it comes at the expense of my international colleagues, a silver lining of the COVID-19 debacle is that the international trip cancellations in 2020 and 2021 prompted those same hunters to replace their trips with hunts in the Lower 48. The shift benefited my business significantly over the last few years. The market adjustment may be temporary, but it has made a difference for outfitters like me during the economic uncertainty surrounding COVID-19.

As anti-hunting groups continue to successfully advance their agendas internationally, rest assured that those pressures and tactics will eventually be applied here in the U.S. We have seen firsthand how the anti-hunting activists look for hunting's soft, vulnerable underbelly as they successfully did with outlawing bear and mountain lion hunting with dogs in Washington, Oregon, and California. We learned that trapping is vulnerable at the ballot box when restrictive laws were passed in California, Colorado, Nevada, and other states. These policy restrictions creep in and add pressure on an already frail body. What may appear to be somewhat innocuous changes within our state and federal policy systems, may actually be part of the long-term strategy of special interest groups to chip away at things, advancing their agendas in an incremental, not-so-noticeable fashion—a classic creep-style approach.

Anti-hunters have learned where the soft spots are and how to patiently carve away hunting, fishing, and trapping allowances. Over time it is death by a thousand cuts. Our hunting community must learn how to counter this movement more effectively. Controlling the narrative surrounding hunting and highlighting its benefits is something that we have not mastered. We are always on defense instead of pressing forward and effectively using media tools to better tell our story and position ourselves in front of anti-hunting initiatives. When it comes to debates and public forums regarding hunting, hunters tend to seek safe haven in the shadows, often electing to avoid confrontation. Retreating to the sidelines cedes control of the narrative to our adversaries. If hunting is going to have a fighting chance of remaining relevant in this country, this must change. And it must change soon. Our hunter numbers are reaching a dire tipping point.

The stakes are high and extend beyond our own backyard. American hunters have not only funded conservation at home, but historically, we have been the largest conservation funders in countries where hunting has been popular. With that said, I sometimes question how our leading conservation groups like the Dallas Safari Club and Safari Club International invest so much in international affairs while overlooking issues on our home soil. Do not get me wrong. I understand the importance of engaging in these international issues and meeting international needs, but if we do not protect our base of American hunters, then global hunting concerns become moot. Personally, I hope our own NGOs will re-prioritize how and where we leverage our resources. The global force for hunting as a conservation tool is stationed here on our own U.S. soil. If we lose the American base, we ultimately lose the battle both domestically and internationally.

The wildlife profession is near and dear to me. While hunting has shaped my wildlife career, I recognize that the wildlife field is much broader than hunting alone. As a college student in the 1980s, I witnessed firsthand how the demographics of students majoring in wildlife science were changing. At the time, about half of them did not come from a hunting and fishing background. This trend has continued. Those wildlife graduates, who largely have no hunting background, are now ascending into regulatory positions that govern our wildlife resources. People's values shape their decisions.

Based on my reading of the current tea leaves, I would encourage young people who are thinking about chasing a wildlife career to focus on non-game industries such as environmental law, urban wildlife, endangered species, natural resource education positions, and other wildlife professions that are not directly tied to hunting. Do not get me wrong, we need good leaders in the wildlife profession to help guide our hunting community; however, from the standpoint of job opportunities, I see it becoming more challenging for young wildlife professionals to establish a career in hunting or a hunting-related business.

Hunting has been good to me. As a kid, it shaped my life and provided immense enjoyment. During my formative years, hunting served as an outdoor classroom for me and continues to do so today. My days afield instilled core values and important virtues, such as patience, focus, commitment, resourcefulness, and

situational awareness. Hunting taught me to rely on my God-given senses, to appreciate life and death, to obtain, process, and properly cook my own foods, and to understand the importance of the ecological function in our natural world. Hunting gave me a platform for bringing my family together where we created memories that are forever ingrained in my heart and mind. Hunting shaped my professional life and continues to do so today. It is not a hyperbole to say that hunting made me the person I am.

Although I am concerned about certain patterns and images that seem to loom in the crystal ball, I also have faith that humans have the capacity to keep what is good. Hunting is good—the products of hunting are largely good. Hunting is an important part of our human DNA and our American culture. Although I have not been blessed with grandkids yet, I would like to think that my descendants will be able to enjoy wild things and wild places as much as I have, and to do so as hunters. For this to happen, I believe hunting must remain a part of the conservation equation because it is integral to the future success of wild things and wild places.

This book, *The Hunting Business*, has been a labor of love and sheer drudgery. I started this project 12 years ago and worked on it for three consecutive summers; I shelved it when I became an officer with TWA. After the six years as a TWA officer, my writing style changed, a lot of water had run under the bridge, and my perspective on many things had evolved. I completely started over, ditching a roughly 50,000-word manuscript. My restart is now three-plus years in the process.

This book reflects the knowledge and opinions that I have gained over the 36 years that I have been working full-time in the hunting industry, and I would like to think that it will serve as a significant part of my professional legacy. I hope that those who read any portion of this book will find a tidbit or two that they can apply to their own lives and undertakings with a meaningful outcome. If that ends up being the case, then my

efforts will have proved to be worthwhile. As I put these final words on this manuscript in December 2022, I will admit that I am awash in a flood of emotions because the book represents a long and amazing journey. I began to question a few years ago whether I would ever see this project to fruition, but there is now visible light at the end of the tunnel, which brings me great joy. I am not sure if I will ever completely retire from the hunting business, but knowing that this book will allow my work to leave an indelible mark gives me peace; I have passed a milestone that I targeted many years ago.

So once again, what do I see as I peer into the crystal ball and look at the future of hunting? As I have said repeatedly, we must learn to play this game smarter. Although we appear to be losing the game right now, our hunting community has proved to be filled with fighters. Some 110 to 130-plus years ago, in the face of seeming futility, our hunting community reinvented itself using imagination and creativity. Today, we have more information than ever before to inspire our thinking, our imagination, and our creativity. Back then, it took political bloodshed to right the ship and it will likely require the same today. It is unlikely that another Theodore Roosevelt will emerge to serve as hunting's change agent, but the world is full of decent people. Collectively, hunters and non-hunters have too much at stake for today's brightest minds not to be put to work on behalf of wildlife.

The future no longer rests in the hands of my generation, as we have done a pretty good job of screwing things up. Rather, the future of hunting rests in the hands of the younger generations of today—and tomorrow. I pray that the good Lord will enable them to make astute choices and be strong leaders, ensuring that our important hunting heritage is preserved forever.

Cheers to a proud past—and to a great future!

ACKNOWLEDGMENTS

Anytime you begin acknowledging people by name, you run the risk of leaving people out who also deserve mention. Unfortunately, that truism applies here..

While *The Hunting Business* is the result of about 12 years of writing, including a false start that lasted several years before I threw out the entire manuscript and started over in 2018, the contents are based on 59 years of first-hand experience. As a result, my acknowledgments have less to do with those who contributed to this project and more to do with those who shaped my career (and me) in various ways. The list of people who have touched my life as a fellow professional, volunteer or outdoor adventurer, would require a second book, so please know you all, regardless of whether your name appears in print or not, have added richness and depth that defies words. I am grateful.

My high school principal, Stephen Fleenor, bridged my transition from Crandall High School to Texas A&M University. Mr. Fleenor recognized the spark in my eye. On graduation day, he sought me out and encouraged me to pursue a degree in the natural resource field. It just so happened that the head of freshman admissions at TAMU, Gayle Wood, was a long-time church friend of Mr. Fleenor. Their relationship proved to be a critical for my acceptance into A&M. I will forever be indebted to Mr. Fleenor for hauling me down to College Station on his own time and dime and spending the day walking around campus, introducing me to campus influencers. Without his personal commitment, I would not have forged a career as a wildlife professional and this book would not have been written.

The second person I met on campus at A&M during my trip with Mr. Fleenor was Dr. Wallace Klussmann, then-department head of Wildlife and Fisheries Sciences. To this day, he claims to have burned a "coupon" to help get me accepted into A&M—and I don't doubt that a bit. Dr. Klussmann has been a cherished mentor since that summer day in 1982 and we have been taking care of the commercial deer hunts at his Longbranch Ranch for approximately 25 years. I treasure our special relationship and am forever grateful for his guidance and investment into my efforts.

I would be remiss if I did not mention Dr. Nova Silvy, my faculty advisor at A&M. Dr. Silvy was my personal giant (or perhaps giant slayer) during my college years. His consistent encouragement pushed me to struggle through my first year of college instead of giving up. Even after all these years, I consider him a "professional father figure" and I'm so lucky that he entered my life when he did.

Outside of my family members who were mentioned in the Dedication, no other people profoundly shaped my early days in the hunting business more than Dick and Norma Laros. Dick was the first industry professional to take a chance on me, eventually investing much time and equity in building a strong foundation for my career.. The wisdom he freely shared with me shortened my learning curve about this unique business and his loyal network of hunters embraced Wildlife Systems Inc. (WSI). Their patronage helped launch my start-up company. In the years after my mom's death, Norma was a mother figure and supported me in the ways that mothers often do. Together, Dick and Norma were vital threads in the fiber of WSI for its first 20 years. Their sense of decency, passion for the outdoors, eye for detail, and professionalism touched everyone around them, including me, in innumerable ways, all of which make the world a better place to call home.

Through the years WSI's support team has been the lifeblood of the business that defined my career. First, Alice Ayers and now Jennifer Jezek, who also handles our special events, collectively managed our office for almost 25 years, making my life easier and more productive in the process. Field managers such as Manuel Garcia, Zach Ehlers, Ruben Fernandez, and Peter Ewald worked behind the scenes to keep things running smoothly, so I could concentrate on growing the business. Guides including Jackie Murphy, Don Richardson, Mike Gray, Mike Lassig, Ted Simpson, Scott Keating, Albert Hernandez, Brown Delozier, and Craig Bowen have been or were a part of our team for 15+ years and have been integral to the WSI's success. There are many other guides who have contributed for numerous years, you know who you are, and I appreciate all that you have done on my behalf. Chefs David Griffith, who has kept our clients well fed for 20 years, and Richard Berry have carried a huge load in our camp kitchens for many years. The husband and wife duos of Cully and Maxine Cullison and Homer and Earlene Hutto helped anchor our culinary efforts during WSI's early days. As with the guides, there are many others chefs who shared their talents and enthusiasm in the kitchen to ensure our clients and camp staff eat well during our hunts. Buce Bearden, whose untimely death left a hole in our ranks, was also instrumental in developing the business during our formative years. We currently have more 40 support team members serving as guides and chefs and I consider myself fortunate to play on their team.

I tip my hat to the landowners and their personnel who have placed their trust in WSI over the years. Frank Price is our longest tenured landowner and our ongoing relationship dates back to 1988. We began working with Bill Wilson in 1990 and continue to work with Bill's family today. Lou Carter, with the La Rucia Ranch and now his son, James Pettus, have been landowner-clients since 1997. Danny Butler with the H. Yturria Ranches has placed an immense amount of trust in me and our team for almost 25 years. Almost 20 years ago, the owners of the A.S. Gage Ranch provided us an opportunity to become deeply involved in the Texas Trans-Pecos region, as did Susan Combs and Marshall Miller. The Cargile family in San Angelo and their general manager Charley Christensen have granted us the privilege of working with them on multiple properties for almost 20 years.

I have been blessed to work with any, many other private landowners through the years. They have collectively created opportunities for me and our team that are too broad and deep to adequately describe. Private landowners are the true stewards of the lands across this country and they are the ones who hold the keys to the future health of our natural resources. As Aldo Leopold put it some 80+ years ago, "Conservation will ultimately boil down to rewarding the private landowner who conserves the public interest." His observation is just as relevant today as it was back then.

Over the years, we have been privileged to host more than 10,000 hunters on WSI-led excursions. The list is too long and the task too complex to mention individuals, but these hunting clients have been the life of WSI since day one. Our clients come from all walks of life, some blue-collar workers and some successful business owners and corporate CEOs. Collectively, they have been a source of continuing education. As they've shared their knowledge and experiences, I have gathered valuable tidbits from which I have pieced together my own strategies for professional and personal success. Thank you all for placing your trust in us to deliver hunts that are worth your time and your money. Your continued support has allowed WSI and me to enjoy a good, long run in the hunting business.

Within the hunting industry, there are many individuals who have invested personal equity into WSI's efforts including serving as mentors and teachers for me. The list is too long to include in its entirety, but folks like Larry Weishuhn, Rob McCanna, Bob Foulkrod, Tom and Betty Lou Fegely, Joe Graham, Blake Barnett, Kim Hicks, Dave Fulson, Dave Richards, Art and Jimmy Browning, Eddie Stevenson, Gary Turner, Ronnie Eckel, Matt Bettersworth, and many others are industry friends whose relationships have elevated my efforts in this arena.

From an NGO standpoint, I must mention my involvement with the Texas Wildlife Association (TWA). My volunteer work with TWA has been an amazing opportunity. In the process of moving the needle forward for conservation through this organization, I have worked alongside many generous and capable people who motivated me further with their passion. For me, TWA is the "who's who" of great people who have been instrumental in my development as a conservation advocate. They include David K. Langford, Tina Buford, Dr. Bill Eikenhorst, Charles Davidson, Tom Vandivier, Dr. Don Steinbach, Karla Welch, Dr. Neal Wilkins, David Brimager, Sarah Biedenharn, Marko Barrett, Alan Curry, Warren Blesh, the late Randy Rehmann, and so many others. Within this league of colossal movers, shakers and difference makers, Steve Lewis has been my personal giant. Steve embodies the true meaning of volunteer and philanthropist, and he, as my colleague and friend, has gone out of his way to lift me up in so many ways. In these ranks, I have learned so much that has served me well in all facets of my life. These people made me a better businessman, volunteer, and conservationist, and have enriched my life beyond measure.

In recent years, I have also become more active in the Dallas Safari Club and the National Deer Association. My volunteer work with those organizations helps further inspire me and allows me to better understand how the broad conservation NGO community should be working together more closely to advance the important missions of all these groups and to ultimately serving as a stronger, united voice for hunters and hunting. The Stacy family, Tim Fallon and others with DSC have inspired me with their amazing generosity and commitment to DSC as well as with their valued friendships. With NDA, I've immensely·enjoyed my relationship with Nick Pinizzotto, Kip Adams, and the dedicated volunteer crew that is part of the NDA leadership team, as they continue to inspire me with their commitment to an important mission.

In the professional natural resource world, I have been blessed to work alongside of and affiliate with many great professionals worthy of emulation who have motivated me to continue to learn and work to make a difference for wildlife. This cohort includes Dr. Nova Silvy, Dr. Neal Wilkins, Dr. Roel Lopez, Dr. Louis Harveson, Carter Smith, Mitch Lockwood, Clayton Wolf, the late Dr. Bob Dittmar, Dr. Don Steinbach, Dr. Fred Bryant, Ruben Cantu, Tamara Wood, Dr. Jim Cathey, Jenny Sanders, John Silovsky, Alan Cain, Jimmy Fontenot, Dr. Doug Slack, Dr. Ray Telfair, Jeff Gunnels, Misty Sumner, Marc Bartoskewitz, Ty Bartoskewitz, Donnie Drager, Kent Mills, Ricky Linex, Justin Dreibelbis, David Synatzke, Linda Campbell, Corey Mason, Helen Holdsworth, Dr. Dale Rollins, Steve Nelle, Ken Cearley, Gene Miller, and many others. In recent years, Shane Mahoney, who honored me by providing comments for the back cover of this book, has reignited my passion through his work in the global conservation space and through his friendship.

Terry Anderson, my business partner in WSI and Conservation Equity Partners, LLC since 2019, has been integral to my professional development in recent years. Terry is one of the most instinctive people I have ever met and his ability to spot opportunities in the confluence of natural resource conservation and investment is unparalleled. My business relationship with Terry rekindled the fire in my belly for business , which likely kept me from beginning to wind down my career a few years ago; I'm now as super-charged as ever.

Regarding this book project, Lorie Woodward with Woodward Communications, has been a wizard with her editing work. I have known Lorie since our college days and her mastery of "wordslinging" is second to none. I am forever grateful for her willingness to serve as the main editor of *The Hunting Business*. Lorie has been a patient and steady force behind this book project over the last year and I cannot thank her enough for her outstanding efforts to bring this project to fruition. Similarly, a big thank you to Christina Tewes and Lauren Carswell for copy editing this book and making sure that everything was tight and tidy. They are both young talents who have bright futures. Lauret Jarvis also deserves high praise for designing this book and pushing it across the finish line as its production manager. I could not have finished this book without her invaluable help.

I must pay my most sincere gratitude to my brother, Robby Simons, who has been one of my biggest supporters for many years. Robby inspires me in ways beyond description.

And lastly, thank you to Larry Weishuhn for writing the Foreword of *The Hunting Business*. I have known Larry for more than 30 years. As an industry icon for several decades, Larry has always been a respected leader and consummate gentlemen, representing our profession well. Thank you, Larry, for penning some words for this book and thank you even more for all that you have done for the hunting industry—you are a giant among giants.

These people mentioned here, along with many others, represent an amazing community of friends, colleagues, business associates, and clients who all have played a part in shaping my time and work in the hunting and wildlife business. They have lifted me up, inspired me, made me look better than I am, and been part of my journey. The material found in *The Hunting Business* is a product of my relationship with these incredible people.

PHOTO CREDITS

CHRIS DOUGLAS→ chrisdouglas.photography • IG *@chrisdouglasphoto*

COVER

GREG SIMONS→ wildlifesystem.com • IG *@wildlifesystems* • FB *@wildlifesystems*

ALL PHOTOS UNLESS CITED OTHERWISE

BLAKE BARNETT→ IG *@trailing_the_hunters_moon* • FB *@blakebarnettofficial*

PG 3 & PG 63—Guide and hunter glassing
PGS 4-5—Harvest Moon
PG 9—Woman glassing across field
PGS 16-17—Guide, hunter and pronghorn
PGS 20-21—Rifle and antlers
PG 116—Tent camp
PG 118—Hunters and guides around campfire
PG 135—Guide packing out aoudad
PG 141—Hunter and guide glassing
PG 146—Tractor setting up deer stand
PG 164—Hunter at gun range
PG 199—Game warden with gator hunters
PG 200—Cutting out dates on license
PGS 272-273—Hunters walking through field

CHASE PHILLIPS→ Fair Chase Creative • IG *@fairchasecreative*

PG 278—Chase with camera

DAVE RICHARDS→ richardsoutdoorphotography.com • IG *@richardsoutdoorphoto* • FB *@richardsoutdoorphotography*

PG 47—Deer in good habitat
PG 226—Elk with mountain backdrop

ALDO LEOPOLD FOUNDATION AND UNIVERSITY WISCONSIN-MADISON ARCHIVES→

aldoleopold.org • IG *@aldoleopoldfoundation* • FB *@aldoleopoldfoundation* | library.wisc.edu/archives • FB *@UWMadLibraries*

PGS 88-89—Aldo Leopold
PG 266—Aldo Leopold looking across landscape

SAFARI CLASSICS→ safariclassics.net • IG *@safari_classics* • FB *@safariclassicsproductions*

PG 40-41—Packstring of horses with hunters

TEXAS YOUTH HUNTING PROGRAM→ tyhp.org • IG *@texasyouthhuntingprogram* • FB *@texasyouthhuntingprogram*

PG 91—TYHP group

VERMEJO→ tedturnerreserves.com/vermejo • IG *@tedturnerreserves* • FB *@tedturnerreserves*

PG 119—Vermejo lodge

OTHER CREDITS

INSIDE COVER; INSIDE BACK COVER; ENDSHEETS—Deer footprint in sand/LFRabanedo/Shutterstock.com
PGS 2-3—Autumn Leaves/Kateryna Bukuros/Shutterstock.com
PG 3—Rifle Scope/Krasula/Shutterstock.com; Protesters/Grant Rooney Premium/Alamy Stock Photo
PGS 10-11—Whitetail buck/Thejake/Shutterstock.com
PG 35—Posted sign/John Rob/iStockphoto.com
PG 46—Deer in pen with no habitat/Alan Cain
PG 61—Hunting club sign/Ruben Cantu
PG 125—Guide cooking over open fire/Gaspr13/iStockphoto.com; fresh vegetables/Bill Oxford/iStockphoto.com
PG 128—Food allergies/Piotr Malczyk/iStockphoto.com
PG 208—Denuded landscape with browse line/Steve Nelle
PG 211—Book cover/m.media-amazon.com/images/I/51EYCPsHvDL.jpg
PG 219—Cow in shute/David F/iStockphoto.com; vet with calf/123 Ducu/iStockphoto.com; fallow deer behind fence/Bargais/
iStockphoto.com; bottle feeding fawn/S. Stan/iStockphoto.com;
PG 229—Gib Surles and Bobby Jarvis with buck/Gib Surles
PG 243—Empty airport/Napat Wesshasartar/iStockphoto.com
PG 258—Bottle feeding fawn/1000 Words Everyday/iStockphoto.com
PG 261—Hanging deer carcass/Akchamczuk/iStockphoto.com
PG 265—Protesters/Jim Wood/Alamy Stock Photo; Voting Booth/Adam Kaz/iStockphoto.com

"NOT ONLY ARE HUNTING AND ANGLING KEY COMPONENTS OF OUR FOOD
SECURITY SYSTEM, BUT THEY ARE LINKED TO ALL OTHER ASPECTS OF
FOOD PRODUCTION EQUALLY ENGAGED IN SUSTAINABLY HARVESTING
THE BOUNTIES OF NATURE. THERE ARE 40-45 MILLION AMERICANS AND
CANADIANS WHO HUNT AND FISH. HOW MUCH DO THEY ACTUALLY HARVEST?
AND WHAT WOULD BE THE COST TO SOCIETY IF HUNTING AND FISHING
WERE TO GO AWAY?"

—SHANE MAHONE

"UNLESS WE PRACTICE CONSERVATION, THOSE WHO COME AFTER US WILL
HAVE TO PAY THE PRICE OF MISERY, DEGRADATION, AND FAILURE FOR THE
PROGRESS AND PROSPERITY OF OUR DAY."

—GIFFORD PINCHOT

"HUNTING FORCES A PERSON TO ENDURE, TO MASTER THEMSELVES, EVEN TO
TRULY GET TO KNOW THE WILD ENVIRONMENT. ACTUALLY, ALONG THE WAY,
HUNTING AND FISHING MAKES YOU FALL IN LOVE WITH THE NATURAL WORLD.
THIS IS WHY HUNTERS SO OFTEN GIVE BACK BY CONTRIBUTING
TO CONSERVATION."

—DONALD TRUMP, JR.

"TO SUM UP, ONE DOES NOT HUNT IN ORDER TO KILL; ON THE CONTRARY,
ONE KILLS IN ORDER TO HAVE HUNTED. IF ONE WERE TO PRESENT THE
SPORTSMAN WITH THE DEATH OF THE ANIMAL AS A GIFT HE WOULD REFUSE
IT. WHAT HE IS AFTER IS HAVING TO WIN IT, TO CONQUER THE SURLY BRUTE
THROUGH HIS OWN EFFORT AND SKILL WITH ALL THE EXTRAS THAT THIS
CARRIES WITH IT: THE IMMERSION IN THE COUNTRYSIDE, THE HEALTHFULNESS
OF THE EXERCISE, THE DISTRACTION FROM HIS JOB."

—JOSE ORTEGA Y GASSET

"A TRUE CONSERVATIONIST IS A MAN WHO KNOWS THAT THE WORLD IS NOT
GIVEN BY HIS FATHERS, BUT BORROWED FROM HIS CHILDREN."

—JOHN JAMES AUDUBON

"THE SINGLE GREATEST SOCIETAL CHALLENGE—REGIONALLY, NATIONALLY,
AND GLOBALLY—IS THE CONSERVATION OF NATURAL RESOURCES AND
PRESERVING THE INTEGRITY OF WILD THINGS AND WILD PLACES. AND WE
SHOULD NEVER UNDERESTIMATE THE INTEGRAL AND IMPORTANT ROLE THAT
HUNTERS AND ANGLERS PLAY IN THIS EVER-EVOLVING CHALLENGE."

—GREG SIMONS